THE NAZIS

A WARNING FROM HISTORY

The Nazis

A Warning from History   Laurence Rees

Foreword by Professor Ian Kershaw

THE NEW PRESS

for Oliver and Camilla

ISBN 1-56584-445-9

Published in the United States by The New Press, New York
Distributed by W.W. Norton & Company, Inc., New York

The New Press was established in 1990 as a not-for-profit alternative
to the large, commercial publishing houses currently dominating
the book publishing industry. The New Press operates in the public interest rather
than for private gain, and is committed to publishing, in innovative ways, works
of educational, cultural, and community value that might not be considered
sufficiently profitable. The New Press's editorial offices are located
at the City University of New York.

First published in 1997 by BBC Books, an imprint
of BBC Worldwide Publishing, BBC Worldwide Limited,
Woodlands, 80 Wood Lane, London W12 0TT.
Published to accompany the television series *The Nazis:
A Warning from History*, first broadcast on BBC 2 in 1997.
Writer and producer: Laurence Rees.

Designed by AB3. Picture research by Joanne King.
Maps by Barking Dog Art. Set in Palatino and Optima by BBC Books.
Color separations by Radstock Reproductions Limited, Midsomer Norton.
Printed in the United States of America.

9 8 7 6 5 4 3 2 1

Contents

'If you gaze for long into an abyss,
the abyss gazes also into you.'

Friedrich Nietzsche, *Jenseits von Gut und Böse*

FOREWORD

'A Warning from History'. The subtitle of Laurence Rees's book is a fitting one. It may be that in the eyes of God all historical epochs are of equal importance but, in the eyes of mortals, the Nazi era has a unique place. Nazism cannot be regarded with detachment or seen as simply the arena for scholarly debates. Its history belongs to all of us. Its lessons should be heeded by all of us.

What happened under the Nazis took place in Europe and not very long ago. In a modern, highly cultured society, the German people voted out a democracy that had failed. Only then could a backstairs intrigue bring Adolf Hitler to power. Once in control of the state, the Nazis were able to dismantle – with widespread popular support – all safeguards of human rights and to bring about a collapse of civilized values more rapid than any seen in history. Exploiting nationalist aims, with massive backing, they could prepare for war in pursuit of racist, imperialist goals. Their quest for ethnic purity, once more with general approval, would lead ultimately to the gas chambers of Treblinka and Auschwitz. History does not directly repeat itself. But 'ethnic cleansing' and racist-nationalist war in the former Yugoslavia, and the potential for catastrophe in the unstable remnants of the one-time Soviet Union, give scant grounds for comfort in today's Europe.

Only in knowledge, as the philosopher Karl Jaspers declared, can the recurrence of the evils which Nazism embodied be prevented. Perhaps we ought to add: together with the readiness, coming from knowledge, to defend inroads into freedom and to reject nationalist and racist intolerance before it is too late.

This book, and the television series on which it is based, make an important contribution to this aim. They make a crucial period of history highly accessible. The testimony of contemporaries and eye-witnesses that Laurence Rees has assembled is important for an understanding of the mentalities which Nazism exploited. These mentalities in turn help to explain how the terrible events perpetrated by the Nazis could come about. Such mentalities have, regrettably, by no means altogether died out. The book deserves, therefore, to have a wide impact, not least on the younger generation – the hope of the future – for whom it is particularly important to heed the 'Warning from History'. I welcome the book most warmly and wish it every success.

Ian Kershaw
Professor of Modern History
University of Sheffield

Introduction

Last summer I sat in an army fort in Lithuania and listened as a mass killer explained how he had murdered defenceless men and women for the Nazis. Only now, with the fall of Communism and the democratization of his country, was he free to tell his story. What this man said (and he was just one of the many, many interviewees we filmed over the last three years) was repugnant, but it was important. We must listen to what such people say in an attempt to understand how Nazism was possible. In the words of the German-born philosopher Karl Jaspers: 'That which has happened is a warning. To forget it is guilt. It must be continually remembered. It was possible for this to happen, and it remains possible for it to happen again at any minute. Only in knowledge can it be prevented.'

It has never been more important than now, as the twentieth century ends, for us to remember Nazism and listen to the memories of those who experienced it. For nearly fifty years Europe lived with the legacy of Nazi rule – a divided Germany, a cold war and the Communist oppression of eastern Europe. Now all that is history too. One of the most frightening remarks made to me by a former Nazi was his assertion, spoken after our formal interview, that he used to feel ashamed of being German as a result of the damage the Nazis inflicted on the world 'but now that Germany has united again that shame is diminishing'.

The written record of our interviews amounts to more than a million words. Most of those we talked to had never before spoken this way to journalists. Many of our interviewees were initially reluctant to appear, but they were open to persuasion. Some were persuaded because they respected the BBC, others in the Eastern bloc countries because the fall of Communism meant that they were free to speak out at last, but many had a simpler reason for agreeing to be interviewed. One eminent German put it this way when I remarked to him after his interview that he had said provocative things that would upset other Germans: 'I don't care. Ten years ago I could not have spoken like this but now, well…I will be dead soon. It is time to tell all of the truth.'

But this is not just an oral history. A key motivation for this book and the television series on which it is based was the desire to tell the story of the Nazis through the functioning of the Nazi state. For many years, certainly in the arena of 'popular' history, there has been a concentration on the character of Hitler (there are more biographies of Hitler than any man who has ever lived) and an approach to the history of this period through his psychological make-up. But this has meant that, for many, the Nazi period can be easily dismissed; since there will never be another human being with the same genetic constituents as Hitler, they argue, we are all safe. Many Germans have been able to say, in effect, 'We fell under Hitler's spell' and so absolve themselves of responsibility. By looking at the workings of the Nazi state, and, only where relevant, the character of Adolf Hitler, a very different and more disturbing picture emerges – a picture in which there was massive voluntary collaboration with the Nazi regime; in which many Germans were happy and content under Nazi rule in the 1930s; in which members of the Nazi élite lied when, after the war, they claimed they were 'acting under orders'; in which thousands eagerly profited from the downfall of the Jews; in which a majority of Germans in 1932 knowingly voted for parties committed to overthrowing German democracy.

Individual Germans and their allies must take responsibility for all this and more. In our interviews many did. The story they told is not a comfortable one and it cannot easily be brushed aside, for in the end Nazism, a creed born in Germany, brought into the world new knowledge of how low human beings can sink. Hitler did not do this on his own.

Could something similar happen again somewhere in the world? I am with Karl Jaspers: 'it remains possible for it to happen again at any minute'.

Laurence Rees
London, January 1997

Right: 1 April 1933: the Nazis organize a boycott of Jewish shops and the Storm Troopers fix hate-filled slogans on shop windows.

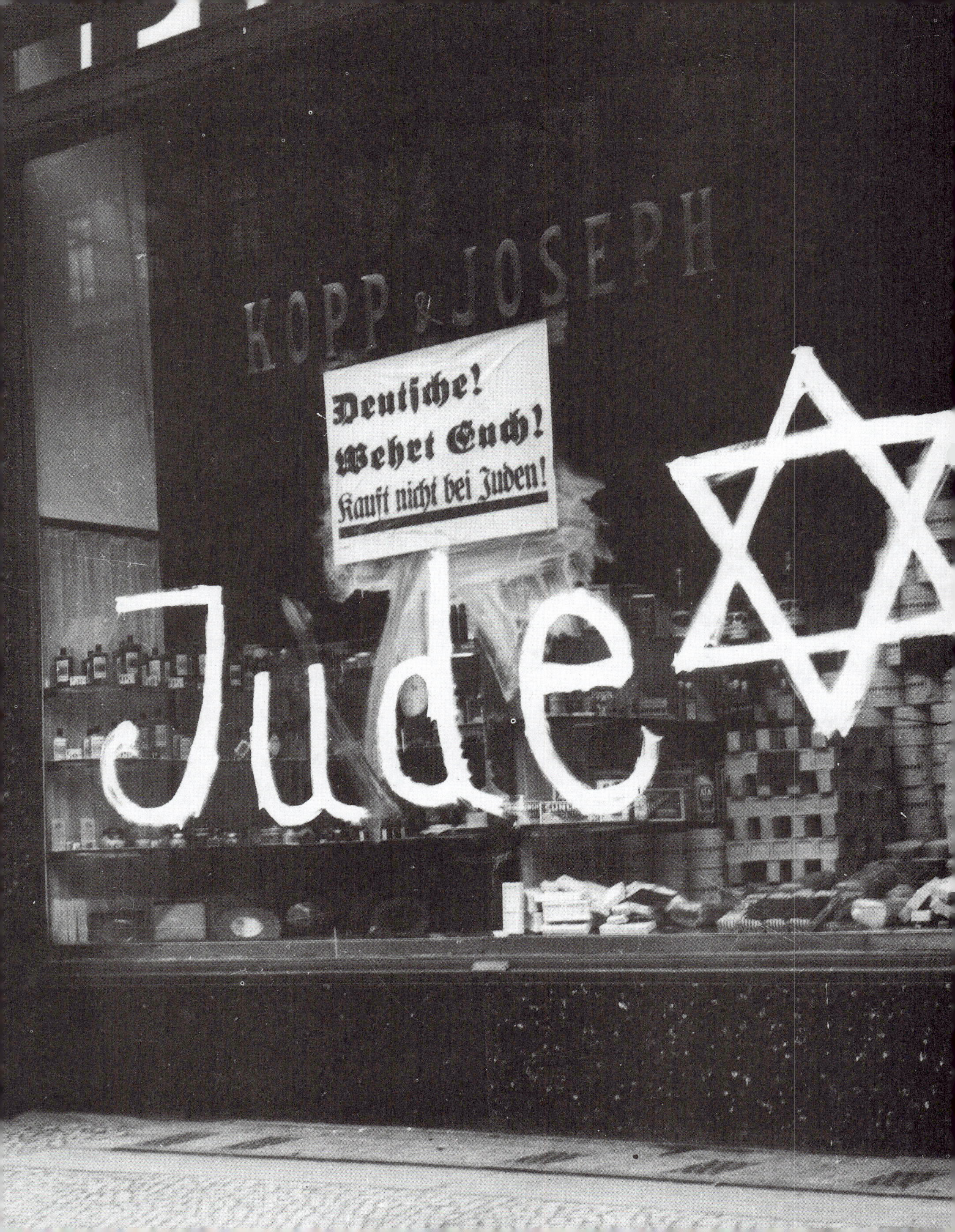
KOPP & JOSEPH
Deutsche!
Wehrt Euch!
Kauft nicht bei Juden!
Jude

CHAPTER ONE

—

HELPED INTO POWER

Near what was the East Prussian town of Rastenburg and is now the Polish town of Ketrzyn lies a tangled mass of reinforced concrete hidden in a forest. Today, in this remote part of eastern Poland near the border with Russia, it is hard to imagine a place more distant from the heart of power. But if you had stood on this spot in the autumn of 1941 you would have been inside the command centre of one of the most powerful men in history – Adolf Hitler. His soldiers stood on the beaches of Brittany and in the wheatfields of Ukraine. More than 100 million Europeans, who only months previously had lived in sovereign states, were now under his rule. In Poland one of the most bestial ethnic rearrangements of all time was in full swing. And, transcending all of this in evil, Hitler had just conspired with Heinrich Himmler to order the elimination of an entire people – the Jews. The decisions Hitler took in this now-ruined concrete city touched all our lives and shaped the course of the second half of the twentieth century – all for the worse.

How was it possible that a cultured nation at the heart of Europe ever allowed this man and the Nazi Party he led to come to power? Knowing as we do the suffering and destruction the Nazis were to bring to the world, the idea that Adolf Hitler could have become Chancellor of Germany in 1933 by constitutional means seems today almost incomprehensible.

One popular way of explaining the Nazis' rise to power is through the character of Hitler. No human being's personality has been more discussed; there are more than twice as many biographies of Hitler than of Churchill. The Nazis themselves pursued this biographical route to extremes in their own search for

Left: One of a series of portraits of Hitler taken by the photographer Heinrich Hoffmann. This one is dated 1938, when Hitler was 49 years old.

an explanation of their success. Hitler's own disciples in the Nazi Party concluded that he was not a mere mortal but a superman. 'Hitler is lonely. So is God. Hitler is like God,' said Hans Frank, Reich Minister of Justice, in 1936. Julius Streicher, a Nazi with a particular fondness for hyperbole, went further: 'It is only on one or two exceptional points that Christ and Hitler stand comparison, for Hitler is far too big a man to be compared with one so petty.' A new prayer was read in German kindergartens in the 1930s: 'Dear Führer, we love you like our fathers and mothers. Just as we belong to them so we belong to you. Take unto yourself our love and trust, O Führer!'

This is the explanation of the Nazi rise to power that Josef Goebbels, the Nazi propaganda minister, wanted the whole world to have. (He himself asked of Hitler after reading *Mein Kampf* (My Struggle): 'Who is this man? half plebeian, half god! Truly Christ, or only St John?') In the Nazi version of history, Hitler, the man of destiny, came to power in Germany in much the same way as Christ came to save the world two thousand years ago. In both cases their careers were pre-determined by their superhuman destiny. This reasoning, although seldom taken to this superhuman extreme, is still popular in some quarters today as an explanation of how the Nazis came to power. It fits with the desire many people have to understand the past simply in terms of the story of 'great men' who carve the world to their will regardless of the circumstances around them. There is just one problem with this as an answer to the question 'How did the Nazis come to power?' – it's wrong.

The Nazi Party took part in the German general election of May 1928. Hitler had then been leader of the party for nearly seven years. The German people had by now had ample opportunity to witness his superhuman qualities and to fall under his hypnotic spell. In that election the Nazi Party polled precisely 2.6 per cent of the popular vote. In a secret Reich report of 1927 there is, in the context of the time, a sensible judgement on the Nazis; the Nazi Party has, according to this report, 'no noticeable influence on the great masses of the population'. Thus the idea of Hitler having hypnotic or quasi-divine influence on the Germans regardless of circumstance is nonsense. Of course, Hitler was an extraordinary individual and his impact on events should not be underestimated, but the content of his character is not a sufficient explanation either for how the Nazis came to exist or for how they went on to gain power. The reality is that Hitler and the Nazis were just as much trapped in the circumstances of their time as we all are. Regardless of who Hitler was, only with the collaboration, weakness, miscalculation and tolerance of others could the Nazis come to power. Indeed, without a crisis that shook the world, the Nazi Party would not even have been born in the first place.

When Germany surrendered and World War I ended in November 1918, there were those in the German Army who couldn't understand why this disaster had happened. 'We did wonder,' says German war veteran Herbert Richter, 'because we didn't feel beaten at all. The front-line troops didn't feel themselves

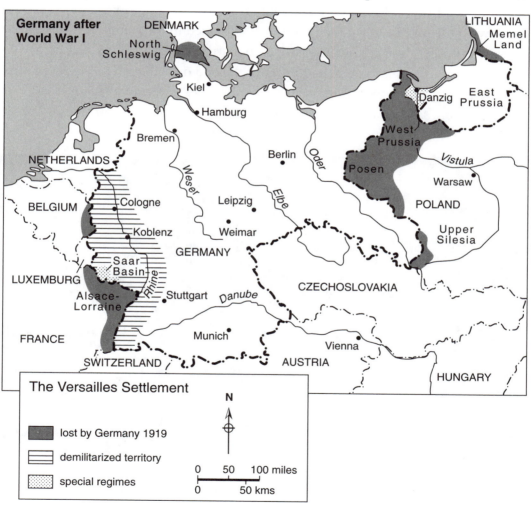

Germany after World War I

The Versailles Settlement

- ▓ lost by Germany 1919
- ▤ demilitarized territory
- ░ special regimes

N

0   50   100 miles
0   50 kms

beaten, and we were wondering why the armistice was happening so quickly, and why we had to vacate all our positions in such a hurry, because we were still standing on enemy territory and we thought all this was strange.' Herbert Richter's memory of how he and his friends felt about the surrender is still vivid: 'We were angry because we did not feel we had come to the end of our strength.' This anger was to have dangerous consequences. Those who felt it quickly looked around to blame someone for the sudden and, to them, suspicious circumstances of the armistice. The myth of the 'stab in the back' grew – the idea that while German soldiers had been laying down their lives, others, behind the lines, back in the Fatherland, were betraying them. Who were these 'others'? They were the politicians of the Left who had agreed to the humiliating armistice in November 1918 – the so-called 'November criminals'. Germany had turned to democracy for the first time in its history at the end of 1918, and to the politicians it was obvious that continuing the war was pointless – Germany must lose. But many soldiers saw it differently; to them the circumstances of Germany's defeat in November 1918 brought only shame and dishonour.

Left-wing demonstration in Munich in February 1919. The socialist (and Jewish) politician Kurt Eisner is the prominent figure in hat and beard to the left of the red flag. He was assassinated a few days later.

In Bavaria, part of southern Germany, this feeling of betrayal was keenly felt among many of the returning soldiers and civilians on the right of the political spectrum. Munich, the capital of Bavaria, was in political chaos in 1919. The socialist politician Kurt Eisner was assassinated in February and this led to the Räterepublik (the councils republic), eventually a Communist government of Bavaria, in April 1919. In the violence and disorder of that spring the military forces of the Right, in part consisting of Freikorps troops (armed mercenaries supported by the government) brutally suppressed the Communists in Munich on 1 and 2 May. The very existence of this final, Communist-led, government of Munich made it plain to many in this traditionally conservative part of Germany that their fear of Communism was well founded. 'Long Live the World Revolution!' ends one of the pamphlets from this period by the Communist Party of Germany – just one of the many pieces of propaganda that fed the Right's paranoia and created an atmosphere in which radical parties opposed to the Communists could flourish.

There was another, more sinister, reason why the Munich Räterepublik was to have a lasting effect on the consciousness of the Right. The majority of the leaders of this left-wing coup were Jewish. This served to reinforce the prejudice that the Jews were behind all that was wrong in Germany. Rumours spread of how Jews had shirked their war service and of how it had been a Jew in the government – Walther Rathenau – who had deviously inspired the humiliating armistice. Even now, so the lies continued, German Jews were selling the country out as part of a worldwide conspiracy organized by international Jewry.

These lies were effective partly, and ironically, because there were surprisingly few Jews actually living in Germany. In June 1933 they numbered only 503,000, a mere 0.76 per cent of the population, and, unlike the Jewish populations of other European countries, such as Poland, they were relatively assimilated into the general population. Paradoxically, this worked in the German anti-Semites' favour, for in the absence of large numbers of flesh and blood Jews, a fantasy image of Jewishness could be spread in which the Jews became symbolic of everything the Right disliked about post-war Germany. 'Politically it was very easy for lots of people to focus upon the Jew,' says Professor Christopher Browning. 'The Jew became a symbol for left-wing politics, for exploitative capitalism, for avant-garde cultural kinds of

experimentation, for secularization, all the things that were disturbing a fairly large sector of the conservative part of the political spectrum. The Jew was the ideal political buzz-word.'

German Jews had been the victims of prejudice for hundreds of years and banned from many walks of life. Not until the latter half of the nineteenth century were they free even to own land and farm it. Germany after World War I was a country in which anti-Semitism was still common. Eugene Leviné, a German Jew brought up in Berlin in the 1920s, suffered as a child simply because he was

Eugene Leviné, the Communist leader of the Räterepublik. He was executed in June 1919.

The boy holding the red flag is his son, also called Eugene.

Jewish. Until he was four or five he used to play with other, non-Jewish children; then, when their older brothers came home, they began to say, 'Dirty little Jew, you can't play here, you've got to go.' 'The other children were quite sad,' says Eugene Leviné, 'but these boys were already full of anti-Semitism. Once, one of the bigger boys beat me up, and as a 6-year-old you're not much match for a 14-year-old.' Other than that brutal experience, the anti-Semitism he experienced had a bizarre ritual to it: 'In any new school in the first mid-morning break

Previous pages: A Freikorps detachment march into Munich in 1919. Even though the Nazi Party was not yet in existence, many wear swastikas on their arm – a traditional right-wing emblem that pre-dated the Nazis.

somebody would pick on you because you were a Jew and see what you were made of, and you'd have a fight. And if you could fight back – you didn't even have to win – but if you could fight back adequately, they'd leave you alone.'

Yet one must be careful not to be guilty of overstatement. As everyone knows the reality of Auschwitz, it is all too simple to leap to the conclusion that at this time Germany was a uniquely anti-Semitic country. It wasn't. While anti-Semitism existed, it was generally, in the words of Eugene Leviné, 'not the kind of anti-Semitism that would get people to burn synagogues'. Tragically, given what was to happen in Germany under the Nazis, a number of Jews fled from Poland and Russia to Germany after World War I partly in order to *escape* anti-Semitism at home. These 'eastern Jews' tended to be less assimilated than other German Jews, and so attracted more anti-Semitism. Bernd Linn, who later became an SS officer, grew up in Germany in the early 1920s and his anti-Semitism was fed by what he perceived as the 'foreign' behaviour of the 'eastern Jews' in his father's shop: 'We had many Jewish customers. They took so many liberties. After all, they were our guests and they didn't behave as such. The difference was obvious between them and the long-settled Jews with whom we did have a good relationship. But all those eastern Jews that came in, they didn't get along at all with the western Jews, the settled ones. And how they behaved in the shop, that increased my antagonism all the more.' Bernd Linn happily confessed to us that as a child he threw fireworks at the Jews in the school playground and, in one trick which was a personal favourite, he and his schoolmates would post pretend one-way tickets to Jerusalem through Jewish letterboxes.

Fridolin von Spaun was old enough, immediately after World War I, to have joined one of the Freikorps. Like Bernd Linn, he too was to support the Nazi Party and he too had a personal problem with Jews. 'If the Jews had brought us something beautiful, that would have been OK,' he says. 'But they cheated us. When they make a fortune they go bankrupt and disappear with their pockets full. So I find it very natural that a generally anti-Jewish attitude became widespread.' Fridolin von Spaun goes on to add, without irony: 'Throughout my life I've had a lot to do with Jews, even as a child, and I must make this personal reproach to the Jews: among all those people whom I have met, not one has become my friend. Why? Not because of me. I had nothing against them. I always noticed they only want to use me. And that annoyed me. That is, I am not anti-Semitic. They are simply not my cup of tea.'

Eugene Leviné's reaction to all this is straightforward: 'I can't be very outraged by something that is so pointlessly unreasonable. To say it's unjust is to give it too much pride. It's a form of ignorance, isn't it? If two people have the same fault, then if it's a Jew they say, "Well typical – what would you expect. Bloody Jews." And if it's an Englishman, you say, "That's odd, that's not the English way of behaving." There are, after all, a hundred stories about this very attitude. About how the anti-Semite says, "This is another outrage by the Jews, and quite apart from that you Jews sank the *Titanic*." And the Jew says, "But excuse me, that's ridiculous, the *Titanic* was sunk by an iceberg." And he says, "Iceberg, Greenberg, Goldberg, you Jews are all the same."'

Against this background, on 12 September 1919, a 30-year-old German Army corporal called Adolf Hitler walked into a meeting of the German Workers' Party in the Veterans' Hall of the Sterneckerbräu beer hall in Munich. Hitler had been sent to observe the party by Captain Mayr, head of press and propaganda in the Bavarian section of the army. At the meeting Hitler turned on one speaker who was calling for the secession of Bavaria from Germany and, showing an immediate rhetorical gift, demolished his arguments. Anton Drexler, a locksmith, who had founded the right-wing party only nine months previously, immediately asked Hitler to join.

Who was this man who walked into history that night at the Sterneckerbräu? Nothing in his first thirty years had marked him out as anything more than an oddball. A failure at school, a failure in Vienna where he had been rejected by the Academy of Graphic Arts, his only success in life had been as a soldier in World War I where his bravery had won him an Iron Cross First Class.

Sources for Hitler's life before that meeting in the Sterneckerbräu are sketchy. One of the chief ones is Hitler's own writing, dating from 1924, in *Mein Kampf*. Here he writes how, as he travelled through Vienna before World War I, 'I began to see Jews, and the more I saw the more sharply they became distinguished in my eyes from the rest of humanity…Was there any form of filth or profligacy, particularly in cultural life, without at least one Jew involved in it?' These familiar words confirm the idea Hitler wanted us to have – that here was a human being who had been set in his anti-Semitic views from the first. But is it true? Some of the most intriguing new work on Hitler's time in Vienna has recently been completed by Dr Brigitte Hamann. She set herself the task of minutely checking the registration details of the people with whom Hitler had come into contact at the Viennese men's hostel where he lodged. This led her to a startling conclusion: 'The picture which Hitler gives of Vienna in *Mein Kampf* is not correct. He says he became an anti-Semite in Vienna, but if you check the contemporary sources closely, you see that, on the contrary, he was very good friends with very many, extraordinarily many Jews, both in the men's hostel and through his contact with the dealers who sold his pictures.' She found that none of those many Jews with whom Hitler had good relations during his time in Vienna said that he was an anti-Semite in the period before 1913. Indeed, says Dr Hamann, Hitler 'preferred' selling his paintings to Jewish dealers 'because they took risks'.

Jews demonstrating in Vienna in 1911. The image of Orthodox Jews like this stayed in Hitler's mind and was recalled by him in *Mein Kampf* (1924).

This is an important discovery. It demonstrates that Hitler, far from being the certain, quasi-divine individual he wanted us to think he was, had actually been buffeted around by circumstances as much as anyone else. In Vienna, according to Dr Hamann, Hitler 'didn't harm anybody, he was law-abiding, he painted fairly good paintings to make ends meet. He was an innocuous person.' The events that turned this 'innocuous person' into the Hitler which history was to know were the same events that traumatized the rest of Germany – World War I and its immediate aftermath. After his time in Vienna, in order to make sense of the new circumstances around him, Hitler, according to Dr Hamann, remembered the prophecies of the rabid Austrian anti-Semites and began spouting them himself.

A common thread in almost all of Hitler's political philosophy is theft. Most often he simply stole his arguments from others. But perhaps he knew that a 'great man' does not steal ideas, something which led him to place the origins of his vicious anti-Semitism in Vienna rather than in the commonplace feelings of betrayal and hatred felt by millions in 1918 and 1919.

Hitler falsified his own early history in other ways. Once he became famous, he was eager to show that he had been one of the earliest members of the German Workers' Party – member number seven. The fact that Hitler had been party member number seven was expressed to us by a number of former Nazis, proud of the fact that the Führer had been in at the start, shaping the fledgling Nazi Party from the very beginning. But it's not true. Anton Drexler wrote a letter of complaint to Hitler in January 1940: 'Nobody knows better than yourself, my Führer, that you were never the seventh member of the party, but at best the seventh member of the committee when I asked you to step in as propaganda representative. A few years ago I was forced to complain

Hitler's membership card for the German Workers' Party, numbered 555.

about this at a party meeting, that your first German Workers' Front card which carried Shüssler's and my own signature had been falsified, whereby the number 555 had been deleted and the number seven inserted…How much better and more valuable it would be for posterity if the course of history had been portrayed as it really had happened.'

However, during 1919 Hitler discovered he did have one genuine and original talent – a gift for public speaking. So effective was he at the kind of rabble-rousing speeches then necessary to distinguish one far-right party from another that the German Workers' Party began to grow in membership. One of the earliest to join was Ernst Röhm, a Reichswehr (German Army) captain, who rapidly came to recognize the crowd-pulling attraction of Hitler's personality. Röhm was a man who liked action. 'Since I am an immature and wicked man,' he said, 'war and unrest appeal to me more than good bourgeois order.' The party Hitler wanted could use a thug

Captain Ernst Röhm, who was to lead the Nazi Storm Troopers.

like Röhm. 'Brutality is respected,' Röhm once stated. 'The people need wholesome fear. They want to fear something. They want someone to frighten them and make them shudderingly submissive.'

Within two years of joining the German Workers' Party Hitler had become its most valuable asset. His speeches attracted new members and his personality began to shape its growth. After a power struggle within the party in August 1921, Hitler emerged victorious, confirmed as the absolute ruler of the renamed National Socialist German Workers' Party, or Nazis for short (a change of name made in February 1920 in an attempt to appeal both to nationalists and socialists). From the first this was a party that traded less in detailed political manifestos than emotional commitment, rejecting democracy, preaching revolution. 'I joined

Hermann Göring in the early 1920s before his
looks were ruined by over-indulgence.

the party because I was a revolutionary,' Hermann Göring was later to say, 'not because of any ideological nonsense.' The mission of the party was and would remain plain – to right the wrongs done to Germany at the end of World War I, to punish those responsible and to 'annihilate the Marxist world view'.

In terms of this general policy there was little to distinguish the embryonic Nazi Party from the host of other small, extreme right-wing groups that flourished in the turmoil of post-World War I politics in southern Germany. The first party programme, presented on 24 February 1920, was a mish-mash of vague economic promises intended to protect the middle class and small businesses, coupled with a clear commitment to exclude Jews from full German citizenship. In none of this was the party unusual. Indeed, in its published programme of action it did not go as far as some other right-wing groups of the time. In the *Marktbreiter Wochenblatt*, the party newspaper of the German Protection and Defiance League, there appeared the following statement: 'It is absolutely necessary to kill the Jews.' Another pamphlet read: 'What shall we do with the Jews? Don't be afraid of the slogan "No violent anti-Semitism" because only through violence can the Jews be driven away.'

The symbols of the young Nazi Party were as unoriginal as its ideas. The swastika was already popular with other German right-wing groups before it was adopted by the Nazis. The skull and crossbones, which would become infamous on the caps of the SS, had been used by the German cavalry. Even the stiff-armed Roman salute was taken from the greeting used by Mussolini's Fascists.

In one respect, however, the Nazi Party was different. Though these were violent times, this was, from the first, an exceptionally violent movement. In 1921 'Storm Detachments' were formed from the innocuously named 'Gymnastic and

Sports Section' of the party to protect Nazi meetings and to disrupt the gatherings of rival parties. Battles between Nazi Storm Troopers and the followers of other political parties would be a common feature of German political life until 1933.

Since the Nazis were preaching that they were the 'salvation' to Germany's problems, it followed that their own fortunes would depend on the extent of the difficulties the country faced. The party had been born out of the trauma following the end of World War I and could flourish only in an atmosphere of political instability. Thus the Nazis benefited when a new crisis occurred involving the French. Angry at Germany's failure to keep up with reparation repayments, France sent troops to occupy the Ruhr at the beginning of 1923. For a nation already dismayed by the loss of honour that accompanied the armistice of November 1918 and the harsh terms of the Versailles peace treaty this was a grave humiliation. The German sense of shame was further increased by the behaviour of the French Army of occupation. 'That was when we found out that the French ruled with an iron hand,' says Jutta Rüdiger, the woman who was later to head the BDM, the female equivalent of the Hitler Youth. 'Perhaps they simply wanted their revenge. Revenge is an emotion I do not know at all.' Frau Rüdiger then adds the following assessment of the French; more than ironic given what the Nazis were later to do, but none the less revealing: 'But the French have a slightly different character, don't they? Perhaps there is a tiny bit of sadism there.'

Bernd Linn was 5 years old when he witnessed the French occupation of the Ruhr. As the French soldiers marched past, he stood on the pavement by his grandfather's house, wearing a child's army uniform and carrying a toy gun: 'I turned round and then a Frenchman came and he disarmed me – apparently he needed this for his children. And I felt very hurt.' Bernd Linn, the little boy from whom the French took a child's pop gun, later became a colonel in the SS.

The Ruhr crisis coincided with Germany's massive economic problems – most notoriously, runaway inflation. 'I once paid 4 billion marks for a sausagemeat roll,' says Emil Klein, who attended his first Hitler meeting in 1920. 'And this collapse naturally supported the Hitler movement and helped it grow, because people said, "It can't go on like this!" And then slowly emerged the discussion about the need for a strong man. And this stuff about a strong man grew more and more because democracy achieved nothing.'

Putschists behind a street barrier during the march and demonstration in Munich on 9 November 1923. The young Heinrich Himmler is in the centre of the picture with the moustache and glasses, holding the flag.

In the political crisis caused both by the French occupation and Germany's economic difficulties, the right-wing Bavarian authorities clashed with the government of Gustav Stresemann in Berlin. The central government in Berlin tried to make the Bavarian authorities censor attacks by the Nazi paper, the *Völkischer Beobachter*, on Stresemann and his government. Kahr, the newly appointed state commissioner of Bavaria, refused, as did General von Lossow, the local military commander. In this atmosphere of internal conflict, Hitler attempted to hijack a meeting at the Bürgerbräukeller in Munich at which both Kahr and von Lossow were speaking. Hitler called for a Putsch (national revolution) to overthrow the central government. The Putschists began a march the next morning, intending to press on to Berlin. Emil Klein took part in that Nazi march through Munich; alongside him were Hitler, Göring and Himmler. 'We shone as marchers that day,' he recalls with fervour. 'But then we turned on to the Maximilianstrasse and as I came to the corner of the Residence [the palace of the former kings of Bavaria] we heard the shots ahead. What's going on?'

When confronted with the choice of cooperating in armed revolution or supporting the Bavarian authorities the police made a clear decision; they rejected the Nazis and shots were fired (it is unclear who fired the first shot – the marchers or the police). Thus, the Putschists' march through Munich came to a violent end. 'You asked me what emotions I felt,' says Emil Klein. 'I'd like to say that actually those were the first political emotions that I ever had. The way things can go wrong. That in itself was a blow to me and to many of my comrades. That such a thing could happen.' Hitler, too, was to learn from this experience. From now on the Nazis tried to gain power from within the democratic system.

Hitler, meanwhile, was arrested and his trial began on 26 February 1924. He was charged with high treason and the evidence against him was damning; not only had the Nazis committed armed robbery during the Putsch, but the violent confrontation had resulted in the death of three policemen. But unlike the others implicated in the failed Putsch, such as the World War I hero General Ludendorff, Hitler stood up and took full responsibility for his actions. His speeches to the judges made him known throughout Germany and he became, for the first time, a national figure. 'Gentleman,' Hitler told the court, 'it is not you who pronounce judgment upon us, it is the eternal court of history which will make its

The famous trial of February 1924 in which Hitler stood accused of high treason.
Judge Georg Neithardt is third from the left on the judges' bench.

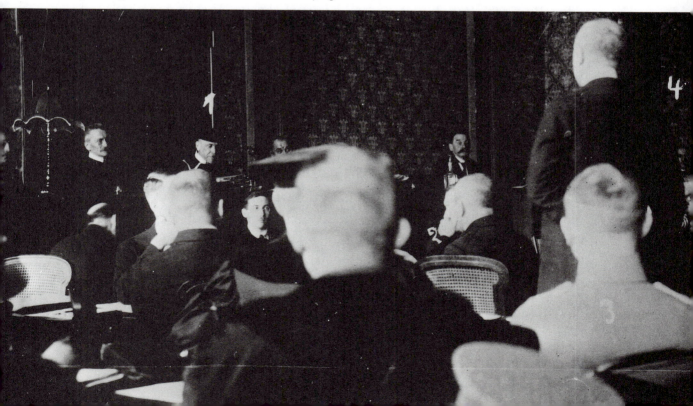

pronouncement upon the charge which is brought against us...You may pronounce us guilty a thousand times, but the goddess who presides over the eternal court of history will with a smile tear in pieces the charge of the Public Prosecutor and the verdict of this court. For she acquits us.' Brave words, but based upon deceit. What the vast majority of Germans did not know at the time was that as Hitler gave that speech he had every reason to suppose that he would be treated extremely leniently by the court, and a man is not courageous when he knows there is virtually no risk. For the judge who presided at the Putsch trial, Georg Neithardt, was the same judge who had sat at another lesser known trial in January 1922. On that occasion the defendants had been accused of violently breaking up a meeting in the Löwenbräu cellar the previous September. They had been charged with the minimum possible offence, breach of the peace, then given the minimum possible sentence, three months in prison. Yet Georg Neithardt wrote to the superior court, saying that he wanted the sentence to be even more lenient, believing that the 'purpose of the imprisonment could be achieved by the imposition of a fine'. One of the defendants at that trial was Adolf Hitler. Judge Neithardt was so taken with him that he managed to press his superiors to allow Hitler's sentence of three months in prison to be commuted to one month in prison with a period on probation. Hitler was standing in front of this selfsame judge during the Putsch trial, a man he knew to be extremely sympathetic to his cause. It was in the courtroom of Georg Neithardt that Hitler made his impassioned speech to the 'eternal court of history'. It is hardly surprising then, that after they came to power the Nazis seized almost all the documents relating to this first trial and burnt them. The sentence in the second, famous case was therefore predictable: five years' imprisonment – the minimum possible – but with the assumption that Hitler would soon be out on probation.

The Bavarian government and its administrators have a great deal to account for. The Nazi Party had been banned in most German states in 1922, but not in Bavaria: there the Nazis were tacitly encouraged. After his conviction for high treason, Hitler was imprisoned in relative comfort at Landsberg Prison, near Munich, where he occupied himself by working on *Mein Kampf*.

While Hitler was in Landsberg, the Nazi Party split into factions. It was only after his release in December 1924 (after serving less than nine months of his five-year sentence) that the party could be put back together again. The Bavarian authorities acted true to form and allowed the party to be refounded on 27 February 1925 at the Bürgerbräukeller in Munich. But by now events in Germany were against the Nazis. The hyper-inflation was over and the future appeared full of hope. The middle years of the 1920s were the Weimar Republic's so-called 'golden' period. But this new prosperity was financed on credit; the German government used borrowed money to pay the Allies their reparations. Still, at the time, everything looked idyllic. The Nazis could never flourish in such sunlight and they were reduced to a tiny rump of fanatical support. Without a crisis to feed on, they were lost. Until the end of the 1920s they were active only at the margins of German political life.

Yet it was during these quiet years that the party evolved structurally into the Nazi Party which was eventually to govern much of Europe. Hitler's position became increasingly secure. He easily brushed away a small internal challenge to his absolute authority in 1926 by a simple appeal to loyalty. The collapse of the party during his absence in prison had demonstrated that it was only his presence as leader that held the movement together.

The Nazis were not a political party in the sense that we today understand the concept. Little in the way of detailed Nazi policy was ever published. A commitment to the Führer (as Hitler became known around this time) and a general belief in the aims of the movement was enough to prove one's loyalty. This was a party not of talk but of action, not of policy but of emotion. As a philosophy, this appealed particularly to the young; research shows that during this period the average age of those joining the party was less than thirty. One young man who joined at the age of twenty-five was a failed novelist called Josef Goebbels. Looking back fondly on the 1920s, after the Nazis had come to power, he spoke emotionally to a group of young people about these years of struggle: 'Then there were young people who wrote the word "Reich" on their banners, against a world of hatred and calumny and malice. They were convinced that a lost war was not enough to push a people into permanent servitude.'

'It was exciting,' says Wolfgang Teubert, who joined the Nazi Storm Troopers in the 1920s. 'There was the comradeship, the being-there-for-each-other, that's for a young man something outstanding – at least it was then.' Something else the party offered a man like Teubert, who wore the Storm Trooper's brown shirt with pride, was a sense of importance. In that shirt he may have been young, but he

Adolf Hitler and followers in 1926, photographed by Heinrich Hoffmann. Already, even
in a supposedly 'naturalistic' picture like this, Hitler sports his 'man of destiny' look.

was still a somebody: 'We marched behind the swastika flag, marching through
the towns. Outside working hours there was nothing but the Storm Troopers.'
And then there was the factor which perhaps appealed most to these youths –
fighting. 'There was the danger, the threats from other people. Night after night
we increasingly provided protection at hall meetings not just in our town but in
many other towns to strengthen the Storm Troopers there. We had no weapons,
the most we could do was defend ourselves with our fists and only work the
enemy over with our fists – where it was necessary. And it was necessary more
often than not!' Teubert and his friends in the Bochum Storm Troopers would
regularly fight the youths of the Communist Party. 'Breaking up the chairs in the

hall and then fighting with the chair legs, that happened quite a lot.' Teubert smiles at the memory. 'Both sides did that, each as much as the other.'

Bruno Hähnel came into the Nazi Party at the same time via another popular route – from the Wandervogel, a 'folklorical' group which sought a return to nature and its values. At weekends, as a young Wandervogel, Herr Hähnel would wander with friends through the countryside. He dates his decision to join the Nazi Party to a discussion evening held in a youth hostel in 1927: 'There was one about the subject of internationalism and among other things it was said that one had to reach the point of being able to marry a Negress. And I found that thought very uncomfortable.' In so far as other reasons influenced Herr Hähnel in his decision to join the Nazi Party, they were the usual negative feelings about Versailles and the 'November criminals' of 1918. As a result, he had a strong 'resistance' to any international movement such as Communism. 'Many of us said simply, "We are Germans first",' says Herr Hähnel, 'and now there was a group who said "Germany first". They shouted, "Germany awake!"'

Recruits like Herr Hähnel were not concerned that they were joining an anti-Semitic party: 'I still remember those statements which frequently occurred, that 50 per cent of all Berlin doctors were Jews, 50 per cent of all Berlin lawyers, that the whole press in Berlin and in Germany was in the hands of the Jews and this had to be done away with.' While tacitly supporting this anti-Semitic idea in principle, Herr Hähnel had no problem in reconciling it with the realities of his own family life: 'I had relatives who were Jews and we would meet at family gatherings. I had a very warm relationship with two cousins who were Jewish. It didn't stop me from agreeing with the other things which the party demanded.'

For other young people at the time, such as Alois Pfaller, this anti-Semitic attitude proved a barrier to joining the Nazis: 'That was something very strange,' he says, 'this extreme anti-Semitism, the Jews being held responsible for everything. I knew Jews and I had friends with whom I used to spend time and I absolutely didn't understand what difference there was supposed to be – we're all humans…I have always stood up for justice – what is just and reasonable, that was my problem, and also fighting injustice, that was my problem, and not somehow persecuting other races or other people.' Alois Pfaller turned his back on the Storm Troopers, but, still looking for a radical solution to the country's problems, he joined the German Communist Party.

Hitler saw his personality as the Nazi Party's greatest strength; he cultivated 'great man' mannerisms, such as staring straight into the eyes of whoever was speaking to him. Fridolin von Spaun remembers just such an encounter with the Führer at a party dinner: 'Suddenly I noticed Hitler's eyes resting on me. So I looked up. And that was one of the most curious moments in my life. He didn't look at me suspiciously, but I felt that he is searching me somehow...It was hard for me to sustain this look for so long. But I thought: I mustn't avert my eyes, otherwise he may think I've something to hide. And then something happened which only psychologists can judge. The gaze, which at first rested completely on me, suddenly went straight through me into the unknown distance. It was so unusual. And the long gaze which he had given me convinced me completely that he was a man with honourable intentions. Most people nowadays would not believe this. They'd say I am getting old and childish, but that's untrue. He was a wonderful phenomenon.'

Hitler had a similar effect on many others. Herbert Richter watched him in 1921 when he walked into a student café behind the university in Munich: 'He was wearing an open-necked shirt and he was accompanied by guards or followers. And I noticed how the people with whom he arrived – there were about three or four of them – how their eyes were fixed on Hitler. For many people there must have been something fascinating about him.' But whatever it was that these others found so entrancing had no effect on Herbert Richter. 'He started to speak and I immediately disliked him. Of course I did not know then what he would later become. I found him rather comical, with his funny little moustache. I was not at all impressed by him.' Nor did Hitler's speaking style have the desired effect: 'He had a kind of scratchy voice,' remembers Herr Richter. 'And he shouted so much. He was shouting in this small room. And what he was saying was really simple. You couldn't say much against it. He mostly criticized the Versailles Treaty – how it had to be set aside.'

Aldous Huxley wrote, 'The propagandist is a man who canalizes an existing stream. In a land where there is no water he digs in vain.' Hitler was no exception to this rule. To those like Herbert Richter, who were sophisticated in their political judgements, he seemed a comical character who spoke the obvious. To those who were predisposed to believe in such solutions, he was a 'wonderful phenomenon'. It is all too easy in retrospect for Hitler's charisma and speaking

Left: A formal portrait of Hitler by Hoffmann from the mid-1920s. Many supporters remarked on the power of Hitler's stare, a trick he attempts to pull on the camera here.

talents to be used as an excuse. 'He hypnotized a nation' it has often been suggested. No, he didn't. A hypnotist does not make speeches which convince only those who like what they hear, as Hitler did.

The Nazis prided themselves on the fact that their party lacked democratic principles. (After all, had democracy not been brought in by the 'November criminals' and produced Versailles?) Towering over the structure of the party was the figure of Adolf Hitler. Unlike other political organizations, which relied on committees or policy discussions, in the Nazi Party only Hitler could arbitrate – he was the only man capable of making a final decision. Even in embryonic form, a dictator-led party like this should have collapsed under the weight of work the leader had to shoulder. Yet not only was Hitler not deluged with the burden of decision-making but, paradoxically, he seems scarcely to have been stretched by administrative tasks at all. An understanding of the reason for this apparent paradox gives an insight into not just how the Nazi Party was structured, but why it was so attractive to the young. For Hitler relied heavily on his own interpretation of the work of one dead Englishman to tell him how to govern the party – Charles Darwin.

'The idea of struggle is as old as life itself,' Hitler said in a speech at Kulmbach on 5 February 1928. 'In this struggle the stronger, the more able, win while the less able, the weak, lose. Struggle is the father of all things…It is not by the principles of humanity that man lives or is able to preserve himself above the animal world, but solely by means of the most brutal struggle.' Hitler sought to apply the Darwinian theory of the survival of the fittest to human action. 'God does not act differently,' he said over dinner on 23 September 1941. 'He suddenly hurls the masses of humanity on to the earth and he leaves it to each one to work out his own salvation. Men dispossess one another, and one perceives that, at the end of it all, it is always the stronger who triumphs. Is not that the most reasonable order of things? If it were otherwise, nothing good would ever have existed. If we did not respect the laws of nature, imposing our will by the right of the stronger, a day would come when the wild animals would once again devour us – then the insects would eat the wild animals and finally nothing would exist on the earth but microbes.'

It should be no surprise, then, to learn that Hitler ran the Nazi Party according to pseudo-Darwinian theory. When Gustav Seifert wrote to Nazi

Party HQ and asked to be reappointed as leader of its Hanover branch, he received this reply, dated 27 October 1925, from Max Amann, editor of the Nazi paper the *Völkischer Beobachter*: 'Herr Hitler takes the view on principle that it is not the job of the party leadership to "appoint" party leaders. Herr Hitler is today more than ever convinced that the most effective fighter in the National Socialist movement is the man who wins respect for himself as leader through his own achievements. You yourself say in your letter that almost all the members follow you. Then why don't you take over the leadership of the branch?' Why don't you *'take over'*? What command could be more exciting to a young man? If you don't like it, change it, don't come to us for orders, if you are stronger than your enemies, you'll win. Equally, if you aren't stronger than your enemies and you lose, then that's simply the way it should be. Such a mindset helps to explain the bizarre utterings of Hitler towards the end of the war when he remarked that Germany 'deserved' her fate at the hands of the Soviet Union.

When the Nazis came to power, Goebbels' film propaganda hammered the same point home – the fittest should thrive and the weak should perish. In one of his later propaganda films, scientists are shown filming an experiment in which two stag beetles are fighting each other. The laboratory technician expresses some doubts about what she sees. 'It is a shame really,' she says to her professor, 'to catch these beautiful, strong animals for a fight between life and death. And to think back in the forest they could have a quiet life.' 'But my dear,' the professor tells her, 'there is no such thing as a quiet life anywhere in nature…They all live in a constant struggle, in the course of which the weak perish. We regard this struggle as completely natural, but we would think it unnatural if a cat lived peacefully with a mouse or a fox with a hare.'

In any attempt to understand the ideology of Nazism the significance of such views can scarcely be understated. Nazi ideology placed man as an animal with an animal's values. The bully who wins *ought* to win if he is stronger. The child who dies *ought* to die if he is weak. If one country is stronger than another, it *ought* to conquer its neighbour. Traditional values, like compassion and respect for the law, are nothing but man-made shields behind which the weak can cower and protect themselves from the fate that is naturally theirs. (It was no accident that the two professions Hitler hated above all others were lawyers and priests.) The Nazis were first and foremost a racist party who believed that nation states, just like individuals, were locked in a permanent amoral struggle to see who should govern the largest portion of the Earth.

However, if Hitler had been applying his Darwinian theory to the Nazi Party in 1928, he should have despaired, for in the general election of that year the Nazis polled only 2.6 per cent of the vote. Germany did not want them because it saw no need for them – yet. Shortly after the election, the economic and political situation in Germany radically changed. First an agricultural depression hit home and then the Wall Street Crash triggered the most serious economic crisis ever encountered in Germany, as the United States called in its loans.

Unemployment started to grow and the effects were deep and bitter. 'In those days,' remembers Bruno Hähnel, 'our unemployed would stand in huge queues in front of the labour exchange every Friday, and they would receive 5 marks at the counter. This was a new and different situation – there were many who simply didn't have the means to buy food.' 'It was a hopeless business,' recalls Alois Pfaller. 'People walked around with spoons in their pockets because they got a meal for 1 mark [from the charity soup kitchens].'

The suffering hit middle-class families, such as Jutta Rüdiger's: 'My father did not become unemployed but he was told he had to agree to work for a lower salary.' Jutta Rüdiger thought she would have to 'kiss goodbye' to the chance of going to university, until a kindly uncle stepped in and gave her an allowance. A family experience like the Rüdigers' would not have appeared on any unemployment statistic, yet they suffered and feared further suffering. As German unemployment grew in the early 1930s to over 5 million, the longing for a radical solution to the nation's economic troubles was not confined to the unemployed – it also extended to millions of middle-class families like the Rüdigers.

The election of September 1930 was a breakthrough for the Nazi Party: their share of the vote increased to 18.3 per cent. Just as worrying for those looking for a life without conflict was the increase in the German Communist Party's vote from 10.6 per cent to 13.1 per cent. Germany seemed to be splitting towards the extremes. With a Reichstag (Parliament) in which the Nazis and Communists were now heavily represented, the German Chancellor, Heinrich Brüning, began to bypass it and issue emergency decrees, signed by President Hindenburg under Article 48 of the Constitution, in order to govern Germany. German democracy

German jobless in Hanover in the early 1930s. These men are not wastrels –
look at the shine on their shoes – yet they are full of despair.

did not suddenly die with the arrival of Hitler; it began its slow death under Brüning.

Social unrest grew along with unemployment. 'You had to sign on every day at the dole office,' remembers Alois Pfaller. 'Everybody met there, the Nazi people, the SPD [German Socialist Party], the Communists – and then the discussions would start and the fights.' Gabriele Winckler gives a young woman's perspective: 'You felt uneasy when you crossed the road, you felt uneasy when you were alone in the woods and so on. The unemployed lay in the ditches and played cards.' In this atmosphere of danger and despair Jutta Rüdiger heard Hitler speak for the first time: 'There was a huge crowd and you got the feeling that he was aiming for electrifying tension. Today, I can probably only explain it with the poverty the people had been suffering and were suffering…In that context Hitler with his statements seemed to be the bringer of salvation. He said, "I will get you out of this misery, but you all have to join in." And everybody understood that.'

During this period the Nazis developed new forms of propaganda to push their message across – famously the 'Hitler over Germany' presidential campaign of April 1932, which saw Hitler speak to twenty-one meetings in seven days, travelling between them by light aircraft. But the importance of Nazi propaganda should not be overstated. Academic research conducted by Dr Richard Bessel shows that in the district of Neidenburg in East Prussia, where the Nazi Party did not build a firm organizational base until 1931, the Nazi vote still increased over the three years leading up to that time. In May 1928 the Nazis received only 360 votes (2.3 per cent) but this increased to 3831 (25.8 per cent) in September 1930. The voters of Neidenburg did not vote Nazi because they were entranced by Hitler or swamped with Nazi propaganda; they supported the Nazis because they wanted fundamental change.

Hitler was open about the nature of the change the Nazis intended to bring to German political life once they gained power. In a speech he gave on 27 July 1932 at Eberswalde in Brandenburg he openly wallowed in his contempt for democracy: 'The workers have their own parties,' he said, 'and not just one, that wouldn't be enough. There have to be at least three or four. The bourgeoisie, which is more intelligent, needs even more parties. The middle classes have to have their party. The economy has its party, the farmer his own party, and here

Left: A clear illustration of the split in German politics in the early 1930s with swastika banners flying from the same block of flats as the Communists' hammer and sickle. The only policy both Communists and Nazis had in common was their commitment to end democracy in Germany.

again three or four of them. And the house-owners also have to have their particular political and philosophical interests represented by a party. And the tenants can't stay behind, of course. And the Catholics too, their own party, and even the Württembergers have a special party – thirty-four in one little land. And this at a time when before us lie the greatest tasks, which can only be undertaken if the strength of the whole nation is put together. The enemy accuses us National Socialists, and me in particular, of being intolerant and quarrelsome. They say that we do not want to work with other parties…So is it typically German to have thirty parties? I have to admit one thing: the gentlemen are quite right. We are intolerant. I have given myself one aim: to sweep the thirty parties out of Germany.'

This speech illustrates a crucial point – Hitler and the Nazis wanted a revolution in Germany and they were open in saying what they planned. In this the Nazis had common cause with the German Communist Party; both thought that democracy had failed. Democracy, after all, was relatively new in Germany; its arrival had virtually coincided with the disastrous peace settlement of Versailles, and in the early 1930s democracy appeared to many to be responsible both for the continuing crippling reparation payments and for massive unemployment. Incredible as it may seem to us today, by 1932 the majority of the German people, in supporting either the Communists or the Nazis, were voting for political parties openly committed to the overthrow of German democracy. Most of them, having seen what democracy had delivered, felt that it was time not just for another party to be given a chance, but for another *system*.

On 30 May 1932 Brüning resigned as Chancellor after losing Hindenburg's support. The aristocratic Franz von Papen was appointed Chancellor on 1 June, but his government immediately ran into problems; at the Reichstag elections held on 31 July the Nazis gained 37.4 per cent of the vote and won 230 seats. They were now the biggest party in the Reichstag. Hitler claimed the right to be Chancellor and saw President Hindenburg to press his claim on 13 August 1932. Otto Meissner, chief of the Reich Chancellery, described what happened: 'Hindenburg declared that he recognized Hitler's patriotic conviction and selfless intentions, but given the atmosphere of tension and his responsibility before God and the German people, he could not bring himself to give government power to a single party which did not represent the majority of the electorate, and which,

Von Papen, wearing a top hat and the Iron Cross, shortly before he lost the Chancellorship in November 1932. He was about to play a key part in helping Hitler to the Chancellorship. On his right is Otto Meissner, Chief of the Reich Chancellery.

furthermore, was intolerant, lacking in discipline and frequently even appeared violent. In foreign affairs, it was of the utmost importance to proceed extremely cautiously and to allow matters to mature. We should at all cost avoid conflicts with other states. As far as domestic affairs were concerned, any widening of the chasm between the opposing sides must be prevented and all powers should be concentrated in order to alleviate economic disaster.'

Given what we know happened once Hitler did gain power, Hindenburg's concerns about him and the Nazis have a prophetic ring to them. Such sentiments clearly show that the aged President knew the dangers Germany faced under Hitler's Chancellorship. So that could have been that; Hitler's political demands had been crushingly rejected. Yet five months later, and at a time when the Nazi Party, wracked by internal crisis, had lost many votes in the November Reichstag election, Hitler was made Chancellor by the selfsame President Hindenburg. Why? The Nazi Party's popularity appeared to have peaked in the summer of 1932. Its support was inherently unstable, the party held together more by emotion and notions of its leader's charisma than by any coherent manifesto of concrete policy. Its rapid growth in popularity owed much to the crisis in which Germany found herself and over which the Nazis had no control. If the German economy began to pick up, success could vanish as rapidly as it had appeared, and the signs were that the economy *was* about to improve given the political agreement at the Lausanne conference in June 1932 that effectively ended German reparation payments.

At the elections in November 1932 the Nazi Party vote dropped from 37 per cent to 33 per cent. Goebbels had seen the danger to the party when he wrote in his diary the previous April: 'We must come to power in the foreseeable future. Otherwise we'll win ourselves to death in elections.' (This failure in the November elections of 1932 was, as Dr Bessel points out, despite a massive propaganda effort – yet more evidence that the 'party's fortunes were not determined primarily by its propaganda'.) The party was in financial trouble, the seemingly endless round of elections having shaken its finances. Worse, Gregor Strasser, leader of the north German wing of the Nazis, resigned amid emotional scenes on 7 December 1932. Strasser had been offered the Vice-Chancellorship by the new Chancellor, General von Schleicher (who had succeeded von Papen on 2 December 1932), but Hitler had insisted he turn the offer down. Strasser did so but quit politics after giving a stinging indictment of Hitler's intransigence in holding out for the chancellorship. It appeared that Hitler might lose control of a Nazi Party that was nervy and on edge. (Hitler never forgave Strasser for his 'treachery' and he was murdered on the 'Night of the Long Knives' on 30 June 1934.)

In parallel with these developments was a series of events which persuaded the aged President Hindenburg to change his mind and appoint Hitler. In November 1932 Hjalmar Schacht, the former head of the Reichsbank, was one of a number of financiers and industrialists (though few apart from Schacht were prominent figures) who signed a petition to President Hindenburg asking him to appoint Hitler as Chancellor. The letter was respectful but clearly influenced by the fact that the November 1932 elections showed another increase in the Communist vote; many of Germany's industrial élite may have disliked the Nazis but they feared the Communists above all. Equally, it was obvious that the aristocratic cabinet of von Papen commanded little public support. 'It is clear,' said the letter, 'that the oft-repeated dissolution of the Reichstag, with the growing number of elections that exacerbate the party struggle, has had a bad effect, not only political, but also on economic calm and stability. But it is also clear that any constitutional change which is not supported by the broadest popular currents will have even worse political, economic and spiritual consequences.' The letter went on to call for the transfer of the political leadership of the Reich to 'the leader of the largest national group'. This was Hitler. Such a course of action 'will arouse the millions of people who today stand at the margins, making of them an affirmative and approving force'.

Hitler and President Hindenburg shortly after Hitler had become Chancellor. A rare picture of Hitler smiling, but then, unlike Hindenburg, he had a lot to smile about.

Hitler had not been a figure whom these people had wanted to embrace in the past, but the economic crisis and huge popular support for the Nazi movement now made them feel that an accommodation must be reached. Key figures on the conservative Right also wanted an authoritarian solution to Germany's problems, and without Hitler no proposal they could initiate would have a base of mass-support. Johannes Zahn, the distinguished German banker, says that since young people at the time were joining either the Storm Troopers or the Communists, those in business preferred the Nazis because of their 'discipline and order'. In addition, 'At the beginning,' he says, 'you really have to say this today, at the beginning, you couldn't tell whether National Socialism was something good with a few bad side-effects, or something evil with a few good side-effects, you couldn't tell.' There was talk of a strategy of 'taming' Hitler. Such a policy was to be enthusiastically proposed by von Papen once he had been forced to step down as Chancellor in favour of General von Schleicher on 2 December 1932.

Then, more worrying news came to Hindenburg. The results of an army war-game, 'Planspiel Ott', were discussed at a cabinet meeting at the start of December 1932. The Armed Forces had examined a number of hypothetical scenarios of civil unrest in an attempt to gauge their ability to respond if called upon during a state of emergency. Major Ott presented their conclusion: '…all preparations have been made to be able to introduce an immediate state of emergency, if ordered. But after careful consideration, it has been shown that the forces of order of the Reich and the Länder [German states] are in no way sufficient to maintain constitutional order against National Socialists and Communists and to protect the borders.' The army was effectively saying it could not control the country if there was a civil war between the Nazis and the Communists. General von Schleicher tried to make the best of it at the cabinet meeting but to no avail: 'Even when Schleicher tried to dampen the effect of what was said at the end by stating that a war-game would always have to be based on a worst-case scenario, and that one would not always have to expect such a worst-case scenario to happen, the deep impression that Ott's discourse made on the cabinet, even on the Chancellor who kept on wiping his eyes during the talk, was unmistakable.'

On 4 January 1933 von Papen and Hitler met at the house of the Cologne banker Kurt von Schröder to discuss the way forward. It was the first of a series of meetings which led to von Papen agreeing that he would push for Hitler's appointment as Chancellor, but only on condition that he, von Papen, was made Vice-Chancellor and there were only two other Nazis in the cabinet apart from Hitler (Göring as Minister without Portfolio and acting Prussian Minister of the Interior, and Wilhelm Frick as Reich Minister of the Interior). Hitler agreed. As a result, on 30 January 1933, following these intrigues, and once von Papen's influence on President Hindenburg had finally opened the door, Hitler was appointed Chancellor of Germany.

Bruno Hähnel, a committed Nazi, describes his reaction to the news as 'elation'. But the reaction from the Nazis' political opponents was less straightforward. Josef Felder, a German Socialist Party (SPD) MP at the time, tells how the SPD believed that since Hitler was now the legally chosen Chancellor, then they were the legal opposition; the SPD could carry on as if in a normal, stable democracy. 'We hadn't fully realized what it would mean,' says Herr Felder. 'We believed that we could still control him through Parliament – total lunacy!'

When Eugene Leviné heard the news that Hitler was Chancellor he was concerned less because he was Jewish than because he was a Communist. He remembers that 'there were quite a few Storm Troopers who had Jewish girlfriends and therefore a lot of Germans just thought, "Oh well, it's not going to be so bad – they have Jewish girlfriends they can't hate us all."' He also had personal reasons to suppose that the Nazis were capable of exercising their anti-Semitism with a degree of restraint: 'At one of the schools I was in there was a Nazi and he said to me, "You really should be one of us." I said, "Look, I can't, I'm a Jew," and he would say, "We don't mean you, decent chaps like you will be perfectly all right in the new Germany."'

As for the Communist Party, their attitude to the news of Hitler's Chancellorship was scarcely a call to world revolution: 'It all happened so fast in those days, after one had seen it coming gradually,' says Eugene Leviné. 'The Communist Party line, to which I still belonged, was that it didn't matter if Hitler gets to power. That's good. He'll soon have proved himself incompetent and then it's our turn…For some extraordinary reason they didn't realize that he was going to change the law once he came to power.'

To Alois Pfaller the lesson of Hitler's appointment is clear: 'The danger is always here, when crises are happening, that people come who say they have the wisdom and the answer, and they can bring salvation to everybody.'

Adolf Hitler had come to power legally within the existing constitutional system. Now he was to keep his promise and sweep democracy away.

CHAPTER TWO

—

CHAOS AND CONSENT –
THE NAZI RULE OF GERMANY

In popular mythology there is one quality above all others that the Germans possess – efficiency. Their cars are sold by advertisements that trumpet it ('If only everything in life was as reliable as a Volkswagen'). Their national football team performs with it ('There go the Germans with typical efficiency'). Hardly surprising then, that this one attribute, more than any other, is ascribed to the Nazis. Since efficiency is the one quality that Fascists are popularly supposed to have (Mussolini is alleged to have 'made the trains run on time'), a combination of being German and Fascist ought, so the logic goes, to have produced the most efficient state of all time. The propaganda images of Nazi parades, most famously in Leni Riefenstahl's film *Triumph of the Will* (1936), certainly support this idea. The propaganda confirms that German society, under Nazi rule, was run with clarity and order. But it wasn't.

'The Führer marches alone along the front,' says Dr Günter Lohse, a former Foreign Office official and member of the Nazi Party, talking of these *Triumph of the Will*-type images. 'This is propaganda and it is impressive. They're all standing in one line! But one simply mustn't look behind the scenes. There was no order there – it was total chaos.' Dr Lohse had to deal with liaison between the Foreign Office and other government departments during the 1930s. He estimates that at least 20 per cent of his day was spent fighting the other departments over jurisdiction. One former Foreign Office official, he claims, estimated that 60 per

Left: The crowd at the Olympics in Berlin in August 1936, a picture that could have been taken at any one of a hundred triumphal Nazi parades in the 1930s.

cent of his day was wasted in this way. Many words can be used to describe the Nazi rule of Germany in the 1930s, but 'efficient' isn't one of them.

In the first seventeen months of Hitler's Chancellorship there were plenty of opportunities to see the radical, chaotic and destructive nature of Nazi rule. Once in power, Hitler quickly called new elections, but made it clear that they were simply a vote of confidence; neither the cabinet nor the government would change as a result of them. (Even with bans imposed on newspapers and public meetings attacking the new state, and with thousands of political opponents

Prisoners at the newly opened concentration camp at Dachau outside Munich in 1933.

already rounded up, the Nazis gained only 43.9 per cent of the vote in March 1933 and failed to acquire the absolute majority they had hoped for.) After the Reichstag had been set on fire on the night of 27 February (almost certainly by the Communist sympathizer, Marinus van der Lubbe), there were mass arrests of Communists the next day, and the Reichstag Fire Decree was inaugurated, which suspended indefinitely all personal rights and freedoms. Under its provisions, political prisoners could be held indefinitely in 'protective custody'. In March the

Reichstag passed an Enabling Act, which gave Hitler absolute power. Outside on the streets, according to one Nazi Storm Trooper, there was chaos: 'Everyone is arresting everyone else, avoiding the prescribed official channels, everyone is threatening everyone else with protective custody, everyone is threatening everyone else with Dachau…Every little street cleaner today feels he is responsible for matters which he has never understood.'

In those first months of power the chaotic terror was directed mainly at the Nazis' former political opponents. Josef Felder was an SPD member of the Reichstag who was picked up by the Nazis and taken to the newly built concentration camp at Dachau, outside Munich. He was thrown into a cell and chained to an iron ring, and his Nazi jailers removed the straw palliasse which was lying on the concrete floor, saying: 'You won't be needing this because you'll only be leaving here as a corpse.' The abuse continued as the guard took a rope and demonstrated the best way Felder could use it to hang himself. Felder told him, 'I have a family. I'm not going to do that. You'll have to do it yourselves!' He was eventually released after more than eighteen months in Dachau, having contracted a lung disease.

The pragmatists among the Nazis' political opponents either escaped Germany or tried to conform to the wishes of the new regime; only the exceptional, like Alois Pfaller, tried to resist. In 1934 he tried to re-start his old Communist youth group. It was a heroic act but, against a ruthless regime which singled out Communists as a particular enemy, failure was inevitable. Pfaller was betrayed by a double agent – a woman who worked for both the Communist Party and the Gestapo. He was arrested, taken to a police station and brutally interrogated; his nose was broken and he was beaten unconscious with leather belts: 'And when I came to again, they did it a second time, again unconscious, the fourth time, again unconscious, then they stopped because I hadn't said anything.' Now the interrogation tactics changed. One man sat at a typewriter to take down Pfaller's 'confession', while the other smashed his fist into Pfaller's face every time he failed to answer a question. The interrogation grew worse after the violent policeman sprained his right hand and began using his left. Now he hit Pfaller on the side of the head and split his ear-drum. 'Then I heard an incredible racket,' says Pfaller. 'It was a roaring, as if your head was on the sea-bed, an incredible roaring.' Pfaller resolved to kill the man who was beating him,

Nazi Storm Troopers enjoy themselves by shaving a young Communist's hair, March 1933.

even though it would also mean his own certain death. He had learnt judo when he was young and he intended to stretch out and stick his fingers into his interrogator's eyes. But just as he decided on this course of action, he haemorrhaged. The interrogation stopped and Pfaller was given a bucket and cloth and ordered to clean his own blood off the floor. Then he was taken to a cell for the night and subsequently transferred to a concentration camp. He was not released until 1945.

In a period of history rich in stories of collaboration and weakness, Alois Pfaller's own personal history is uplifting. Here is a man who was tortured to betray his comrades and refused: 'It's a question of honour,' he says. 'I'd have let them beat me to death but I never would have betrayed anyone. I would rather have died miserably.'

Most Germans did not confront the regime. More common was the experience of Manfred Freiherr von Schröder, a banker's son from Hamburg, who welcomed the new regime and joined the Nazi Party in 1933. He thought himself an idealist and believed that 1933 was the beginning of a wonderful new period for Germany: 'Everything was in order again, and clean. There was a feeling of national liberation, a new start.' Like most Germans, von Schröder knew that Socialists and Communists were imprisoned in concentration camps, but he dismisses this as unimportant in the context of history: 'You have never had anything of this kind since Cromwell in England. Closest is the French Revolution, isn't it? To be a French nobleman in the Bastille was not so agreeable, was it? So people said, "Well, this is a revolution; it is an astonishing, peaceful revolution but it is a revolution." There were the concentration camps, but everybody said at that time, "Oh, the English invented them in South Africa with the Boers."' Although these remarks are unacceptably dismissive of the horror of Nazi concentration camps, it should be remembered that the camps which sprang up in 1933 were, for all their horror, not identical to the extermination camps of the Holocaust which were to emerge in 1941. If you were imprisoned in Dachau during the early 1930s, it was probable that you would be released after a brutal stay of about a year. (Alois Pfaller's experience is unusual for a political opponent arrested in 1934, in that he had to endure eleven years in a concentration camp.) On release, former inmates were compelled to sign a paper agreeing never to talk about the experience, on pain of immediate re-entry to the camp. Thus it was possible for Germans to believe, if they wanted to, that concentration camps were 'merely' places designed to shock opponents of the regime into conforming. Since the terror was mostly confined to the Nazis' political opponents, or to Jews, the majority of Germans could watch what Göring called the 'settling of scores' with equanimity, if not pleasure.

On 6 July 1933 Hitler announced that he wanted an end to arbitrary violence on the streets. 'Revolution is not a permanent state,' he declared. He realized that the Storm Troopers posed a threat to the stability of the new Germany. One group of powerful Germans agreed with him wholeheartedly – the army. The professional soldier Johann-Adolf Graf von Kielmansegg remembers: 'One rejected the Storm Troopers because of their behaviour, the way they looked, the way they were…they were hated by most soldiers.' Von Kielmansegg confirms that the regular army believed that Ernst Röhm, leader of the Storm Troopers, was trying to take over the armed forces of Germany. They thought he wanted to integrate the Nazi Storm Troopers into the regular army and become supreme commander of them all. This was not in the interests of either the army or of Hitler.

Von Kielmansegg emphasizes the importance of making a distinction between support for the Nazis and support for Hitler himself. He maintains that the Nazis were 'rejected' by professional soldiers like him, but that Hitler, the individual, wasn't. Given that Hitler epitomized his party in a way that few political leaders have ever done, such a distinction seems tenuous today. It was also a distinction Hitler adamantly denied, declaring: 'The Führer is the party and the party is the Führer.' Notwithstanding this, von Kielmansegg's separation of Hitler from the Nazis was a distinction some officers clearly felt able to make at the time. To the uncharitable mind, it can be seen as one way in which professional soldiers could reconcile any disquiet they might have felt about the abuses committed by rampaging Storm Trooper thugs, with their own approval of Hitler's rearmament programme.

Hitler himself soon felt compelled to act against the Storm Troopers. In addition to learning of the concerns of the Armed Forces, he also spotted what he took to be a deterioration in Röhm's behaviour. Röhm had talked of a 'second revolution' so that the Storm Troopers could receive the rewards they felt had been denied them. For Hitler, this was not to be countenanced. Heinrich Himmler seized the moment and made up a story about Röhm – that he was planning a coup – and Hitler believed him. Himmler, whose SS (Schutzstaffeln – originally the personal bodyguard of Hitler in 1920s) were still technically under the umbrella of the Storm Troopers, moved his men against Röhm on 30 June 1934 – the 'Night of the Long Knives'. Hitler also used this occasion to settle old scores against Gregor Strasser (who had quit the Nazi Party in December 1932) and General von Schleicher (the former German Chancellor) who both lost their lives. In all, around eighty-five people were killed.

General von Blomberg, the Minister of Defence, was delighted at the news, so much so that he ensured the army publicly thanked Hitler for the action. Only a few weeks later (after Hindenburg's death on 2 August 1934) he arranged for all soldiers to swear an oath of allegiance to Hitler personally. All the soldiers we interviewed from that time emphasized the importance of this oath in the context of what was to happen; for this was an oath sworn not to an office-holder but to a man – Adolf Hitler. Karl Boehm-Tettelbach took the oath in 1934 as a young Luftwaffe officer. For him, like many others, the oath was sacred and accompanied him to the very end of the war. He felt, and still feels, that if he had

Left: Hitler and Röhm in the summer of 1933. One year later Röhm would be dead, murdered on the orders of the man standing next to him.

broken the oath, he might have had to 'commit suicide'. For Boehm-Tettelbach this was to have clear consequences when he was at Hitler's headquarters in East Prussia, the Wolfsschanze (the 'Wolf's Lair') in 1944 and witnessed the results of Count von Stauffenberg's attempt to blow up Hitler. Boehm-Tettelbach had not been approached to take part in the bomb plot himself, but had he been he would have refused. He would never break his oath.

Karl Boehm-Tettelbach served as an attaché to the Minister of Defence, General von Blomberg, who was 'like a father' to him. 'Blomberg was a good

soldier,' says Boehm-Tettelbach, 'but he also saw good things for the army in Hitler.' In 1933, Blomberg later said, he had been given three things as a result of Hitler's appointment as Chancellor: faith, veneration for a man and complete dedication to an idea. A kind remark from Hitler could bring tears to Blomberg's eyes and he used to say that a friendly handshake from the Führer could cure him of colds. Boehm-Tettelbach witnessed how much Blomberg venerated Hitler when he regularly drove him back from his audiences with the Führer: 'There was hardly a trip back when he didn't praise him, and said that he had a good idea.'

Karl Boehm-Tettelbach as a young Luftwaffe officer.

Once Hitler had removed Röhm, become head of state as well as Chancellor (on Hindenburg's death) and been the subject of a solemn oath of allegiance from the army, his hold on power was secure. He and his Nazi Party were masters of Germany. Now he pursued one simple policy – rearmament. As for the day-to-day domestic considerations which weigh heavily on most political leaders, Hitler either delegated or abnegated them. Chaos may have disappeared from the streets but it became rampant inside the Nazi administration and government.

Fritz Wiedemann, one of Hitler's adjutants, wrote that Hitler 'disliked the study of documents. I have sometimes secured decisions from him, even ones about important matters, without his ever asking to see the relevant files. He took the view that many things sorted themselves out on their own if one did not interfere.' The result was, in the words of Otto Dietrich, Hitler's press chief, that 'in the twelve years of his rule in Germany Hitler produced the biggest confusion in government that has ever existed in a civilized state.'

Nor does Hitler's daily routine at this time sound like that of a political workaholic. Fritz Wiedemann wrote, 'Hitler would appear shortly before lunch, read through the press cuttings prepared by Reich press chief Dietrich, and then go into lunch. When Hitler stayed at the Obersalzberg [the mountain in southern Bavaria on whose slopes Hitler built his house – the Berghof], it was even worse. There he never left his room before 2.00 p.m. Then he went to lunch. He spent most afternoons taking a walk; in the evening straight after dinner, there were films.'

Albert Speer, the architect who was to become the Nazi armaments minister, tells how, when Hitler was staying in Munich, there would be only 'an hour or two' a day available for conferences: 'Most of his time he spent marching about building sites, relaxing in studios, cafés and restaurants, or hurling long monologues at his associates, who were already amply familiar with the unchanging themes and painfully tried to conceal their boredom.' The fact that Hitler 'squandered' his working time was anathema to Speer, a man who threw himself into his work. 'When,' Speer often asked himself, 'did he really work?' The conclusion was inescapable: 'In the eyes of the people Hitler was the leader who watched over the nation day and night. This was hardly so.'

Hitler was not a dictator like Stalin who sent countless letters and orders interfering with policy, yet he exercised as much or more ultimate authority over the state and was at least as secure as a dictator. How was this possible? How could a modern state function with a leader who spent a great deal of time in his bedroom or in a café? One answer has been provided by Professor Ian Kershaw in a careful study of a seemingly unimportant speech given by Werner Willikens, State Secretary in the Ministry of Food, on 21 February 1934. Willikens said: 'Everyone who has the opportunity to observe it knows that the Führer can hardly dictate from above everything he intends to realize sooner or later. On the contrary, up till now everyone with a post in the new Germany has worked best

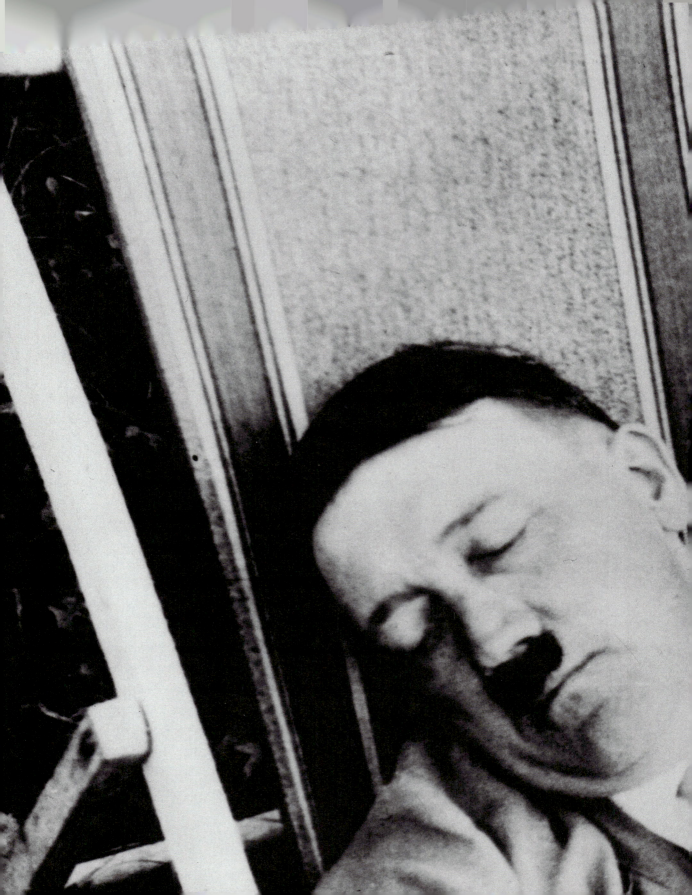

when he has, so to speak, worked towards the Führer...in fact it is the duty of everybody to try to work towards the Führer along the lines he would wish. Anyone who makes mistakes will notice it soon enough. But anyone who really works towards the Führer along his lines and towards his goal will certainly both now and in the future one day have the finest reward in the form of the sudden legal confirmation of his work.'

'Working towards the Führer' suggests a strange kind of political structure. Not one in which those in power issue orders but one in which those at the lower end of the hierarchy initiate policies themselves within what they take to be the spirit of the regime and carry on implementing them until corrected. Perhaps the nearest example we have in British history occurred when Henry II is supposed to have said, 'Who will rid me of this turbulent priest?' and the barons rushed to Canterbury to murder Thomas à Becket. No direct order was given, but the courtiers sensed what would please their liege lord.

Professor Kershaw believes that the practice of 'working towards the Führer' is a key insight into understanding how the Nazi state functioned, not just in the 1930s, but also during the war, and is particularly relevant when examining the provenance of many of the administrative decisions taken in the occupied territories. It gives the lie to the excuse offered by so many Nazis that they were just 'acting under orders'. Often, in fact, they were creating their own orders within the spirit of what they believed was required of them. Nor does the idea of 'working towards the Führer' excuse Hitler from blame. The reason Nazi functionaries acted as they did was because they were trying to make an informed judgement about what Hitler wanted of them and, more often than not, the substance of their actions was retrospectively legitimized. The system could not have functioned without Hitler or without those subordinates who initiated what they believed were desired policies.

'Working towards the Führer' can be used to explain the decision-making process in many of those areas of domestic policy which Hitler, through temperament, neglected. Most political parties, for example, have a carefully conceived economic policy at the core of their manifesto. The Nazis did not. Indeed, one academic joked to me that the question, 'What was Hitler's economic policy?' was easy to answer – 'He hadn't got one.' Perhaps that is unfair in one respect, for despite a lack of policy, Hitler always had economic *aims*. He

Previous pages: Hitler asleep in Bavaria in the early thirties, before he came to power. After he became Chancellor in 1933 he slept just as much.

promised to rid Germany of unemployment, and, less publicly trumpeted but, in his eyes, more important, to bring about rearmament. Initially he had only one idea how to achieve this and that was to ask Hjalmar Schacht, a former president of the Reichsbank and a brilliant economist, to 'sort it out' (see Chapter Three). Apart from rearmament and strengthening the army, Hitler had little detailed interest in domestic policies.

Surprisingly, for those who believe that a successful economy has to be guided by a political leader, in the short term Hitler's delegation of the economy to Schacht seemed to work. Schacht pursued a policy of reflation financed on credit, and alongside this implemented a work-creation programme based on compulsory work service for the unemployed. For average citizens, unless they were among the regime's racial or political enemies, life began to improve. They knew little of the economic theory behind the reflation of the economy. Nor did they suspect Hitler of indolence when it came to details of domestic policy. Instead they looked around and saw with their own eyes what the regime had done – and most liked what they saw. Almost everyone we talked to emphasized the Nazi achievement of reducing unemployment and clearing the streets of the desolate-looking jobless. (Unemployment, with some massaging of the figures, dropped from a high of 6 million in January 1932 to 2.4 million by July 1934.) The programme of public works – particularly the high-profile building of the autobahns – was seen as proof of Germany's new dynamism. 'Everybody was now happy,' says Karl Boehm-Tettelbach (in what is plainly an exaggeration). 'People now said, "My wife and all my daughters can walk through the park in darkness and not be molested." Today it's really dangerous again but at that time it was safe and this made them happy.'

Unlike most officers, Boehm-Tettelbach had the opportunity in the 1930s of getting to know the top Nazis. As Field-Marshal von Blomberg's aide, he sat alongside them at dinner parties and was impressed with what he saw. Göring was admired as a man who knew how to speak to pilots thanks to his exploits in the Richthofen fighter squadron during World War I. Goebbels had a 'pleasant' manner and would enquire, while drinking a glass of champagne, what films the Field-Marshal had seen so that he could then recommend his own favourites, such as *Gone with the Wind* (a film Goebbels was obsessed with). But it was another Nazi leader for whom Boehm-Tettelbach has the kindest words –

Heinrich Himmler, head of the SS and by 1936 chief of the political and criminal police throughout Germany: 'He was a very nice and agreeable guest because he always involved younger people like me and would enquire about the air force, how I was getting along, how long I would be with Blomberg, if I liked it, what I had seen the last trip to Hungary and things like that.' All these people, Boehm-Tettelbach thought, were good at their jobs. When, much later, he learned of the horrors Himmler perpetrated, he found them hard to reconcile with the considerate man he had met across the dinner table. Unpalatable as it may be to accept today, it was not just the Nazi regime that was popular during the 1930s, but also many of the Nazi élite, whose names were later to become synonyms for evil.

Erna Kranz was a teenager in the 1930s and is now a grandmother living just outside Munich. She remembers the early years of Nazi rule, around 1934, as offering a 'glimmer of hope…not just for the unemployed but for everybody because we all knew that we were downtrodden'. She looked at the effect of Nazi policies on her own family and approved: salaries increased and Germany seemed to have regained its sense of purpose. 'I can only speak for myself,' she emphasized a number of times during our interview, conscious no doubt that her views are not politically correct. 'I thought it was a good time. I liked it. We weren't living in affluence like today but there was order and discipline.' Ask Erna Kranz to compare life today with life in the 1930s under the Nazis and she says, 'I thought it was a better time then. To say this is, of course, taking a risk. But I'll say it anyway.'

Erna Kranz speaks fondly of the amusements the Nazis organized for young people, such as pageants and celebrations. One of the most famous 'artistic' processions was the 'Night of the Amazons' held in Munich each year for four years, starting in 1936. Surviving colour film of this extraordinary event recorded for posterity the sight of topless German maidens on horseback. The semi-naked young women were arranged to represent historical tableaux, including hunting scenes from Greek myths. Erna Kranz took part in the parade, not as one of the topless girls, but as a Madame Pompadour with a hooped skirt and a plunging neckline. She did not see the event as pornographic – far from it: 'The girls were there the way God created them, but the real purpose was, I think, a feast for the eyes and the edification and joy of the people who went there.' After all, she

The centre of Würzburg, an ordinary bustling market town; one of the few German towns where Gestapo records survived the war.

points out, 'In the Sistine Chapel, they're all naked, aren't they?'

There was more to an event like the 'Night of the Amazons' than a pageant designed to fulfil the fantasies of the watching Nazi leaders. According to Erna Kranz, the purpose of events like this was to present the Germans as an élite: 'People had the conceit to say that a German is special, that the German people should become a thoroughbred people, should stand above the others.' This idea was contagious: 'You used to say that if you tell a young person every day, "You are something special," then in the end they will believe you.'

Knowing as we do the unique horrors perpetrated by this regime, people who claim to have been happier under Nazi rule than they are today are, at best, likely to attract ridicule. But it is vital that people like Erna Kranz speak out, for without their testimony an easier, less troublesome view of Nazism might prevail – that the regime oppressed the German population from the very beginning. Academic research shows that Erna Kranz is not unusual in her rosy view of the regime during this period. Over 40 per cent of Germans questioned in a research project after the war said they remembered the 1930s as 'good times'. As this survey was conducted in 1951, when the Germans knew the full reality of the wartime extermination camps, it is a telling statistic.

All this may seem incomprehensible now, or perhaps only comprehensible by relying on a cultural view of the Germans as a uniquely odd people peculiarly susceptible to a crazed authority figure. But there is another explanation, and to grasp it fully one must try to imagine oneself in the same position as Erna Kranz and her family in 1934. What did they have to look back on over the previous twenty years? A war which had drained the country of young men and resulted in national shame; a peace treaty which had economically crippled the country and taken away much of its territory; raging inflation which had destroyed people's savings; a plethora of political parties who appeared to bicker constantly with each other; street fights between the paramilitary supporters of rival political parties; unemployment on a scale never seen before. Is it surprising that the apparent stability of the Nazi regime from 1934 onwards was welcomed?

Unexpected as it may be to discover that many Germans were content during the 1930s, this news is as nothing compared to recent revelations about the infamous Nazi secret police – the Gestapo. In popular myth the Gestapo have a secure and terrifying role as the all-powerful, all-seeing instrument of terror which oppressed an unwilling population. But this is far from the truth. To uncover the real story you have to travel to the town of Würzburg in southwest Germany. Würzburg is a German town much like any other, except for one special attribute: it is one of only three towns in Europe where Gestapo records were not destroyed by the Nazis at the end of the war. Resting in the Würzburg archive are around 18,000 Gestapo files, which exist more by luck than design; the Gestapo were in the process of burning them as the American troops arrived. They had begun to burn them alphabetically, so there are relatively few A–D files left; otherwise the files are complete.

Professor Robert Gellately of Ontario was the first person to uncover the secrets of the files. As he started work on them, an old German man saw what he was studying and said to him, 'Perhaps you'd like to interview me, because I lived here during that time and I know a lot about it.' Professor Gellately talked to him over a cup of coffee and asked him how many Gestapo officials there had been in this part of Germany. 'They were everywhere,' the old man replied, confirming the conventional view of the Gestapo.

Yet after studying the files, Professor Gellately discovered that the Gestapo simply couldn't have been 'everywhere'. Würzburg lies in the administrative area of Lower Franconia, a district covering around a million people. For that whole area there were precisely twenty-eight Gestapo officials. Twenty-two were allocated to Würzburg, and almost half of those were involved only in administrative work. The idea that the Gestapo itself was constantly spying on the population is demonstrably a myth. So how was it possible that so few people exercised such control? The simple answer is because the Gestapo received enormous help from ordinary Germans. Like all modern policing systems, the Gestapo was only as good or bad as the cooperation it received – and the files reveal that it received a high level of cooperation, making it a very good secret police force indeed. Only around 10 per cent of political crimes committed between 1933 and 1945 were actually discovered by the Gestapo; another 10 per cent of cases were passed on to the Gestapo by the regular police or the Nazi Party. This means that around 80 per cent of all political crime was discovered by ordinary citizens who turned the information over to the police or the Gestapo. The files also show that most of this unpaid cooperation came from people who were not members of the Nazi Party – they were 'ordinary' citizens. Yet there was never a duty to denounce or inform. The mass of files in the Würzburg archive came into being because some non-party member voluntarily denounced a fellow German. Far from being a pro-active organization that resolutely sought out its political enemies itself, the Gestapo's main job was sorting out the voluntary denunciations it received.

The files teem with stories that do not reflect well on the motives of those who did the denouncing. One file tells of a Jewish wine-dealer from Würzburg who was having an affair with a non-Jewish woman who had been a widow since 1928. He had been staying overnight with her since 1930 and they had declared their intention of getting married. The file demonstrates how Hitler's becoming Chancellor coincided with the widow's neighbours starting to voice objections to the presence of the Jewish man and confronting him on the communal stairs. As a result, he stopped staying overnight with the widow, but continued to help her out financially and to eat with her. Then, a 56-year-old woman who lived in the same house sent a denunciation to the Gestapo. Her main complaint was that she

Ilse Sonja Totzke as she appears in her Gestapo file.

objected to the widow having a relationship with a Jew, although it was not then an offence. From correspondence between the party and the police it becomes clear that she and a male neighbour pressurized the party into taking action. The local Nazi Party then put pressure on the SS, who, in August 1933, marched the

Jewish man to the police station with a placard around his neck. The placard, with its despicable message painted in blood red, is still carefully preserved in the file. In neatly stencilled letters it reads, 'This is a Jewish male, Mr Müller. I have been living in sin with a German woman.' Herr Müller was then kept in jail for several weeks before leaving Germany altogether in 1934. He had broken no German law.

The German cartoonist Erich Ohser (better known by his pen-name E.O.Plauen) with his family on holiday on the Baltic. He was arrested by the Gestapo and killed himself in his prison cell in March 1944.

Denunciations became a way in which Germans could make their voices heard in a system that had turned away from democracy; you see somebody who should be in the army but is not – you denounce them; you hear somebody tell a joke about Hitler – you denounce them as well. Denunciations could also be used for personal gain; you want the flat an old Jewish lady lives in – you denounce her; your neighbours irritate you – you denounce them too.

During his many months of research in the Würzburg archive Professor Gellately struggled hard to find a 'hero' – someone who had stood up to the regime, an antidote, if you like, to the bleak aspect which the study of the Gestapo files casts on human nature. He believed he had found just such a person in Ilse Sonja Totzke, who went to Würzburg as a music student in the 1930s. Her

Jubilant crowds greet Hitler at the Party Congress in Nuremberg in 1938.

Gestapo file reveals that she became an object of suspicion for those around her. The first person to denounce her was a distant relative, who said that she was inclined to be too friendly to Jews and that she knew too much about things that should be of no concern to women, such as military matters. This relative said that he felt driven to tell the Gestapo this because he was a reserve officer (though there was nothing in being a reserve officer that required him to do so). Totzke was put under general surveillance by the Gestapo, but this surveillance took a strange form: it consisted of the Gestapo asking her neighbours to keep an eye on her. There follows in the file a mass of contradictory evidence supplied by her neighbours. Sometimes Totzke gave the 'Hitler greeting' (Heil Hitler) and sometimes she didn't, but overall she made it clear that she was not going to avoid socializing with Jews (something which at this point was not a crime). One anonymous denouncer even hinted that Totzke might be a lesbian ('Miss Totzke doesn't seem to have normal predispositions'). But there is no concrete evidence that she had committed any offence. Nonetheless, it was enough for the Gestapo to bring her in for questioning. The account of her interrogation in the file shows that she was bluntly warned about her attitude, but the Gestapo clearly didn't think she was a spy, or guilty of any of the outlandish accusations made against her. She was simply unconventional. The denunciations, however, kept coming in, and eventually the file landed on the desk of one of the most bloodthirsty Gestapo officials in Würzburg – Gormosky of Branch 2B, which dealt with Jews.

On 28 October 1941 Totzke was summoned for an interrogation. The Gestapo kept an immaculate record of what was said. Totzke acknowledged that 'If I have anything to do with Jews any more, I know that I can reckon on a concentration camp.' But despite this, she still kept up her friendship with Jews and was ordered once more to report to the Gestapo. She took flight with a friend and tried to cross the border into Switzerland, but the Swiss customs officials turned her over to the German authorities. In the course of a long interrogation conducted in southwest Germany, she said: 'I, for one, find the Nuremberg Laws and Nazi anti-Semitism to be totally unacceptable. I find it intolerable that such a country as Germany exists and I do not want to live here any longer.' Eventually, after another lengthy interrogation in Würzburg, Totzke was sent to the women's concentration camp at Ravensbrück, from which we have no reason to believe she ever returned. Her courage cost her her life.

We decided to follow up Professor Gellately's research with this file by trying to find living witnesses to Totzke's denunciation. Eventually we traced Maria Kraus, who had lived with her parents less than a hundred metres from Totzke. At the time we interviewed her, she was 76 years old and no different in appearance from any of the respectable elderly ladies one sees on the streets of Würzburg, itself a solid, respectable town. But lying in Totzke's Gestapo file there is a denunciation signed by a 20-year-old Maria Kraus on 29 July 1940. The statement begins: 'Maria Theresia Kraus, born 19.5.20, appeared in the morning at the Secret State Police.' During our own interview with her we read her the statement, which includes the section: 'Ilse Sonja Totzke is a resident next door to us in a garden cottage. I noticed the above-named because she is of Jewish appearance...I should like to mention that Miss Totzke never responds to the German greeting [Heil Hitler]. I gathered from what she was saying that her attitude was anti-German. On the contrary she always favoured France and the Jews. Among other things, she told me that the German Army was not as well equipped as the French...Now and then a woman of about 36 years old comes and she is of Jewish appearance...To my mind, Miss Totzke is behaving suspiciously. I thought she might be engaged in some kind of activity which is harmful to the German Reich.' The signature 'Resi Kraus' is under the statement. We asked Frau Kraus if it was her signature. She agreed that it was but said that she did not understand how the document could exist. She denies having given the statement and has no recollection of ever visiting the Gestapo. 'I do not know,' she told us. 'The address is correct. My signature is correct. But where it comes from I do not know.' Whether Resi Kraus's amnesia was genuine or merely diplomatic is impossible to say. Of course, it is scarcely in anyone's interests today to confess to having denounced one's neighbour to the Gestapo. In a telling remark at the end of our brief interview with her she said: 'I was talking to a friend of mine and she said "Good God! To think that they rake it all up again fifty years later"...I mean I did not kill anyone. I did not murder anyone.'

I still have the image in my mind of Frau Kraus as we left her, after the interview, standing in the cobbled town square of Würzburg; a profoundly unexceptional figure and thus a deeply troubling one. If you want to believe there is a difference in kind between those who may have aided the Nazi regime and those who definitely did not, then a meeting with Frau Kraus is a shocking one, for in all respects, other than the denunciation signed with her name which lies in the Gestapo file, she appears an ordinary, decent woman – someone who kindly enquired how old my children were and where we planned to go for our holidays.

If Frau Kraus is the sort of person who signed a denunciation (which she cannot now remember), what does this say about the Gestapo itself? On examination, it transpires that just as the notion that the Gestapo were 'everywhere' is a myth, so is the idea that Gestapo officials themselves were fanatical SS members who, when the Nazi regime began, managed to oust decent law-abiding officers from the police and substitute themselves. What actually happened was that most of the police remained in their posts when the Nazi regime began, but they did not have to carry on as usual; they were now off the leash. Under the Nazis, the German police could act in ways which, for many of them, must have been liberating – disregarding the rights of suspects and pursuing what in their view was a strong law and order policy.

Heinrich Müller, the notorious head of the Gestapo from 1939, was no exception to this rule. He had been a policeman before the Nazis came to power, working in the political department, where he concentrated on left-wing parties. Indeed, Müller was so far from appearing to be a committed Nazi that the local party headquarters recommended that he should not be promoted in 1937 because he had done nothing of merit for the Nazi cause. Their appraisal, referring to his actions against left-wing groups before the Nazis came to power, contains the words: 'It must be acknowledged that he proceeded against these movements with great severity, in fact partially even ignoring the legal

Heinrich Himmler takes aim at an SS sports day. On 17 June 1936 Hitler appointed Himmler (already in command of the SS) head of the German police force, including the Gestapo.

regulations and norms. It is not less clear, however, that Müller, had it been his task, would have proceeded just the same against the right.' The report goes on to contain a chilling insight into Müller's motivation for serving the Nazis: 'With his vast ambition and relentless drive, he would have done everything to win the appreciation of whoever might happen to be his boss in a given system.' Despite this negative evaluation, Müller still won promotion. His superiors, Heinrich Himmler and Reinhard Heydrich, must have felt that it was more important to give the job to someone ruthless, ambitious and qualified rather than to someone who was merely politically correct.

Most Germans, of course, would never have come into contact with the Gestapo. If you were law-abiding (in Nazi eyes), you were safe. The terror was rarely arbitrary, unless you had the misfortune to belong to one of the regime's target groups – beggars, social misfits, Communists or Jews.

The chaotic nature of the Nazi administration of Germany was one factor which meant that Nazi anti-Semitic policy, until the start of World War II, was less consistent than one might have expected from a party committed to hating Jews. The basic anti-Semitism, particularly among the hardline Nazis, never changed, but the nature of the persecution varied wildly.

There were a series of uncoordinated attacks against Jews immediately after the election of March 1933. We have already seen one form this took in Würzburg – the public humiliation and imprisonment of a Jewish man for having an affair with a non-Jew (something, it bears repeating, which was not then against the law). But unofficial anti-Semitic action could be even more violent. Arnon Tamir was a 15-year-old Jewish boy when Hitler became Chancellor, and was told by a friend that, shortly after Hitler gained power, Storm Troopers from outside his village came in and thrashed all the Jews so badly that they were 'unable to sit down for weeks'. Elsewhere in Germany there were reports of Jews being subjected to a variety of humiliating measures, such as having their beards shorn or being forced to drink castor oil.

Rudi Bamber and his family, part of the Jewish community in Nuremberg, quickly learned about the arbitrary way in which Nazi Storm Troopers could act against Jews: 'In 1933 the Storm Troopers came and took my father away, and together with many other Jews in Nuremberg, they were taken to a sports stadium where there was a lot of grass and they were made to cut the grass with their teeth by sort of eating it…It was to humiliate them, to show them that they were the lowest of the low and simply to make a gesture.'

None of these actions was formally ordered by Hitler, though he must have sympathized with the motives of those involved. On 1 April he authorized a boycott of all Jewish shops and businesses. When it was planned, the boycott was intended to be indefinite but, after pressure from Hindenburg and others

Storm Troopers stand outside a Jewish shop on 1 April 1933 to harass potential customers and enforce the boycott.

(concerned about the danger of foreign trade reprisals), it was limited to one day. Nonetheless, for the Jewish population of Germany it was a day of great symbolic importance. Arnon Tamir saw Storm Troopers daub paint on Jewish shop windows and then stand intimidatingly outside to enforce the boycott. The Storm Troopers shouted slogans such as, 'Germans do not buy in Jewish shops' and 'The Jews are our misfortune'. He saw one or two brave Germans force their way into Jewish shops but witnessing their bravery only showed him how desperate the position of Jews in Germany had become. 'I felt like I was falling into a deep hole,' he says. 'That was when I intuitively realized for the first time that the existing law did not apply to Jews...you could do with Jews whatever you liked...a Jew was an outlaw.' From that moment on he resolved to try and distance himself from non-Jewish Germans. In a sense, he reacted as the Storm Troopers hoped all Jews might. The Nazis wanted the Jews to separate themselves from other Germans, creating their own Jewish state within Germany. Jews consequently formed their own schools, their own youth clubs, their own sports clubs – they began voluntarily to segregate themselves. This was all the more tragic given that so many Jews in Germany had taken such pains to integrate themselves into the population as a whole. Even though they remained physically within Germany's borders, they felt expelled.

There were still Jews, Arnon Tamir's parents and their friends among them, who clung to the hope that the boycott was directed not against them – loyal German citizens – but against 'international' Jewry. Indeed, with the segregation of Jews and the announcement of the Nuremberg Laws in the autumn of 1935, which codified the extent of Jewish exclusion from normal German life (including stripping them of Reich citizenship and banning them from marrying 'Aryans'), many Jews thought the regime had finally controlled its hatred. A combination of pressure from Hjalmar Schacht, Minister of Economics and President of the Reichsbank, over the economic consequences of persecuting Jews and the necessity of presenting Germany in a good light for the Olympic Games of 1936 meant that 1936 and 1937 were relatively quiet years for German Jews. This is not to say that the persecution disappeared – merely that compared with the harassment meted out in earlier years, life was not quite so bad.

However, there was still great suffering. The 'Aryanization' programme – the forced exclusion of Jews from the owning of businesses – meant that many Jews were deprived of a livelihood. Even those in businesses not initially forbidden to Jews could face ruin. Shortly after the boycott of 1 April 1933, Arnon Tamir's father experienced problems in running his small cigarette factory. The town's cigarette dealers, with whom his father had previously had very good relations, told him one after the other that they were 'sorry' but that since he was known to be a Jew they were no longer able to sell his cigarettes. Within one or two months of this unofficial 'boycott', he was forced to close down his factory. 'That came as a heavy blow to him,' says Arnon Tamir, 'because after the war and after the inflation, this was the third time that he had lost the basis of his livelihood. After that he lay on the sofa for weeks staring into space.'

Thousands of other Jews lost their livelihood not through an unofficial boycott, like Arnon Tamir's father, but through the raft of legislation in the 1930s which prohibited Jews from certain professions, like the Civil Service. Thousands more were so desperate that they fled the country.

Karl Boehm-Tettelbach accepts that it was wrong that many Jews felt forced to leave Germany, but says he 'understood' why the Nazis felt as they did, given their claim that '90 per cent' of lawyers in Berlin were Jews. Former banker Johannes Zahn puts it this way: 'The general opinion was that the Jews had gone too far in Germany,' and he too mentions the perceived problem that certain professions (such as the law) were dominated by Jews. These are significant remarks since it is easy to assume, given where this anti-Semitism was to lead, that Nazi anti-Semitic policy was pushed through against the wishes of the majority. From the variety of different witnesses we talked to it is clear that many Germans at the time supported the restrictions the Nazis placed on Jews.

Of course, the reason why Jews were concentrated in certain professions was the legacy of hundreds of years of exclusion from other areas of employment. 'The Jews were actually pushed into a particular sector,' says Arnon Tamir. 'Until 200 years ago they were not allowed to be farmers or craftsmen.' But logical explanation does not prevail over prejudice.

For non-Jews it was easy to look the other way. I asked Karl Boehm-Tettelbach how it was possible in the 1930s that someone could respect Hitler and what he was doing for Germany when Jews were forced to lose their jobs and leave the country. In his reply he spoke, I believe, for millions of other Germans: 'That never came up. Everybody thought the same, that you were in a big team and you didn't separate from the group. You were infected. That explains it a little bit.' Thinking back to his own enjoyable experiences in the Luftwaffe in the 1930s, he says: 'A young pilot flying all day long, he didn't want to discuss these problems and they never came up in the officer's mess. We came home, had a nice dinner and then went to bed or went out dancing.'

Arnon Tamir suffered as he grew to adulthood in this atmosphere of 'infectious' anti-Semitism. He would look into the mirror and stare at his nose – was it too big? And his lower lip – did it protrude too much? As for his attitude to non-Jewish German girls, 'The mere idea of becoming friendly, or more, with a German girl was poisoned right from the start by those horrible cartoons and headlines which claimed that the Jews were contaminating them.' Arnon Tamir discovered that, to the committed Nazi, the Jews weren't just different, they were diabolical. When he was at work on a construction site he listened in horror as a young Storm Trooper told a story, in all seriousness, about a Jewish woman in his village who was a sorceress. He claimed she had been able to turn into a foal and then change back again. One day the blacksmith caught her while she was still a foal and shod her with horseshoes so that she stayed a foal. 'I was deeply dismayed,' says Arnon Tamir, 'that it was possible he believed something like this.' The ludicrous prejudice of this Storm Trooper could more easily flourish in a society where there were very few Jews – remember that only 0.76 per cent of the German population was Jewish. It is sometimes easier to be frightened of an unseen, almost supernatural enemy, than the ordinary neighbour who lives next door.

After escalating throughout the summer and autumn of 1938 in a third big wave of anti-Semitic outrages to follow those of spring 1933 and summer 1935, violence against the German Jews exploded in an unprecedented manner on the night of 9 November – Kristallnacht, the night of broken glass. Two days earlier, Ernst vom Rath, a German diplomat in Paris, had been shot by Herschel Grynszpan, a Polish Jew angry at the Nazi treatment of Jews, particularly his own family, who had been among those recently deported with great brutality across the Polish border. Josef Goebbels heard the news of vom Rath's death and, when the Nazi hierarchy met in Munich to commemorate the anniversary of the Putsch, asked Hitler to let loose the Nazi Storm Troopers. Hitler agreed.

Rudi Bamber (right) and his parents. Respectable German citizens all.

The first Rudi Bamber and his family knew about Kristallnacht was when their front door crashed open: 'In the early hours of the morning they sort of broke the front door down and started to smash the place up

– the Storm Troopers. We had two lots: one lot just concentrated on smashing things up and left, but then the second lot arrived.' He tried to ring the police but saw that the people perpetrating the violence were in uniform themselves. 'We had three elderly ladies who were living on the first floor with us. One was dragged out and beaten up, for no reason except she probably got in the way or something. And I was knocked about and finally ended up in the cellar which was where the kitchens were…Then I was arrested and put under a guard outside the front door while they finished off what they were doing inside.' In a typical example of their arbitrary behaviour, the Storm Troopers suddenly changed their mind and decided not to detain Rudi Bamber: 'A great many people were arrested that night and it was obviously their intention to arrest me as well. But after a while they found that the leader of the group had gone home. He had obviously had enough and they were very irritated by this. They weren't going to waste any more time, so they gave me a swift kick and said 'Push off,' or words to that effect, and they walked out and left me to it.' But a terrible sight awaited Rudi Bamber when he re-entered the house: 'I went upstairs and found my father dying, dead. I tried as far as I could to give artificial respiration but I don't think I was very good at it and in any case I think it was too late for that…I was absolutely in shock. I couldn't understand how this situation had arisen…uncalled-for violence against a people they didn't know.'

For Germans like Erna Kranz, Kristallnacht 'was a shock because from that moment on you thought about things more. You see, at first you let yourself be carried along by a wave of hope; we had it better then, we had order and security in the country. Then you really started to think.' We asked her if she therefore became an opponent of the regime. 'No, no,' she replied hastily, 'that, no. When the masses were shouting "Heil", what could the individual person do? You went along. We went along. We were the followers. That's how it was. We were the followers.'

The reaction of ordinary Germans to Kristallnacht varied. Many were shocked, disgusted or stunned by the violence and destruction. Often the extent of the material damage was criticized. Sometimes people felt ashamed that a cultured nation could stoop to this. Sometimes expressions of human sympathy, albeit muted, could be heard. Most people, however, appear to have approved of ridding Germany of Jews. The Jews were friendless.

Eberswalde synagogue on fire as a result of Kristallnacht.

The morning after Kristallnacht, in Nuremberg, local Germans demonstrated what they felt about the suffering Rudi Bamber and his family had experienced: they threw stones at the windows of their house.

There is no reliable record of how many Jews were murdered as a result of Kristallnacht, nor how much property was destroyed. Recent research by Professor Meier Schwarz (a biologist from Tel Aviv, whose own father was killed by the Nazis) suggests that more than a thousand synagogues were destroyed and at least four hundred German Jews died.

The circumstances of Kristallnacht demonstrate once again how momentous events could occur within Nazi Germany with little advanced planning, and how violence, always near the surface, could explode once Hitler gave the nod. Hitler's own reputation suffered little as a result of Kristallnacht. He never spoke openly about the affair and, for those Germans who wanted to, it remained

A passer-by surveys the damage to a Jewish shop in Berlin after Kristallnacht, 10 November 1938.

possible to believe that such violence could once again be laid at the door of
Goebbels and the party's rabble.

In 1938, the same year as Kristallnacht, a grand new Chancellery was built (to
a design by Albert Speer) to symbolize the power and authority of Nazi rule. But
within its walls Hitler's style of government could still only lead to chaos.
According to Dr Günter Lohse, of the German Foreign Office, the basic problem
was that Hitler would appoint two people in two separate departments to do
relatively similar tasks without making it clear who was working for whom. Then

they would fight between themselves. Alternatively, Hitler would issue an instruction and then 'everyone made an institution out of the instruction'. When it came to resolving the inevitable disputes, Hitler rarely made a decision as to the merits of a case or said who was right. He would say to his ministers, 'Now you should sit down together and when you've made up, you can come and see me.'

In this spirit of competition Hitler's working life within the Chancellery was organized not by one private office but by *five*. There was the office of the Reich Chancellery under Hans-Heinrich Lammers; the office of the Chancellery of the Führer under Philipp Bouhler; the office of the Presidential Chancellery under Otto Meissner; the office of Hitler's personal adjutant under Wilhelm Brückner; and the office of the Führer's deputy under Martin Bormann. Since all these people claimed to represent Hitler, much of their time was spent fighting with each other over jurisdiction. All of them looked for ways of pleasing their Führer as a means of increasing their influence. The result was a system in which chance events could provoke radical policies. The most chilling example of how this

The new Reich Chancellery in Berlin designed by Albert Speer.
It symbolizes a fiction – the order of Nazi rule.

could happen within the Chancellery is the origin of one of the most repugnant policies of the Third Reich – the Children's 'Euthanasia' Programme.

Sometime in late 1938 or early 1939 the father of a deformed child wrote a petition to Hitler, one of hundreds received by the Chancellery of the Führer every week. (In a system that lacked democratic representation, writing to the Führer, like offering a petition to the King in medieval times, became one of the few ways individuals could try to influence their fate.) This father wrote that his child had been born blind, appeared to be an idiot and was also lacking a leg and part of an arm. He wanted the child to be 'put down'. Officials in the Chancellery of the Führer, under the ambitious Philipp Bouhler, now decided that this should be one of the few petitions which they actually put in front of Hitler rather than responded to themselves or passed to other government departments. (The process of selecting letters always involved 'working towards the Führer', namely deciding in advance which of the petitions would be most likely to please Hitler.) Knowing Hitler's obsessive pseudo-Darwinian views, it must have been obvious that this particular petition would feed his prejudice (laws had already been passed by the Nazis which ordered the compulsory sterilization of the mentally ill). Hitler read the petition and then asked his own physician Dr Karl Brandt to go and examine the child and, if the father's statement proved to be correct, to kill the child. According to the post-war testimony of Dr Hans Hefelmann, a leading functionary in the Chancellery of the Führer, the Knauer case, as it became known, prompted Hitler to authorize Brandt and Bouhler to deal with similar cases in the same way.

Philipp Bouhler, the ambitious Nazi who organized the child 'euthanasia' policy

There then followed a period in which doctors and other medical officials, drew up detailed criteria for children who were to be 'referred for treatment' under the new policy. Diseases which had to be referred included 'idiocy and mongolism…deformities of every kind, in particular the absence of limbs, spina bifida, etc'. Forms were returned to a Reich committee, from whence they were sent to three paediatricians who acted as assessors. They marked each form with a plus sign if the child were to die, or a minus sign if the child were to survive. None of the three doctors who made the judgement saw any of the children: they decided on the information of the forms alone.

Gerda Bernhardt's family was one of the thousands to suffer once the 'euthanasia' policy was in full swing in the early years of the war. Her younger brother, Manfred, had always been retarded. When he was ten he was still speaking like a 3-year-old. He could say 'Mama' and 'Papa' but little else except 'Heil Hitler' – something he was pathetically proud of being able to pronounce. Some unpleasant neighbours in their block of flats said that it would be for the best if the boy was 'put away', but Manfred's mother always tried to resist the idea. Eventually, though, her husband convinced her that their son should be sent to a nearby children's hospital in

Gerda Bernhardt and Manfred, her younger brother.

Dortmund called Aplerbeck. Manfred was 12 years old now and becoming a strain for all the family. There was a farm at Aplerbeck and Herr Bernhardt comforted his wife with the thought that Manfred would be able to spend time around animals.

Manfred was duly admitted to the hospital and his parents went to visit him once a fortnight – all the regulations would allow. Gerda also visited her brother as often as she could, taking him little gifts of food. Then, around Christmas of Manfred's first year in Aplerbeck, Gerda noticed a change in him. He was brought into the anteroom where they normally met dressed only in his underpants and he seemed apathetic and weak. Gerda hugged him goodbye. That was the last time she saw him alive.

Nazi banners on the Brandenburg Gate in Berlin in celebration of Hitler's birthday on 20 April 1939.

The hospital authorities said that Manfred had died a natural death of measles, but Gerda Bernhardt noticed that a lot of children were dying at Aplerbeck around this time. She asked to see the body of her brother and in one room saw the bodies of fifteen little children all wrapped in white sheets. The nurse asked her as they moved from one body to another, 'Is this your brother?' and at each body Gerda said, 'No.' Manfred's body was not one of these fifteen corpses, but lay in another room on a hospital trolley.

After the burial his father said to the family, 'They killed our son,' but he had no evidence to prove it. Only in the last few years has it been possible to piece the true story together and to be able to say with certainty that staff at Aplerbeck murdered children who were put into their care.

Paul Eggert was a patient at Aplerbeck around the time Manfred was there. His father was a violent drunkard and he was one of twelve children. With this family history, classed by the Nazis as 'delinquent', Paul Eggert was forcibly sterilized at a hospital in Bielefeld when he was 11 years old and then sent to Aplerbeck for 'assessment'. As he was not mentally disabled, he was given odd jobs to do, such as fetching clean linen or pushing trolleys containing dirty washing. Once he thought the trolley he was pushing felt unusually heavy, so when no one was looking, he pulled back the washing and saw the bodies of two girls and a boy.

The similarity between life at Aplerbeck and a horror story continued in the nightmare world that was the children's evening meal. Dr Weiner Sengenhof, one of the senior doctors at Aplerbeck, would come into the dining-room with a nurse. They would then select the children who had to go to the doctor's consultation room in the morning for 'immunization' injections; the children, however, had noticed that those selected for such 'immunization' in the past were never seen again. Outside the consultation room, a child hung on to Paul Eggert screaming for help as the nurse tugged him away. Paul Eggert told us, 'These pictures would swim in front of my eyes when I lay in bed at night and they are still before my eyes today.'

Piecing together the historical evidence for what happened at a hospital like Aplerbeck has been extremely difficult. Almost all the papers which could have established clear proof about what went on there were burned in the last months of the war. After 1945 nothing was said by those who had perpetrated or witnessed these terrible acts. Dr Theo Niebel, the doctor who had been in charge of the Special Children's Unit at Aplerbeck under the Nazi regime, still worked there as a doctor until his retirement in the 1960s. According to local historian Uwe Bitzel, 'It became possible to uncover something only when the direct participants were no longer at the hospital.' To Herr Bitzel this compounds the crime: 'I do find it totally awful that after 1945 none of these people stood up and said: "I have done terrible things. I recognize that we have all done them." But they all remained silent, denied it and lied – trivialized it in some cases.'

Uwe Bitzel took us down into the dusty basement of Aplerbeck and showed us the few remaining records from which he has pieced together the true story of Aplerbeck. The official record of deaths at the hospital shows a large number of children dying from inconspicuous diseases such as measles or 'general weakness'. On the same day Manfred Bernhardt met his death, two other children died. In the previous week eleven children lost their lives. In the following week nine children died. As Uwe Bitzel concludes, 'This is such a high death rate that it can be ruled out that all these children died of natural causes.' The cause of measles or 'general weakness' at Aplerbeck turned out to be either a massive overdose of luminal (a powerful sedative) or morphine.

The origin and practice of child euthanasia in the Third Reich is not just abhorrent, it is instructive. As we have seen, it originated not just out of Nazi racist ideology, but from the chaotic manner in which decisions were taken in the Third Reich. A chance letter to the Führer on a subject dear to his heart resulted eventually in the deaths of more than five thousand children. By the time Manfred Bernhardt met his death, two years after the policy was instigated, doctors in homes such as Aplerbeck did not have to fill in Bouhler's form. In a typical example of how policies could spiral out of control, staff independently selected the children they wanted to kill. The chaotic radicalism inherent in the Nazi system meant that, unlike in the Fascist states of Italy and Spain, German Fascism could never settle to a status quo, however dreadful or repulsive. Any idea, given a leader who spoke in visions and enthusiastic supporters anxious to please, could grow radically to an extreme in almost an instant. The consequences, not just for Germany but for the rest of the world, would be enormous.

Of course, in 1939 the vast majority of Germans would have known nothing of the evil policy of child euthanasia. Nor would they have realized the chaotic structure of Nazi government and the reasons for it. Nor would they have understood just why the Gestapo was so effective. What they chose to see was a dynamic country on the move – and they were part of it.

Neither a study of the documents nor the opinions of academics enabled me to understand how it was possible, before World War II, to actually *like* living in Nazi Germany. But after listening to witness after witness, not hardline committed Nazis, tell us how positive their experiences had been, a glimmer of understanding emerged. If you have lived through times of chaos and humiliation, you welcome order and security. If the price of that is 'a little evil', then you put up with it. Except there is no such thing as a 'little' evil. I am reminded of the old joke about the man who says to a woman, 'Will you sleep with me for £10 million?' The woman says, 'Yes.' The man replies, 'Now we have established the principle, let's negotiate the price.'

For the people of Germany the price of putting up with 'a little evil' would be very high indeed.

CHAPTER THREE

—

THE WRONG WAR

At the Berghof, his house in the shadows of the mountains of Bavaria, Hitler would relax by watching feature films. One of his favourites was a 1930s' Hollywood epic of adventure and conquest, *The Bengal Lancers*, which contained a message of which Hitler approved: it demonstrated how one 'Aryan' nation had subjugated another more numerous but 'inferior' race.

'Let's learn from the English,' Hitler said over dinner on 27 July 1941, 'who with 250,000 men in all, including 50,000 soldiers, govern 400 million Indians.' Here, according to Hitler, was clear evidence of the superiority of the 'Aryan' race: the English could rule India with a relatively tiny force because of their better blood. 'What India was for England,' said Hitler in 1941, 'the territories of Russia will be for us. If only I could make the German people understand what this space means for our future!'

When he became Chancellor in 1933, Hitler wanted close friendship with England (by which he meant Great Britain). Dr Günter Lohse of the German Foreign Office says, 'He wanted England as an ally, a real ally.' Other diplomats agree; Herbert Richter confirms that Hitler saw the English as fellow members of the very select 'master race' club.

Yet in 1939, Hitler ended up at war with Great Britain, the one country in the world he wanted as an ally, while Germany allied herself to the Soviet Union, the one country, as we shall see, he most believed he risked conflict with. This war was not planned. But the combination of Hitler's character, the international tensions of the time and the institutional structures of the Nazi state made a war of some kind inevitable. It was just that the war of 1939 was, from Hitler's initial

Left: The Union Jack and the Tricolour hang above an SS guard of honour outside the 'Führerhaus' in Munich during the conference of September 1938.

point of view, the wrong one. How could he, a man often praised for his political acumen, make such a mess of his own foreign policy?

When he came to power in January 1933 Hitler told the world he wanted to rid Germany of the shackles of the Versailles Treaty in order to make her strong once more. To accomplish this goal the country needed massive rearmament. His reply in February 1933 to a proposal from the Reich Ministry of Transport to build a reservoir demonstrates the extent to which, in his eyes, the policy of rearmament came before anything else: 'The next five years in Germany had to be devoted to rendering the German people again capable of bearing arms. Every publicly sponsored measure to create employment had to be considered from the point of view of whether it was necessary with respect to rendering the German people again capable of bearing arms for military service.'

Rearmament could only be possible if the German economy provided the funds. But Hitler knew next to nothing about economic theory. 'The Nazi movement was really quite primitive,' confirms the banker Johannes Zahn, who knew Hjalmar Schacht, the man who was to be responsible for getting the German economy on its feet in the 1930s. Hitler may have known nothing about how to run an economy but Schacht thought he knew everything. 'It is clear, obviously,' says Zahn discreetly, 'that Schacht was very self-confident.' In 1923, at the age of 46, Schacht was made Reich Currency Commissioner and told to stabilize the economy in the face of runaway inflation; later that year he became head of the Reichsbank. In 1930 he resigned in protest at the Young Plan, a regime of reparation payments to the victors of World War I to which the German government had agreed. He turned to Hitler and the Nazis for the solution to Germany's problems. 'I desire a great and strong Germany,' he said, 'and to achieve it I would enter an alliance with the devil.'

Hjalmar Schacht, the brilliant German economist who masterminded Germany's apparent economic recovery.

Hitler appointed Schacht as Minister of Economics in 1934 and passed a law giving him dictatorial powers over the economy. Unemployment had already started to fall sharply as a result of huge work-creation schemes, such as the autobahn construction programme, and the economy as a whole was beginning to recover from the effects of the Great Depression. Schacht managed to pay for rearmament via the 'Mefo bills' – a form of deficit financing which had two advantages: it allowed the risky early stages of rearmament to be kept relatively secret and meant the Nazis could pay for it on credit. The regime also benefited from an upturn in the world economy and the effective cancellation of reparation payments which had been negotiated by Chancellor Brüning at the Lausanne conference in 1932.

For Hitler this turnaround in the economy must have seemed like magic – simply another exercise of his will. He certainly wasn't concerned with *how* Schacht was working this miracle. He said in August 1942: 'I have never had a conference with Schacht to find out what means were at our disposal. I restricted myself to saying, "This is what I require and this is what I must have." '

The army could not have been more positive about Hitler's actions. He was finally ridding Germany of the 'ignominy' of disarmament. 'This was absolutely welcomed,' says Graf von Kielmansegg, an army officer at the time, 'and he didn't ask about the cost at all. At last, an army was to be formed which, everyone agreed, was truly capable of defending Germany. The Reichswehr [German Armed Forces] were not capable of doing this with their 100,000 men. And don't forget, Germany was surrounded by its main enemies from World War I.' For many of the soldiers we talked to, rearmament also had a symbolic, almost spiritual importance; it was the means by which the country regained its potency. Others thought that if the newly rearmed forces were used to threaten Germany's neighbours so that some of the wrongs of Versailles could be righted, then well and good. Nobody we talked to believed during the 1930s that they were engaged in the preparations for a world war of conquest. Yet in 1924, Hitler had outlined in *Mein Kampf* some clear foreign policy objectives: 'We are taking up where we left off six hundred years ago. We are putting an end to the perpetual German march towards the south and west of Europe and turning our eyes towards the east…However, when we speak of new land in Europe today, we must principally bear in mind Russia and the border states subject to her. Destiny itself seems to wish to point the way for us here.' And how was Germany going to gain this new land? The answer is clear: 'At the present time, there are on this Earth immense areas of unused soil only waiting for the men to till them. However, it is equally true that Nature as such has not reserved this soil for the future possession of any particular nation or race. On the contrary, this soil exists for the people which possesses the force to take it and the industry to cultivate it.'

Mein Kampf (*My Struggle*) was written by Hitler in 1924. Despite being widely bought it was not widely read.

Few people, however, had read *Mein Kampf*, or if they had read it, they had dismissed it. 'Nobody believed *Mein Kampf* was of any importance,' says diplomat Manfred Freiherr von Schröder. 'What would politicians think today of what they have written twenty years ago?'

'But let me digress a little,' says Johannes Zahn. 'If you take Christianity, for example, the demands of the Bible, the demands of the catechisms, do you know anybody who fulfils the demands of Christianity 100 per cent, or even pretends to fulfil them 100 per cent? And one thought the same way about *Mein Kampf* – these are demands, these are ideas, but nobody thought that they were to be taken literally.' Herbert Richter, who worked in the Foreign Office, says, 'I too am to blame. I read the first fifty pages and found it so crazy that I did not read any more of it.'

Had these gentlemen taken seriously what they read in *Mein Kampf*, they would have learnt that Hitler believed Germany lacked *Lebensraum* (living space). If life was a struggle between the fittest races, then in order to triumph the Germans needed the right balance between population numbers and agricultural land. But Germany, according to Hitler's analysis, lacked the land it needed to support a strong population. Germans were thus a 'people without space'.

Right: German troops march in Nuremberg in September 1937. Hitler would shortly reveal what he wanted this new army for.

Hitler looked around and saw one nation which had solved the problem of lack of living space – England. In the early years of Hitler's Chancellorship he pursued the dream of an alliance with England, something which also fitted his desire to deal with European nations one by one rather than through the collective League of Nations.

In parallel with the policy of friendship with England, Hitler attempted to shake off the restraints of Versailles. Germany withdrew from the League of Nations and a disarmament conference in October 1933 after agreement had not been reached on a revision of the Versailles Treaty as it applied to German armaments. Now, Hitler tried to reach an agreement separately with England. At this point in the story one of the oddest Nazis makes his entrance – Joachim von Ribbentrop. Hitler was so impressed by this former wine merchant, who had married into money and society, that he made him his personal emissary and sent him to London to float the question of a non-aggression pact between the two nations. The unspoken idea behind the attempted friendship was, as former diplomat Reinhard Spitzy says, 'that Britain and Germany should practically rule the world. Britain should rule the waves and Germany should rule from the Rhine to the Urals.'

In 1935 the strategy of wooing Britain appeared to work. After meetings between Sir John Simon, the British Foreign Secretary, Anthony Eden, the Under-Secretary, and Hitler and Ribbentrop a naval agreement was signed which allowed Germany to rebuild her navy to 35 per cent of the British surface fleet and 100 per cent of her submarine fleet. An important factor in the British decision to sign the naval agreement was the view that Germany had been punished too much by Versailles and that a reasonable accommodation should be reached with Adolf Hitler.

In March 1935 Germany had announced that it had no further intention of observing the defence limits in the Versailles Treaty. In April the League of Nations had passed a motion of censure against the Germans. The British, by their naval agreement, showed what little store they placed in the League of Nation's collective response to German military expansion. Hitler described hearing news of the naval agreement as the 'happiest day of his life'.

The following year, Ribbentrop was appointed German ambassador to Britain. He did not make a good first impression. When he presented his letters of accreditation to the King, he raised his right arm in a Hitler salute. The British press ridiculed him for it, but having done it once, he felt compelled to do it every time he met the King or he would lose face. Dr Lohse, who worked with Ribbentrop, believes that 'he couldn't and wouldn't forgive the English for his own mistake'.

The atmosphere in the London embassy was not a happy one. According to Reinhard Spitzy, who served there, Ribbentrop was almost impossible to work for, continually postponing appointments; he was 'pompous, conceited and not too intelligent'. More seriously for his reputation, Ribbentrop also mistreated British tradesmen. He would keep tailors waiting for hours, not realizing that they would tell their other aristocratic clients about his thoughless behaviour. 'He behaved very stupidly and very pompously,' says Spitzy, 'and the British don't like pompous people.'

Ribbentrop was intensely disliked by many who crossed his path. Goebbels said, 'He bought his name, he married his money and he swindled his way into office.' Count Ciano, the Italian Foreign Minister, remarked that 'The Duce says you only have to look at his head to see that he has a small brain.' His was the one name guaranteed to raise a negative response from our interviewees. Herbert Richter thought he was 'lazy and worthless' and Manfred von Schröder believed him to be 'vain and ambitious'. No other Nazi was so hated by his colleagues.

Hitler was well aware of the low opinion in which Ribbentrop was held. According to Herr Spitzy, Göring told Hitler that Ribbentrop was a 'stupid ass'. Hitler replied, 'But after all, he knows quite a lot of important people in England.' Göring retorted, 'Mein Führer, that may be right, but the bad thing is, they know him.'

So why did Hitler support Ribbentrop? In essence the answer is simple. Because Ribbentrop knew how to handle Hitler. At one level he was merely a sycophant: 'Ribbentrop didn't understand anything about foreign policy,' says Herbert Richter. 'His sole wish was to please Hitler. To have good relations with Hitler, that was his policy.' In pursuit of this policy Ribbentrop used every device he could think of, including informants. He would ask people who had had lunch with Hitler to report back to him on what Hitler had said. Then, the next day, he would tell Hitler the same opinions but pretend they were his own. Hitler, not surprisingly, felt Ribbentrop had fine judgement. But there is another, more

sophisticated, reason why Ribbentrop was so favoured by Hitler during this period. As Reinhard Spitzy puts it: 'When Hitler said, "Grey," Ribbentrop said, "Black, black, black." He always said it three times more, and he was always more radical. I listened to what Hitler said one day when Ribbentrop wasn't present: "With Ribbentrop it is so easy, he is always so radical. Meanwhile, all the other people I have, they come here, they have problems, they are afraid, they think we should take care and then I have to blow them up, to get strong. And Ribbentrop was blowing the whole day and I had to do nothing. I had to brake – much better."'

Thus, despite his obvious faults, Ribbentrop had found the key to ingratiating himself with Hitler, something which was lost on his more obviously gifted colleagues; he realized that the Führer always smiled kindly on a radical solution. This fact alone meant that Nazi foreign policy must lead to crisis. To Hitler, the most exciting solution to any problem was always the most radical. It did not matter whether the radical solution was adopted – the mere fact of suggesting it proved the true National Socialist credentials of its proposer. The corollary of this was that qualities of intelligence and ability in subordinates were not valued by Hitler as much as loyalty and radicalism, a truth which Hjalmar Schacht, the most intelligent of all the leading figures in the Nazi government, was about to discover.

'The Nazis turned towards the obvious ills,' says Johannes Zahn. 'These were unemployment and disarmament and these things are not really economic questions.' Talking of Schacht's actions during 1933–5, Zahn says: 'The Nazis had solved the problem simply by increasing the circulation of banknotes without having a real understanding of the concept of inflation.' The difficulty with the Nazi policies of rearmament and road-building was that, as Herr Zahn puts it, 'A motorway doesn't sit in a shop window, a motorway cannot be sold, though the purchasing power remains. Rearmament cannot be sold, though the purchasing power remains.' As an economist Zahn knew what Hitler didn't – money is purchasing power and only at your peril do you create purchasing power without having goods to sell.

According to Zahn, Schacht was very clear about the destabilizing and inflationary pressure that had been injected into the German economy by his short-term solution to the problem of financing rearmament. Schacht knew that unless industry soon made goods which people could buy in the shops, or which

Left: Ribbentrop and Himmler at Nuremberg in 1938. Himmler was one of the few leading Nazis not to despise Ribbentrop openly. At least they shared a sense of radicalism.

could be exported for foreign currency, Germany was heading inexorably towards ruin. He made this reality clear in a speech in November 1938 in which he echoed Herr Zahn's point that the economy was creating a demand from those with money to spend which could not be satisfied. Schacht's conclusion was simple: 'The standard of living and the extent of armament production are in inverse ratio.'

Johannes Zahn reveals that by 1938 Schacht was not alone in thinking that Nazi economic policies must fail: 'But we all, me included, we all underestimated what you could achieve with state power through pay freezes, exchange controls and concentration camps.'

Once this deficit financing had been running for several years (rather than the initial 'pump priming' process which trained economists would have favoured, in which deficit financing was used just to start the stalled economy), Schacht must have been asking himself the question – how can Germany get out of this mess? The answer, at least to Herr Zahn, was frighteningly clear: 'One day the Nazi regime would have collapsed economically and Hitler thought, to put it crudely, what I do not get voluntarily I will try and take through war. So the war broke out and was lost.'

Documents show that while Hitler was aware of the economic problems caused by the financing of rearmament, he saw any domestic difficulties palling beside the overwhelming foreign policy problem Germany faced and which only rearmament could solve. In a memo written at Berchtesgaden in 1936, Hitler said: 'Germany will, as always, have to be regarded as the focus of the Western world against the attacks of Bolshevism. I do not regard this as an agreeable mission but as a serious handicap and burden for our national life...The extent of the military development of our resources cannot be too large, nor is its pace too swift...If we do not succeed in bringing the German Army as rapidly as possible to the ranks of premier army in the world so far as its training, raising of units, armaments and above all spiritual education is concerned, then Germany will be lost!' To Hitler it was ludicrous that he must concern himself with the petty realities of economic theory in face of the need to arm the country against the perceived Bolshevik threat. 'Hence all other desires without exception must come second to this task [of rearmament]. For this task involves life and the preservation of life, and all other desires – however understandable at other junctures – are unimportant or even mortally dangerous and are therefore to be rejected.'

At the same time as Hitler wrote this memo, justifying the introduction of the Four-Year Plan, he decided that Schacht should be sidelined and the drive to maximize armaments production be directed by someone interested less in the complexities of economic theory than in the crude philosophy of Nazism – Hermann Göring. Schacht had no further future in Hitler's administration. He finally resigned and left office as Minister of Economics on 26 November 1937.

Schacht is symbolic of those Nazi supporters who saw the new regime as a welcome change from the insecurities and failures of the Weimar period and who were striving for stability in government. They wanted a strong and prosperous Germany. If that could be accomplished only in a dictatorship, then so be it. Germany's brief experience of democracy had not served it well. But Schacht clearly grew uneasy as Hitler's regime progressed, gradually realizing the true realities of Nazism. He believed that rearmament of itself was not something to be opposed. In fact, to some degree it was clearly desirable to help revitalize the economy and in order to set aside the shame of the Versailles Treaty, which had presented Germany to the world as a neutered nation. But Hitler now appeared to have no other goal, and he was ready to pay any price so long as Germany was prepared for war.

During the course of making the television series on which this book is based I met many men who had the same awakening as Schacht, although in most cases their awakening came later. Many thought Nazism would bring good things to Germany and, as they surveyed the initial years of the regime, culminating in the Berlin Olympics of 1936, they were well satisfied with what they saw. Many of these people now try to make sense of their own experience by referring to 'several' Hitlers. There was the Hitler of the 1930s (the 'good' Hitler), the Hitler of the initial war years (the 'warlike' Hitler) and there was the Hitler of the Holocaust (the 'evil' Hitler). It's an understandable attitude, since few people want to believe they were part of something rotten from the first; but they were. The 'Night of the Long Knives', Dachau and the other concentration camps, the racism and anti-Semitism at the core of Nazi ideology – all were present from the early years. I thought more than once after talking to these people that their travels through Nazism had been like a rocket ride. They had started on the journey because they wanted an exciting new experience. Then, when the rocket went up through the clouds, they grew uneasy. 'That was fun, but now it's time

Overleaf: Every year Hitler and leading Nazis retraced the route of the Putsch march through Munich. This picture is from November 1936. The Nazis never hid their radical and violent origins.

to return,' they would have said. But the rocket did not return. It went on and on into the dark, a bleak and horrible place. 'But I only asked for a rocket ride,' they said at the end of the whole horrific journey. 'I never wanted to go into the dark.' But the rocket was always going into the dark if only they had looked ahead.

Many others were to suffer the same fate as Schacht before the outbreak of war, for this was a regime which could not 'settle down'. Leaving aside Hitler's own visionary desires as outlined in *Mein Kampf*, his own sense of power and prestige relied on continual success. After some of the major foreign policy coups – leaving the League of Nations (1933), the reoccupation of the Rhineland (1936) and the Anschluss (unification) with Austria (1938) – Hitler held a plebiscite to gauge public approval for his actions and support was predictably huge. Though not a conventional politician who worried about re-election, Hitler was nonetheless continually anxious lest the regime and the country as a whole lack excitement and movement. 'Instead of increase, sterility was setting in,' he said in November 1937, 'and in its train, disorders of a social character must arise in course of time.'

Did this mean that during the 1930s Hitler planned the war? No single question about the Nazi state in the 1930s has been more debated. Much of that debate centres on one document, known as the 'Hossbach Memorandum'. Colonel Friedrich Hossbach was Hitler's Wehrmacht adjutant and took notes of a meeting at the Reich Chancellery on 5 November 1937 attended by the Commanders of the Air Force (Göring), Army (von Fritsch) and Navy (Raeder), the Reich War Minister (von Blomberg) and the Foreign Minister (von Neurath).

According to Hossbach's notes, the meeting started with Hitler at his most portentous: 'The Führer began by stating that the subject of the present conference was of such importance that its discussion would, in other countries, be a matter for a full Cabinet meeting, but he, the Führer, had rejected the idea of making it a subject of discussion before the wider circle of the Reich Cabinet just because of the importance of the matter. His exposition to follow was the fruit of thorough deliberation and the experiences of his four-and-a-half years in power. He wished to explain to the gentlemen present his basic ideas concerning the opportunities for the development of our position in the field of foreign affairs and its requirements, and he asked, in the interest of a long-term German policy, that his exposition be regarded, in the event of his death, as his last will and testament.'

Left: A child gives the Führer flowers in 1938, the year of his greatest popularity so far.

Even in these few brief lines, one experiences the authentic sense of Hitler's political character – his distrust of cabinet meetings, his fear of an early death which would cheat him of glory and his own belief in himself as a major figure in world history.

According to Hossbach, Hitler went on to outline how he believed it was impossible for Germany to maintain self-sufficiency 'in regard both to food and the economy as a whole' within her current borders. Germany should now seek *Lebensraum* within Europe. There was, however, no mention of a campaign against Russia. Instead, he proposed that by 1943–5 at the latest, Germany should move against Czechoslovakia and achieve unification with Austria even at the risk of war with the Western powers, since after that date Germany's relative strength could only diminish.

At the Nuremberg Trials the Hossbach Memorandum was presented as evidence that a complete blueprint existed of Hitler's expansionist plans. It has proved hard to sustain this position, not least because there is no mention of Russia in the document. Some argue that this omission was deliberate 'in order not to alarm his audience'. On the other hand, the historian A.J.P. Taylor wrote that the Hossbach Memorandum was essentially 'day-dreaming, unrelated to what followed in real life'. The memo should be treated, in his words, as a 'hot potato'. Yet recent study of material not available to Taylor (such as the complete run of Goebbels' diaries) indicates clearly that Hitler knew he could not get what he wanted without conflict. But even to read just the full text of the Hossbach Memorandum is scarcely to learn the intentions of a mere day-dreamer. There could be no clearer statements than: 'The aim of German policy was to make secure and preserve the racial community and to enlarge it. It was therefore a question of space…The question for Germany was where could she achieve the greatest gain at the lowest cost?…Germany's problem could be solved only by the use of force, and this was never without attendant risk.' The Hossbach Memorandum may not be a 'complete blueprint' for war but it is a clear statement of expansionist intention. It is evidence of a foreign policy which would offer the rest of the world a simple choice as to how it could react – capitulate or fight.

One other policy decision is clear from the Hossbach Memorandum: the love-affair with Britain was over. Throughout the meeting, Britain was lumped with France as a potential enemy whose possible reaction to Germany's aggression should be carefully analysed. Ribbentrop had begun to influence Hitler against Britain, and would continue to do so. He wrote Hitler a note in January 1938: 'I have worked for years for friendship with England and nothing would make me happier than if it could be achieved. When I asked the Führer to send me to London, I was sceptical whether it would work. However, in view of Edward VIII, a final attempt seemed appropriate. Today I no longer believe in an understanding. England does not want a powerful Germany nearby which would pose a permanent threat to its islands.'

British coolness towards Germany had also been reported to Hitler from other sources. Karl Boehm-Tettelbach accompanied Field Marshal von Blomberg to London in 1937 for the coronation of King George VI. The German delegation took the opportunity to have talks with senior British politicians. Blomberg told his aide how disappointed he had been with the results of his discussions with Baldwin, Chamberlain and Eden – especially with Eden, whom Blomberg described as 'unfriendly'. But the Royal Family were nicer, even without the presence of the newly abdicated Edward VIII, whose friendliness to the new German regime is infamous. At the coronation dinner in Buckingham Palace Blomberg was honoured to be asked to sit at the King and Queen's table, gaining the impression that the Royal Family wanted to be friends with the new Germany. Unfortunately for the Germans, the politicians appeared not to be so agreeable and this was the news Blomberg reported to Hitler at Berchtesgaden. Boehm-Tettelbach followed behind Hitler and Blomberg on a long walk in the mountains as the bad news was broken to the Führer. On the way back to Berlin, Boehm-Tettelbach asked Blomberg what Hitler had said about the news. 'Nothing,' replied Blomberg. But shortly afterwards more resources still were planned for the army, something which Boehm-Tettelbach believes 'was the answer and reaction from the coronation'.

Blomberg, of course, was also one of the key participants at the Hossbach meeting. Hossbach, in his memoirs, writes that neither Blomberg nor Fritsch, the commander of the army, appeared overenthusiastic after they heard Hitler explain his plans: 'the behaviour of Blomberg and Fritsch must have made it clear to the Führer that his political ideas had simply produced sober and objective counter-arguments instead of applause and approval. And he knew very well that the two generals rejected any involvement in a war provoked by us.'

These two leading army officers were not behaving as Hitler would have liked. There could be no greater contrast than between their sober pragmatism and Ribbentrops's aggressive radicalism. Unfortunately for them, Hitler much preferred the latter's approach. According to diplomat Reinhard Spitzy, Hitler once said, 'My generals should be like bull terriers on chains, and they should want war, war, war. And I should have to put brakes on the whole thing. But what happens now? I want to go ahead with my strong politics and the generals try to stop me. That's a false situation.'

Within a few months of the Hossbach meeting, those senior military officers who had not leapt enthusiastically to support Hitler's plans were removed. Blomberg and Fritsch were forced to resign and Neurath, the Foreign Minister, was also disposed of, appointed to the powerless job of 'president' of a Reich secret cabinet. The linkage of these events to the Hossbach meeting seems obvious, and there is a strong temptation to make the link appear a simple one of cause and effect – as though Hitler had decided that since these men now displeased him, they should be removed. But that is not how it happened. An understanding of the true circumstances surrounding the removal of Blomberg and Fritsch reveals how Hitler and the Nazi élite worked as politicians; for rather than having a preconceived plan, they seized the moment.

Blomberg announced his intention of marrying a commoner called Erna Gruhn. Hitler gladly gave his permission for the match: he liked the idea that an ordinary German girl would marry the grand Blomberg. The marriage was conducted quietly on 12 January 1938, with Hitler and Göring as witnesses. Karl Boehm-Tettelbach, Blomberg's aide, was upset that the wedding was such a small affair and that he himself hadn't been invited: 'I called my other adjutants and said, "Now look, isn't that strange? He's going to marry tomorrow and we don't even get a glass of champagne! Isn't that strange?"' Immediately after the wedding, following pressure from his fellow officers, Blomberg permitted a small wedding announcement to be placed in the newspaper. The next morning the paper was read by a policeman who recognized the bride's name and, checking his files, found that this same woman had posed for pornographic pictures, some of which were even in the file. The file was passed to the chief of Berlin's police, Count von Helldorf. He rang Karl Boehm-Tettelbach and made an appointment to see Blomberg at once, entering the ministry discreetly through a back entrance.

Left: Field Marshal Werner von Blomberg, German Minister of Defence, and Hitler in September 1937; less than six months later Blomberg resigned.

After the meeting he said to Boehm-Tettelbach, 'Well young boy, you'd better look for a new job.'

On the afternoon of 26 January 1938 Hitler accepted Blomberg's resignation. Blomberg had no alternative but to quit, living as he did by the strict honour code of the German officer corps. Blomberg returned to the Ministry of Defence, entered Boehm-Tettelbach's room and asked him to open the safe. 'Here is the last will of Hitler,' Blomberg told him. 'Take that and give it tomorrow to Hitler with my field marshal's baton.' Then, shaking and crying, he said, 'Goodbye, my friend,' and embraced him. To Boehm-Tettelbach 'the world broke down because I believed in him and saw that he had made a big mistake in marrying someone not decent for a field marshal.' Blomberg's decision to hand back his baton is significant because a field marshal usually keeps it into retirement. Perhaps the shame was simply too great.

Hitler could not have predicted these events, but once they occurred, he and his hardline subordinates exploited them. Days after Blomberg's removal, Fritsch was forced to resign after Himmler and Göring instigated a trumped-up charge of homosexuality against him, even hiring a false witness. In addition, sixteen older generals were retired and forty-four transferred. At the same time as Hitler made these changes, he also replaced Neurath with Ribbentrop as minister of foreign affairs.

This radical clearing-out of any restraining element on Hitler stemmed entirely from the resignation of Blomberg – something that could not have been anticipated. But one of Hitler's strengths as a politician was an ability to exploit a situation when it occurred. He hinted at his attitude in July 1924 when he explained, 'The theoretician must always preach the pure idea and have it always before his eyes: the politician, however, must not only think of the great objective but also the way that leads to it.' One reason why so many contradictions appear in German foreign policy during this period is that Hitler was always keen to exploit the immediate situation, sometimes (as in the alliance with the Soviet Union) at the short-term expense of the long-term 'theoretical' goal. One day during a lunch at which Reinhard Spitzy was present, Hitler said, 'If someone is burning a little fire, I would put there my pot with soup and heat it for the good German people, and blow a little bit in the fire.' To Spitzy it was clear he meant that 'he wanted to take the occasions as they came, he wasn't fixed'.

Without, as he saw it, the shackles of the old guard, Hitler now began to pursue a more radical foreign policy, and Austria was his first target. General Alfred Jodl noted in his diary on 31 January 1938: 'Führer wants to divert the spotlights from the Wehrmacht. Keep Europe gasping and by replacements in various posts not awaken the impression of an element of weakness but of a concentration of forces. Schuschnigg is not to take heart, but to tremble.' Kurt von Schuschnigg, the Chancellor of Austria, had been bravely resisting Nazi influence in his country. In 1936 an agreement had been signed in which Austria acknowledged herself to be a German state, but was nonetheless free to run her own domestic affairs. Hitler put pressure on the Austrians for still greater ties with Germany only days after the Cabinet meeting at which the changes following Blomberg's departure had been announced. In January 1938 Franz von Papen, now ambassador to Austria, passed on to Schuschnigg Hitler's invitation to meet him at Berchtesgaden. The meeting revealed Hitler at his most bullying. Dr Otto Pirkham was a member of the Austrian delegation and recalls how 'on the staircase Schuschnigg was already seized by Hitler and taken to his rooms'. Hitler demanded the appointment of the Austrian Nazi, Arthur Seyss-Inquart, as Austrian Minister of Interior and the integration of Austrian economic and foreign policy with Germany's. Schuschnigg was clearly shocked by these demands. At lunch that day, where Hitler played the amiable host and talked about trivial matters, Schuschnigg sat completely silent. At the end of the day, when Schuschnigg had been bullied into giving Hitler what he wanted, he was even more depressed and silent. 'His silence,' says Dr Otto Pirkham, 'was due to the fact that what he had learned at the meeting with Hitler would not have been very agreeable.'

Shortly after the Berchtesgaden meeting, Jutta Rüdiger learnt Hitler's own opinion of Schuschnigg. She was attending an official Nazi dinner in her capacity as a senior figure in the BDM (the Nazi league of young women) when Hitler joined her table and the talk turned to the character of the Austrian Chancellor. 'Hitler said that he reminded him of a butterfly collector and only the botanist's vasculum [collecting case] was missing.' Hitler then described the metaphor he had used to illustrate why Austria and Germany must be together. 'I have told him that we had always said, "a good engine alone is no good. It has to have a good chassis too, but the good chassis on its own won't do either."'

Chancellor Schuschnigg still tried to resist what he knew was the eventual Nazi goal – the subjugation of his whole country. On 8 March 1938 he announced that there would be a plebiscite on 13 March so that Austrians could vote on whether or not they wished to be part of the German Reich. Schuschnigg was forced to drop the planned plebiscite after German pressure, but despite this, Hitler decided to increase the tension still further. He had learnt from Ribbentrop that England would not fight over Austria, so the only obstacle to pursuing a potentially violent policy against his neighbour was Italy.

On 10 March Hitler sent Prince Philip of Hesse to Rome with a letter which explained that the Italians had nothing to fear from any action the Germans might take against Austria; Hitler would always regard the Brenner Pass as the border with Italy. The following day Mussolini's view on the potential invasion of Austria by Germany was conveyed to Hitler in a telephone call from Prince Philip of Hesse:

'I have just come from the Palazzo Venezia. The Duce accepted the whole thing in a very friendly manner. He sends you his regards.'

'Then please tell Mussolini I will never forget him for this,' said Hitler. 'Never, never, never, whatever happens. As soon as the Austrian affair is settled, I shall be ready to go with him, through thick and thin, no matter what happens.'

The tone of Hitler's response shows how anxious he was during the crisis, and perhaps also explains why he remained loyal to Mussolini until the end of the war. The historian Joachim Fest describes 'the mood of hysteria and indecision' that characterized the atmosphere around Hitler during this crisis: 'All reports from members of Hitler's entourage speak of the extraordinary chaos surrounding the decision, the panicky confusion that overtook Hitler on the verge of this first expansionist action of his career. A multitude of over-hasty mistaken decisions, choleric outbursts, senseless telephone calls, orders and cancellation of orders, followed in quick succession during the few hours between Schuschnigg's call for a plebiscite and March 12…Keitel [Chief of Staff of the High Command] later spoke of the period as a "martyrdom".'

This is not a familiar portrait of Hitler. In popular myth (and, indeed, in Nazi myth) one of Hitler's defining characteristics is decisiveness. Yet it was Göring, not Hitler, who coolly called for the most radical action – invasion – and who actually issued the order for the troops to invade. Göring was behaving as Hitler believed a general should, as a 'bull terrier'. (Göring's decisiveness may also have been self-serving; it was in his own interests to keep the German Army distracted by an invasion of Austria from pursuing any investigation into the Fritsch affair and his own role in it.)

Hermann Göring and fellow beer-drinkers in Berlin in 1935. His bullish stance during the Austrian crisis three years later was to prove crucial.

On 12 March 1938 Hitler drove in triumph into Austria, the land of his birth. Film footage captured the wild emotional response of the Austrians. They weep, they scream, they chant: 'One Reich, One People, One Führer!' German troops are pelted with flowers and showered in kisses. To watch this raw footage, without commentary, but accompanied by the sounds of ecstatic Austrians, is still to be affected by the emotions of the time. For the Germans who were the objects of such veneration it was overwhelming. 'It was the nicest day of my life when we entered Austria,' says Reinhard Spitzy. 'I entered with Hitler in the sixth car. I had tears in my eyes.'

For Austrians such as Susi Seitz, the sight of Hitler caused an outpouring of a simple desire: 'All the people were answering Hitler in one way – "Get us to the German country, get us to Germany, let us be with you." And it was as if Hitler really got from all the people the answer to a question he was himself not thinking to have asked, because at that time we knew very well Hitler didn't want to take Austria in.' What we now know is that Hitler, too, was profoundly moved by what he saw – so moved that he altered his plans regarding Austria's political fate. Before entering Austria his only firm plan had been to put a puppet government in place. Now, as he experienced an enthusiastic reception in his former home town of Linz, he simply changed his mind. He decided that Austria deserved not to be a puppet state but a full member of the Reich; Germany and Austria should unite.

It is hard for us today to comprehend the ecstasy with which so many Austrians greeted the Nazis in general and Hitler in particular. In fact, the cause of their joy was clear – the Germans were righting a wrong done to them by the post-World War I settlement. Only twenty years earlier Austria had been a world power wallowing in the grandeur of the Austro-Hungarian Empire, but defeat in the war had reduced the country to the status of Switzerland. Now the Austrians felt they could recover their own greatness in a Germanic Reich.

After the triumphal Linz rally in March 1938, the 14-year-old Susi Seitz managed to shake Hitler's hand, and has never forgotten the moment: 'He came. Everything got quiet. And we were so excited, I felt my heart up here in the throat. And when he came to me I nearly forgot to give him my hand; I just looked at him and I saw good eyes. And in my heart I promised him, "I always will be faithful to you because you are a good man…." That was a dream-like time. And later I kept my promise. All my free time, besides school, I gave to the work because he had called us: "You all," he said to us, "you all shall help me build up my empire to be a good empire with happy people who are thinking and promising to be good people."'

But this was to be a brutal act of union. Hitler had been met on his entry into Austria by Heinrich Himmler, who had crossed the border the night before in

Right: Austrians in Linz greet Hitler's arrival on 12 March 1938. What must this have done to Hitler's already sky-high self-confidence?

order to start 'cleansing' the country of any elements of opposition. Austrian Jews suffered immediately. Walter Kammerling was then a 15-year-old Jew living in Vienna: 'We hear the noises from the streets coming in, the whole Viennese population, that is obviously the non-Jewish population, in jubilation and enjoyment. And then the first problem starts, the Jewish shops get smashed, and when you go on to the street the next day, that was the Saturday, you had already people molesting you...You were completely outlawed, there was no protection from anywhere. Anybody could come up to you and do what they want and that's it, and people came into flats which they wanted and took them.' The SS approved of all the humiliations local Austrian Nazis heaped on the Jews, especially when they made the Jews scour the streets clean: 'I remember I once had to scrub the streets as well,' says Walter Kammerling. 'I can't remember anything except that I saw in the crowd a well-dressed woman, you can't say the uneducated proletariat, and she was holding up a little girl, a blonde lovely girl with these curls, so that the girl could see better how a 20- or 22-year-old man (a Nazi Storm Trooper) kicked an old Jew who fell down because he wasn't allowed to kneel. He

Austrian Nazis, encouraged by their German cousins, make
Viennese Jews scrub the streets in the aftermath of the Anschluss.
The crowds watching were so big that they had to be held back.

had to scrub and just bend down sort of, and he fell and he kicked him. And they all laughed and she laughed as well – it was a wonderful entertainment – and that shook me.'

Susi Seitz accepts that anti-Semitism was widespread in Austria: 'I must say the Jews were not very much liked in Austria…We never had the feeling that they were the same as us, they were different, completely different…We only knew our families made jokes about them and didn't like them. That we knew. But we didn't think much about it because we had other things to think about, and we liked to play games and do sports and liked to hike around in our country. And we knew that the Jews hadn't that feeling for our home country.' With prejudice like this to exploit, Austria became a happy home for the SS. Austrian Jews were forcefully encouraged to emigrate. Within six months of the Anschluss eager SS officers, organized by Adolf Eichmann, had expelled around a third of Vienna's Jews. The emigrants had to leave their wealth behind. The Nazis simply stole it.

Heinrich Himmler realized that territorial expansion meant the potential for a huge increase in power for the SS. In November 1938 he told his SS generals: 'Germany's future is either a greater Germanic empire or a nothing. I believe that if we in the SS are doing our duty, then the Führer will create this greater Germanic empire, this greater Germanic Reich, the biggest empire ever created by mankind on the face of the earth.' The brutal way the SS acted in Austria in 1938 was a foretaste of how the Nazis would rule their empire. Outside the borders of Germany the SS intended to operate with little or no restraint.

The German Foreign Office basked in the glory of the Anschluss. 'The unification of Austria was really a national dream,' Manfred von Schröder told me. 'It was the summit of Hitler's popularity and that influenced everyone in Germany at that time.' The euphoria also affected Hitler, according to von Schröder: 'It must have been an enormous feeling of success and probably it made his megalomania grow.'

Spurred on by the bloodless success of the Anschluss, Hitler now turned to Czechoslovakia. Its strategic geographical position in Europe convinced Hitler that he could not expand further without neutralizing its army. The most obvious way of destabilizing Czechoslovakia was to incite the more than 3 million Germans who lived in the Sudetenland; they had already been calling for greater rights within Czechoslovakia as an ethnic group. Less than three weeks after his

Himmler and two other SS officers pick wild flowers. Himmler, the former chicken farmer, had always said that 'heroes were born in the country'. Now he hoped that Hitler's foreign policy would deliver tracts of new land for the Fatherland – land that he would administer.

triumphant entrance into Austria, Hitler held a meeting in Berlin with the leaders of the Sudeten German Party and told them that he intended to 'settle' the Sudeten problem in the 'not-too-distant-future'. Hitler knew that world opinion would not permit him to attack Czechoslovakia without a pretext, so after approving the Sudeten German Party's tactic of agitation against the Czech government, he left events to escalate without his direct involvement.

The Czechoslovakian government suffered because their country was a creation of the post-World War I settlement. Not only did this mean that the Nazis despised it, but that the country's genesis had created a number of ethnic minorities within it, many of whom were suspicious of each other. To outside observers, such as the British, it seemed that there was some justice in the Nazi dislike of Czechoslovakia and their support for the Sudeten Germans. An editorial in *The Times* on 7 September 1938 even called for the Sudetenland to be given to the Germans.

As problems with the Sudeten Germans escalated, the British Prime Minister, Neville Chamberlain, intervened to try to solve the crisis. He began by making two visits to Germany to meet Hitler on 15 and 22 September. The dispute was finally resolved at the Munich conference on 29 September at which representatives from Italy, Britain and France agreed that the Sudetenland should be ceded to Germany in stages between 1 and 10 October.

The Czechoslovakian crisis allowed the British to see what sort of statesman Hitler actually was. Chamberlain called him 'the commonest little dog' he had ever seen. The British and the French witnessed the rows, the vacillations, the bullying and the changes of mind that characterized Hitler's diplomacy. Nor was Hitler satisfied with the Munich Agreement. He had doubted all along whether the British and French would really have risked everything over Czechoslovakia and now believed he had been badly advised. He suspected that it had not been necessary for Göring and Mussolini to devise any form of compromise at the conference. Manfred von Schröder, who had been present at the signing of the agreement, heard only the day after the Munich conference that Hitler was saying 'They have robbed me of my war.'

Hitler still had not finished with Czechoslovakia. Even though the Nazis now possessed the Sudetenland, and had thus deprived Czechoslovakia of her man-made fortifications and the mountains which were her natural defences, Hitler still saw the rest of Czechoslovakia as a threat. He now used the same tactic to destabilize the remainder of Czechoslovakia that he had used to gain the Sudetenland – he encouraged a minority to revolt. Now he pressed the Slovak leaders to declare full independence from the rest of Czechoslovakia. Their natural inclination to do so was reinforced by threats from Hitler that if they did not do as he wished, he would encourage Hungary to claim Slovakia as *her*

Hitler enters the Sudetenland after the Munich Agreement of September 1938.
The 3 million Sudeten Germans greet him in scenes reminiscent of his entry into Austria.

territory. This was diplomacy the Darwinian way: we are stronger than you and if you don't do what we want, then you will be crushed. Treaties, international law, mutual policing of nations through organizations like the League of Nations – all were devices the weak employed to hide from the strong. Hitler practised not the diplomacy of Bismarck but that of the bully. Up to now he had cloaked his brutal bullying in such a way that it was capable of another interpretation – the Anschluss was Austria's wish, the Sudeten Germans were mistreated – but now he was to demonstrate openly the true essence of Nazi philosophy, in which the strong simply 'take over' the weak.

On 14 March 1939 the Slovaks declared independence (reading from a text prepared by Ribbentrop). That night the ageing Czech President, Emil Hácha, arrived in Berlin for talks. Hitler humiliated him, first by keeping him and his entourage waiting for hours, then by making them tramp through hall after hall of the new Chancellery to reach his office, and finally by meeting them at one o'clock in the morning and announcing that at six o'clock, in five hours' time, German troops were going to invade their country. Hitler was enjoying himself; Hácha was not. As the Czech President tried to telephone Prague, Göring joined in the fun and began describing to him how German planes would bomb the Czech capital. Manfred von Schröder witnessed what happened next: 'Hácha broke down and had a heart failure.' Von Schröder called Hitler's personal physician, Dr Theodor Morrell, who gave Hácha an injection. The Czech President revived sufficiently so that at four o'clock in the morning he signed away the Czech people into Hitler's 'care'.

Manfred von Schröder witnessed the celebrations in Hitler's huge office following the submission of Czechoslovakia: 'It was a sort of victory party with champagne – Hitler had his mineral water. And then I got a very close impression of that man. It was amazing to see how he behaved when he was among friends, alone, and hadn't to behave like a statesman for the public. He was sitting first of all like this…' Here von Schröder demonstrates by tousling his hair, undoing the top buttons of his shirt and sitting across his armchair, his legs dangling over one side. 'He was talking the whole time, dictating to two secretaries; one proclamation to the Czechoslovak people, and a letter to Benito Mussolini. I thought he was behaving like a genius but that was wrong, of course. When I look back today and I have the clear picture of him standing up and then sitting down again I think he was absolutely behaving like a maniac.'

Hitler may have won the immediate prize of the Czech republic, but he had demonstrated, even to his own loyal diplomats, that he had extremely poor judgement. 'That was the most stupid act and he ruined practically everything,' says Reinhard Spitzy. 'There was no necessity to invade Czechoslovakia because all electric lines, the railways, the roads, the water pipes could be cut at the ethnic frontier. After the Munich conference the Czechs were absolutely in our hands and with nice treatment we would have won them all.' To Manfred von Schröder Hitler's actions were diplomatic suicide: 'That changed the whole of history because from that moment on it was clear that Hitler was an imperialist and he wanted to conquer – it had nothing to do with the self-determination of the German people.'

Hitler, of course, did not see his actions in this negative way. Removal of any potential threat from a country as strategically placed as Czechoslovakia was essential if the German Army was to move further east in search of conquest. But still nothing could be accomplished without a common border with Russia. Standing in the way was a country re-created at Versailles – Poland.

Paradoxically, since it was to be the invasion of Poland that would spark the war, Hitler's claims on it were not as unreasonable as his claims on Prague and the remainder of Czechoslovakia had been. Danzig, previously a German city, had been designated a Free City under the Versailles Treaty and sat in a Polish 'corridor' of land between German East Prussia and the rest of Germany. It was easy to argue that in this case Germany had experienced injustice.

Initially, Ribbentrop asked the Poles for the return of Danzig and a strip of German territory across the Polish corridor on which a German-run road and rail link between East Prussia and the rest of Germany could be built. This time Hitler met real resistance. On 31 March 1939 the British and French guaranteed the borders of Poland. Encouraged by the guarantee, the Poles were not about to compromise. Then, as 1939 progressed, the position of the Soviet Union became critical. If Stalin allied himself with Britain, Germany would run the risk of a two-front war if she pushed the world to conflict. British attempts at negotiation with the Soviet Union were, however, lacklustre, for both ideological and practical reasons (Stalin had purged thousands of officers from the Red Army and the Soviets were perceived to be a third-rate military force). Stalin was also unwilling to be pushed into a war which offered him little in terms of his own narrow self-interest. Then the Nazis pulled what Manfred von Schröder calls a stroke of 'courage' and 'genius' – they signed their own treaty with the Soviet Union, their greatest ideological enemy.

The German Foreign Office had noticed the significance of Stalin's speech in March 1939 when he had said, in a clear rebuff to Britain, that he would 'not let our country be drawn into conflict by warmongers, whose custom it is to let others pull their chestnuts out of the fire'.

'That was the turning-point,' says Hans von Herwarth, then a diplomat at the German embassy in Moscow. After Stalin's speech, Germany and the Soviet Union began negotiations on greater economic ties. As the summer progressed, Ribbentrop, with Hitler's blessing, pushed forward with negotiations for a political treaty, a 'non-aggression' pact, which was eventually signed on 23 August. At first sight, the treaty seemed incredible – totally at variance both with Hitler's expressed ideological view of the Soviet Union and the Soviets' own suspicions about the Nazi regime. But there was a secret part of the treaty, not revealed at the time, which shows why both countries, greedy for spoils, would have seen the agreement in their own national self-interest. Hans von Herwarth saw the secret protocol signed, and confirms that within it Hitler 'promised to give back to the Soviet Union all that they had lost through the results of World War I. And naturally that was a prize which France and Great Britain couldn't pay because that meant to sacrifice the freedom of the Baltic states, Poland and even, perhaps, Finland.'

Hans von Herwarth was clear what the consequences of the Non-Aggression Pact would be. 'Now we have lost the war,' he told his colleagues that summer. 'My opinion was that the Americans would come in and we would lose World War II.' But Hans von Herwarth was very much in a minority. The general view was that the Non-Aggression Pact with the Soviet Union was a major foreign policy coup. Britain and France realized that it made a Nazi invasion of Poland more likely. Hitler himself, according to notes of a meeting taken by Admiral Wilhelm Canaris (head of the Abwehr – the military intelligence of the German High Command), admitted to his military commanders: 'Now Poland is in the position in which I wanted her…Today's announcement of the Non-Aggression Pact with Russia came as a bombshell. The consequences cannot be foreseen.

Right: Proof that history can be much stranger than fiction. Ribbentrop shakes the hand of Joseph Stalin, the man who represented the ideology the Nazis despised – Communism. The Hitler-Stalin Pact, signed in Moscow on 23 August 1939, was an act of pure pragmatism by both sides.

Stalin also said that this course will benefit both countries. The effect on Poland will be tremendous.'

This meeting at Berchtesgaden on 22 August 1939 showed Hitler at his most frightening. All the threads of Nazi thought were pulled together: an overwhelming sense of the great Darwinian struggle ahead ('A life and death struggle…On the opposite side they are weaker men'), the importance of individual courage ('It is not machines that fight each other, but men'), and a complete rejection of 'weak' values such as restraint and compassion ('Close your hearts to pity. Act brutally').

Yet as he gave this chilling speech to his military leaders, Hitler had put himself in the position of being allied to the one country in the world he wanted as an enemy – Russia – and was close to war with the one country in Europe he had originally wanted as a friend – Britain. When faced with this reality today, a number of interviewees answered us reproachfully: 'Please don't forget,' says Graf von Kielmansegg, then a Wehrmacht officer, 'England and France declared war, not Germany.'

'I always hoped,' says Karl Boehm-Tettelbach, 'that England – here I'm talking to you as an Englishman – that England would see what Germany was planning to do and would agree and share in Europe, whatever the politics.'

Even at this late stage – August 1939 – officers such as Karl Boehm-Tettelbach did not feel they were about to embark on a world war. 'Hitler's story was that he wanted to help Germans. He didn't want to invade Czechoslovakia. He didn't want to have Czechoslovakia, he wanted to help the Germans there. And it was the same with Poland. He wanted to erase the Versailles diktat that Danzig and Königsberg were separated from Germany. So therefore he had something good in mind: he wanted to help the Germans and to unite Germany…Politically, I approved of it.'

The Nazi leadership knew that Hitler was not limiting himself to 'uniting Germany' again. The tone of his 22 August meeting had shown that his desire for conquest was much more ambitious than that. On 29 August Hermann Göring beseeched Hitler not to 'go for broke'. Hitler replied that 'throughout my life I have always gone for broke'.

On 1 September German troops invaded Poland. Two days later Britain and France declared war. This war had not been planned, but with Hitler and the Nazis pursuing these particular policies, war of some kind was inevitable.

The chaos and rivalries which had characterized so much of the Nazi government were now exposed to the stresses of a world conflict. As Dr Goebbels heard the news that war had been declared, he turned to his hated rival Ribbentrop and said, 'Herr von Ribbentrop, this is your war. To begin a war is easy. To end it is more difficult.'

CHAPTER FOUR

—

THE WILD EAST

On 20 June 1946 there was a celebration in Poznan, western Poland. Crowds gathered wherever they could, climbing fences and trees, all striving to find the best place to witness the much-anticipated hanging of Arthur Greiser, former Nazi ruler of the Polish Warthegau. Anna Jeziorkowska had taken a friend along: 'I can only say that at the moment when Greiser was hanged from the gallows, people were so overjoyed, so overcome by enthusiasm that they were kissing one another, jumping up and down, shouting, bursting into songs.' Anna walked home rejuvenated. 'After one has had to endure such suffering,' she says, 'then one is looking for some form of satisfaction, isn't one?'

No country occupied by Germany in the entire war endured as much as Poland. This was the epicentre of Nazi brutality, the place where Nazism achieved its purest and most bestial form. Six million Poles died in the war – around 18 per cent of the population; by comparison, the British lost fewer than 400,000.

Arthur Greiser was one of the men most responsible for the appalling suffering of the Poles. Along with Hans Frank, who ran the district the Nazis named the General Government, and Albert Forster, the overlord of Danzig/West Prussia, Greiser was one of the absolute masters of Poland. But at his war crimes trial you would never have guessed the individual power he had once possessed. He pleaded with the court that he had really been a friend of the Poles and that Hitler was the man to blame for what had happened. Greiser said that he, too, had been a 'victim of Hitler's policies' and a 'scapegoat for the crimes

Left: A Polish farmer and his family run from their home during the Nazi occupation. An individual scene of panic and suffering that was multiplied in Poland a hundred thousand times.

Hitler with German soldiers in Poland in the immediate aftermath of the invasion, September 1939. He rarely smiled in photographs (see page 45 for the only other example in this book), so we can guess the happiness and relief he felt at this moment of military success.

of his masters'. In essence, he claimed he was simply acting under orders, but there were, in fact, hardly any orders (in the sense of binding instructions) given to men like Greiser.

Hitler referred to such men as a 'race of rulers, a breed of viceroys.' These rulers of the east were allowed tremendous latitude in decision-making. The type of order they received from Hitler was one which went – 'they had ten years to tell him that Germanization of their provinces was complete and he would ask no questions about their methods.' The logical conclusion of a regime where party leaders were told to 'take over power themselves' (see page 37), or where in the absence of orders from the top, party functionaries worked 'towards the Führer' (see page 60) was the terror and chaos of the Nazi occupation of Poland. A letter Greiser had written to Himmler was quoted at the trial. In it Greiser stated his belief that he could effectively treat the Jews of Poland as he liked: 'I, for my part, do not believe that the Führer needs to be consulted yet again about this matter, particularly in view of the fact that it was only recently during our last discussion concerning the Jews that he told me I could proceed with them according to my own discretion.'

Hitler had promised a 'new order' for the east. What happened may have been new, but there was precious little order in it.

As the German troops crossed into Poland on 1 September, their political masters had still not made the most basic decisions about what political shape the newly acquired territory should have. How much of it should be incorporated into the Reich? Indeed, should any piece be left which could still be called 'Poland'? What was clear was what the Nazis wanted to do with the Poles themselves – turn them into slaves, educated only to a level that would enable them to read road signs so that they could keep out of the way of German trucks and tanks as they sped down the highways. Poland was thus about to become the scene of the biggest racial experiment the world has seen. In the process the belief that twentieth-century Europe was home only to civilized people would be shattered.

Sporadic signs showed from the first that this was no ordinary invasion. German SS units displayed terrible and casual brutality as they accompanied the regular army into Poland. Wilhelm Moses served in a regular army transport regiment during the invasion of Poland and what he saw led him to the conclusion that 'an animal isn't as dangerous as the Nazis were in Poland'. As he

Arthur Greiser, Nazi ruler of the Polish Warthegau. The Nazis, especially Greiser, governed Poland with a disregard for human life that is without precedent in Europe in modern times.

drove through one Polish village, he witnessed the brass band of the SS Germania Regiment playing as seven or eight people were hanged from the gallows. He could see that the SS had first tied the victims' feet together and then attached stones to them. This technique led them to die a deliberately slow death. Their

Poles hung by the Germans during the occupation. It was a scene like this that Wilhelm Moses happened upon as he drove his truck around a corner.

tongues were hanging out, their faces blue and green. 'I no longer knew where I was,' says Wilhelm Moses. 'You can't really describe the way I saw it. The music was only playing because people were screaming so much.'

Later in the invasion, Wilhelm Moses and his truck were commandeered by the SS, and he was ordered to transport Polish Jews between towns, delivering them from one SS unit to the next. He is still haunted by their cries as they were loaded: 'Let me get down, don't take me, they will kill us,' he says the families would cry.

'Well, who said that they are going to kill you?' he asked.

'But of course they will kill us, they killed the others too, my mother, my father, my children have all been killed. They will kill us too!'

'Well, are you Jews?' asked Herr Moses.

'Yes, we are Jews,' they replied.

'What could I do?' says Herr Moses. 'I am a tortured person. As a German, I can only tell you that I was ashamed about everything that had happened. And I no longer felt German…I had already got to the point where I said, "If a bullet were to hit me, I would no longer have to be ashamed to say that I'm German, later, once the war is over."'

Wilhelm Moses has no clear idea why those he saw executed were murdered, or how the particular families he transported were selected. Even today, studying the documents, it is hard to make sense of why the terror occurred where it did. Unlike the systematic killing the Einsatzgruppen (Reinhard Heydrich's infamous 'special units') were to embark on in the invasion of the Soviet Union in 1941, the killings following the invasion of Poland were sporadic. The SS probably killed anyone they didn't like the look of – especially any Polish Jews who had in some way 'offended' them. There was no law to prevent their random cruelty.

Aside from individual acts of terror against Jews, or 'partisans' who had been resisting the invasion, the Nazis also victimized another particularly hated section of Polish society, the intelligentsia. Implementing a policy that was to be copied by the Cambodian Communist Pol Pot more than thirty years later, the Nazis proposed genetically engineering a country by killing. They believed that if intelligent people were removed, there would be less resistance to their plans for creating a state consisting of ignorant slaves. And if intelligent people could be prevented from breeding, the next generation would consist of only stupid people. A practical step to the fulfilment of this warped idea occurred in November 1939 at the Jagellonian University in Cracow.

The occupying Germans called the professors of the ancient university to a meeting in one of the lecture rooms. One of those who attended was Mieczyslaw

Brozek, an assistant professor of philology. He expected the representatives of the new German authorities simply to instruct the academics present how they were to carry on teaching. Instead, after he and his colleagues had been sitting in the lecture room for a few minutes, they turned round to see that a row of soldiers had appeared behind them. The Nazis ordered the academics to go downstairs, beating them with rifle butts as they went. Brozek was in shock as he saw elderly professors hit by young German soldiers. 'I had a very Catholic upbringing,' he says, 'and it did not enter my head that something evil could happen…For anyone to imagine anything like this. It was beyond our life experience.'

Professor Stanislaw Urbanczyk was another academic caught up in this diabolical German plan whose intention was, he says, for 'the Poles to remain only at the lowest levels…to be slaves'. In the concentration camps where the professors were imprisoned, 'What was really difficult to survive was the hunger and the cold. It was a particularly cold winter and in the space of one month over a dozen professors died.' Those who transgressed even the most minor camp rule were tortured. 'One of my colleagues had a letter from his mother in his pocket,' says Professor Urbanczyk, 'and when they found it during a search he was strung up on a post and had to hang there with his arms tied tight behind him for an hour or more. Another punishment was to be beaten with a stick.'

For these extremely intelligent men used to making sense of what was going on around them, the sheer injustice of their suffering was almost unbearable. Mieczyslaw Brozek remembers seeing a German guard cuddling his child in his arms and then thinking, 'Crowds of corpses lie in the cellar, and at the same time this man has a heart for his child, his wife and so on. The duality of this is unbelievable.' Brozek suffered the effects of this psychological torture for many years afterwards. His time in the camp persuaded him of 'the complete annihilation of values. After the experiences I had in the camp there are no values. I had a vision of the worthlessness of everything. The senselessness of everything. This tormented me desperately, to the brink of suicide.'

Fourteen months after the meeting at which they had been snatched, almost all the surviving professors were released. News of their abduction had reached the outside world and pressure had been growing, particularly from Italy and the Pope, for them to be freed. That the Nazis were susceptible to outside pressure of this sort may seem surprising given what was to happen during Operation

Barbarossa and its aftermath; but the professors had the 'good fortune' to be victims of the regime in the very first year of the war when, particularly before the fall of France, the Nazis still took some notice of outside pressure.

In those early months of the war some of the German Army leadership also disliked the excesses they learnt had been committed, primarily by the SS. Colonel-General Johannes Blaskowitz, commander of the Ober-Ost region, wrote two memorandums of complaint; this extract is from his second, dated 6 February 1940: 'It is misguided to slaughter tens of thousands of Jews and Poles as is happening at present…The acts of violence against the Jews which occur in full view of the public inspire among the religious Poles not only deep disgust but also great pity…The attitude of the troops to the SS and police alternates between abhorrence and hatred. Every soldier feels repelled and revolted by these crimes which are being perpetrated in Poland by nationals of the Reich and representatives of State authority.'

Colonel-General Johannes Blaskowitz, who complained 'it is misguided to slaughter tens of thousands of Jews and Poles as is happening at present.'

Hitler was not moved by such arguments. The diary entry of his army adjutant, Major Engel, for 18 November 1939 records Hitler's reaction to Blaskowitz's first memo: '[Hitler] starts making serious criticisms of the "childish attitudes" among the army leadership; one can't fight a war with Salvation Army methods. This also confirms his long-held aversion to General Bl. whom he had never trusted.'

There was never any question about which side of the argument Hitler supported. But the very fact that generals such as Blaskowitz still felt able to protest at atrocities witnessed by the army may go some way to explaining why the killings and oppression in Poland were seemingly arbitrary. Less than two years later, following the invasion of the Soviet Union, the army leadership would be much more compliant in the face of Nazi atrocities.

The Division of Poland

Latvia

Lithuania

Kaunas (Kovno)

Vilnius (Vilno)

Minsk

Danzig

East Prussia

West Prussia

Grodno

Bialystok

Bydgoszcz (Bromberg)

Ukraine

Poznań (Posen)

Warthegau

Warsaw

Lodz

Radom

Lublin

GERMANY

General Government

Katowice

USSR

Cracow

Lvov (Lemberg)

CZECHOSLOVAKIA

Galicia

ROMANIA

N

— — Polish boundary before 1.9.39

••••• Dividing line between Germany and Russia until 22.6.41

annexed by Germany

under German civil administration

0   100   200 miles

0   100 kms

Six weeks after the invasion and its initial chaos, the Nazi administrative plans for Poland had taken shape. The country had been split between Germany and the Soviet Union under the secret part of the Nazi-Soviet Pact signed in August 1939 by Molotov and Ribbentrop. The German part (188,000 square kilometres of Polish territory with a population of 20.2 million Poles) was either parcelled off to be part of existing Reich territory like East Prussia, or formed into one of three new districts, each run by a committed Nazi. Albert Forster ran the area called West Prussia, Arthur Greiser ran the Warthegau (an area with Posen – as the Germans called Poznan – at its heart), and Hans Frank ran the remaining occupied territory, now called the General Government. West Prussia and the Warthegau were integrated into the Reich, and the General Government was to be, initially at least, a dumping ground for unwanted Jews and Poles.

Hitler may have had a 'vision' for Poland – to reorder it racially so that West Prussia and the Warthegau became 'German' while the General Government became the dustbin into which the people not wanted elsewhere were thrown. But the enormity of accomplishing this vision at a time of war, plus the chaos endemic within the Nazi hierarchy, meant that those charged with carrying it out had great latitude in decision-making – even, as we shall see, to the extent of contradicting the spirit of the vision altogether.

Central to the task of racially reordering Poland was movement. The Nazis intended to treat the Polish people like so many parcels, throwing them from one place to the next until the pattern pleased them. Heinrich Himmler was charged with organizing this massive task. Space first had to be found in the incorporated territories for the hundreds of thousands of incoming ethnic Germans who, under the secret protocol with the Soviet Union, had been allowed to leave the Baltic states and other territories in the wake of Stalin's occupation. Meanwhile, 'unsuitable' Poles (such as the intelligentsia, or those who might present a 'threat' to the Germans) were to be deported south to the General Government. Simultaneously, the indigenous Polish population was to be assessed and graded according to racial value. Some might be classed suitable as 'additional population', others classed as 'unsuitable'. The Jews (who were certainly 'unsuitable' in the eyes of the Nazis) were to be gathered in ghettos until a decision could be made as to their eventual fate. In a regime within which there was already a predisposition to institutional chaos, this

Himmler examines a child, eyeing up his racial potential. Himmler treated such children as a farmer treats his animals, deciding which should be allowed to grow and breed, and which should be slaughtered young.

gigantic reordering of a population was a recipe for anarchy.

To try to understand the human impact of the Nazis' wild plan for Poland we traced individuals from every level of the Nazis' racial order, from the indigenous Germans of the Warthegau to the Jews of Lodz, from the dispossessed Poles of Posen to the incoming Volksdeutsche (ethnic Germans) of the Baltic states. Together they bear testimony to the consequences of an inhuman scheme.

Parts of Poland had, of course, been German before the Versailles Treaty, and large numbers of ethnic Germans were already living there. They presented no problems to the Nazi administrators in classification terms – they were simply German and therefore they were at the top of the racial pile. Charles Bleeker-Kohlsaat belonged to one of the grand German families who lived in the province of Posen. His grandparents owned an estate of more than 600 hectares with a magnificent house. They kept fifty-four horses and employed twenty-eight Polish families, nearly 300 people altogether. The Bleeker family were proud of their German tradition and had refused to relinquish it after the Versailles Treaty Posen made part of Poland. Long before the German Army arrived, Charles Bleeker's grandmother, who had deliberately never learnt more than a few words of Polish, held the view that the

Germans were superior to the Poles. 'She would say, "After all, we are the Germans, we are more highly evolved. Those are just Poles and there is no need to learn their language,"' says Charles Bleeker. 'We were rich and somehow the Poles were made to feel that.'

The Bleeker family were overjoyed at the news that the German Army was approaching: 'The adults were glad to be German again,' says Charles Bleeker. He remembers, when he was eleven, a German soldier arrived on a motorcycle, the first of an army they all felt would bring their liberation. 'I looked at him,'

German troops enter Lodz in Poland, September 1939. The ethnic Germans in the parts of Poland that had been German before World War I were ecstatic in their welcome.

says Bleeker, 'and said "Good afternoon!" and he looked at me and said, "Good afternoon, lad. What good German you speak!" I said, "But I am German!" Then it was the soldier's turn to be astonished because he had thought that now that he was in Poland, there would only be Polish people living there. I was fascinated by his uniform, by the fact that he spoke German, that he was friendly to me, by his beautiful motorcycle. I was beside myself.' But within days, this feeling of euphoria became mixed with fear. As ethnic Germans the Bleekers were able to keep their grand estate – indeed, the Nazis renamed the whole area Bleekersdorf – but their Polish landowning neighbours suffered a very different fate. 'They were evacuated very early on,' says Charles Bleeker, 'and they came to us and begged us on their knees to intercede on their behalf so that they could stay on their own property. We did no such thing because we simply lacked the courage. Then we suddenly heard things like this person had been dispossessed and that person has been dispossessed, another one has been shot as a hostage, and we told ourselves, good heavens these people must have done something, otherwise the German government would not have dispossessed them or shot them as hostages. They must have done something.'

Still trying to rationalize the suffering they saw around them, the Bleekers went to welcome the trains bringing in ethnic Germans from the Baltic states, Bessarabia and the other regions now occupied by Stalin. At the station they experienced another disappointment: some of the incoming Germans were not the superior race they had expected. 'We were not at all keen on them, at least my family wasn't. These people spoke mostly very poor German. They had a terrible accent which nobody could understand and we almost took them for Poles.'

The Eigis were one incoming family of German ethnic origin. They had chosen to be deported by the Nazis from Estonia once they heard that Stalin was approaching. Irma Eigi was 17 years old when she found herself with the rest of her family on a ship heading towards Poland. 'We were not happy at all,' she says. 'It was like standing next to yourself. It happened, you didn't quite grasp it. It was a bit like being in a state of shock.' Irma Eigi had loved living in Estonia; she and her family had found it a tolerant and beautiful country, but they felt they had little choice but to leave on the German ships when they came. Their only alternative had been to face Stalin and, they were warned, risk being sent to Siberia. Instead, they thought, the German ships would take them to Germany. But, like the Bleekers, they too were disappointed by the harsh realities of the Nazi racial reorganization. When the Eigis learnt that their true destination was not Germany but Poland, they were outraged. 'We hadn't reckoned on that at all. When we were told we were going to the Warthegau, well, it was quite a shock, I can tell you.' The shock increased when, after the boat docked, the Eigis found that their first home was a transit camp, a school strewn with straw. But this was nothing to the surprise they experienced on discovering how the Nazis went about finding somewhere for the incoming ethnic Germans to live. 'Poles had to move out of their houses for us so that we had flats to live in,' says Irma Eigi. 'We had no inkling of that before it happened.'

Right: A child arrives (held by her mother) from Lithuania to be resettled by the Nazis in Poland in the autumn of 1939.

Frau Eigi still remembers with horror the day, just before Christmas 1939, when she went with her family to the Nazi housing office in Posen to ask if there was a flat available for them. The housing officials said there was. The Eigis were given the keys, the address and a map of the city, and told to go off on their own and find it. 'When we went to visit the flat we had terrible feelings,' she says. 'It was a tall apartment building, unrenovated and with strange windows.' They climbed the stairs and opened the front door of the apartment. Inside there was chaos. 'You noticed there had been people here who had had to leave very quickly,' she says. 'Some of the cupboards stood open. The drawers were open. On the table were the remains of food. And then the unmade beds, messed up.' Frau Eigi's father refused to stay in the flat and the whole family went back to the Nazi housing allocation office. There they were told that since it was near Christmas there was no other flat on offer, so the Eigis had to move in. They chose to settle in only one room, huddled together against their fears of what had happened. 'Strangely, I can still see this flat today,' says Frau Eigi. 'And every time I think about it I am still overcome by some fear. It is as if I had goose pimples on my back. Always, when I'm frightened, I see this flat in front of me, even in other situations of fear.'

Now that the Eigi family had a flat, the next stage in the Nazi resettlement programme was to find the head of the family a job. In Estonia Herr Eigi had run a hotel. There were no hotels available in Posen, but there were still some restaurants which had not yet been taken over by the Nazis. Herr Eigi was told to walk around town and see if he liked the look of any restaurant still owned and run by Poles. Off he went, accompanied by his wife and his daughter. 'Most restaurants were in German hands,' says Irma Eigi, 'we were relatively late. And the Baltic Germans had already taken possession of the better restaurants.' Eventually they managed to find a small restaurant still run by Poles, so her father went back to the Nazis and asked for permission to run this restaurant. After signing formal papers of ownership, he simply took over the restaurant. ('Taking over' is a recurrent theme in Nazi ideology. Herr Eigi was behaving as the Nazis believed all Germans, as a superior race, should. He wanted this restaurant, so why not just take it?)

Irma Eigi cannot remember what happened to the Polish owner, or even if she or her father ever met him. 'It could be that the Polish owner had already left,' she says. 'You live in a trance. If you were always thinking about it, you'd have to kill yourself. You can't live with this guilt. You can't even shrug off the guilt on to the government. But on the other hand, every person has an instinct for self-preservation. What else could we have done? Where else were we supposed to go?'

Frau Eigi still tries to imagine the suffering endured by the family evicted from the flat she and her family first inhabited in Posen. Anna Jeziorkowska doesn't have to imagine the suffering because she experienced it. She and her family, all Poles, were quietly at home in their flat in Posen on the evening of 8 November 1939 when Anna's mother looked out of the window and exclaimed 'Germans!' Buses and cars pulled up outside the block of flats and moments later German soldiers banged on the door. 'They burst into the room,' says Anna Jeziorkowska, 'into the kitchen, they were everywhere. Of course, there was great chaos, crying, wailing. The Germans pushed us, they hit father on the face, and we got so frightened that we started crying. My younger brother, he was very delicate, started vomiting.' The German soldiers demanded money and jewellery from her parents before they threw them out of the flat. Her mother gave them all the jewels she had, including her wedding ring. 'I was scared,' says Anna, who was then just 10 years old, 'as much as only a child can be'. The family, along with their neighbours from the same block, was taken to a transit camp where they slept on straw. 'The conditions were unbearable for children,' says Anna. 'The food was cold. There was a turnip soup. For us children it was uneatable.'

After a few days word reached them that Germans had moved into their flat. 'I cried,' says Anna. 'We cried together, my sister and I, cuddled to each other, remembering our toys, the good old days, what we had lost. And it was terrible, it is impossible to describe, even now it hurts to think about it.' After five months in the transit camp, they were herded out and shoved into train wagons which were normally used for transporting animals. They had eight or ten days in the dark and cold of the wagons before they reached their destination, the town of Golice in the General Government. There, an old man saw them huddled in shock in the town square and took pity on them. He took them to his own run-down house and offered them a room. 'The conditions there were also difficult,' remembers Anna. 'There were no beds, we slept on the floor, no comforts, no running water, and everything else was difficult. But at least we had a room, a very small room.'

Evictions and deportations, such as that suffered by the Jeziorkowska family, happened in town and countryside alike. In rural areas whole villages could be uprooted in one action. Franz Jagemann was a German of Polish ancestry who, as an interpreter, helped the Nazis in their dreadful work. He vividly remembers one action which took him to a remote village in the Gnesen district of Poland. Twenty or twenty-five police officers in vans drove to the village and were stopped by local Nazi Storm Troopers just outside the village boundary. The Storm Troopers had been keeping watch but the villagers suspected nothing. Then trucks arrived bearing the SS, members of the Totenkopf (death's head) division. At a little after three o'clock in the morning the police and SS swarmed down the central street of the village, breaking into the homes, while the local Storm Troopers surrounded the village from the outside. 'People were beaten,' says Franz Jagemann, 'people were kicked, there was blood. The worst thing about it for me was to see an elderly couple, they were over seventy and clearly didn't understand what was going on, they were beaten up and thrown on to a truck. One SS man, who was born in Upper Silesia, carried on as if he was berserk, screaming at the villagers and driving them together with violence. People were kicked, punched, pistols waved in their faces. It was like a proper hold-up.'

Stefan Kasprzyk, the son of a Polish peasant, remembers that night when the SS came to call: 'They surrounded the farms so that no one would run away. People took what they could carry. Only a few ever returned. My grandfather was tortured by them and after he was deported, he died. Our neighbour lost two children.'

The Nazis who terrorized this tiny Polish village needed space for the Germans who were arriving that very afternoon, so they solved their problem by simply removing the entire population of a village. Franz Jagemann also witnessed the arrival of the incoming Germans. 'You might say that the beds were still warm when they arrived,' he says. Some of the ethnic Germans expressed surprise that they were expected just to take over someone else's house in someone else's village. They said, "And we're supposed to take it over? It doesn't even belong to us!" I really did hear such comments,' says Franz Jagemann, 'but I would say that the majority were convinced that it was their new property now because the war had been won against Poland and that it was all in order.'

After witnessing the brutality of the SS, Franz Jagemann subsequently tried to get warnings to villagers who were to be deported, but he does not believe he was a hero: 'I was there to assist in what we today euphemistically call ethnic cleansing. I was conscious of that…I didn't immediately go into hiding or run away or join the underground. I displayed a lack of courage.'

There was no chance for any of the villagers caught up in these violent deportations to alter their fate by claiming, 'I am really of German origin – you must reclassify me.' Yet for many thousands of Poles reclassification was a possibility. In pursuit of their aim to 'Germanize' the areas of Poland outside the General Government, the Nazi administrators had huge powers of discretion in deciding who was Polish and who was now German. These powers of discretion led to conflict between the two Gauleiters (district leaders) of the newly incorporated territories of Poland – Arthur Greiser of the Warthegau and Albert Forster of West Prussia – a conflict which shows how in wartime the notion of 'working towards the Führer' could assume arbitrary and contradictory dimensions on a massive scale.

Arthur Greiser was the hardest of the hardline Nazis, a man who had Himmler as a mentor. His aim was to turn the Warthegau into a model Gau (district). He expressed contempt for the indigenous Poles and took care to implement seriously the detailed criteria the Nazis used to determine which of the Poles could be Germanized and which could not. His policy was one of ruthless, uncompromising racial segregation. Albert Forster, ruler of the adjacent Nazi district, Danzig/West Prussia, though also a committed Nazi (and a man later sentenced to death for war crimes), had a very different attitude to racial classification. Forster had been overheard to joke that if he 'looked like Himmler' he wouldn't talk about race so much.

The dispute between Forster and Greiser is personified by the experience of Romuald Pilaczynski of Bydgoszcz, a town in what was then Albert Forster's kingdom. Forster did not enforce tedious individual classification on the population. He decided to reclassify some Poles as Germans *en masse*, without detailed examination. After all, hadn't Hitler said that in the pursuit of Germanizing Poland he would 'ask no questions about their methods'? 'According to materials known to me,' says Mr Pilaczynski, 'about 80 per cent of Bydgoszcz's population responded to Forster's announcement: "If you want to be in Germany, sign the 'Germanization list'." ' The Pilaczynski family signed and became German 'in the third category'. This gave them important advantages denied to ordinary Poles: the right to increased rations, the right to an education and the right to remain in the incorporated territories. But signing the paper didn't make Romuald Pilaczynski feel German: 'We lived the Polish way, we spoke Polish…The 80 per cent who obtained the identity cards of the third group did not consider themselves in any way German.' But Mr Pilaczynski had an uncle who lived in the Posen region, Arthur Greiser's realm: 'The uncle from Posen was not offered the Volksliste (the chance to be Germanized) but was deported.' Of course, as the Pilaczynskis realized at the time, there was no sense to this. They were from the same family and had the same ethnic background. One was no more German than the other. Yet the Pilaczynskis of Bydgoszcz escaped the suffering of deportation while their relatives in Posen had to endure it.

Unlike Forster, Greiser was pursuing a policy of debasing the Poles and Polish culture out of pure ideological zeal. In September 1940 a directive was issued in Greiser's name. It said: 'It will require a long period of education to achieve a state of affairs in which every German citizen adopts an attitude to Poles which corresponds to our national dignity and the aims of German policy.' In other words, Germans were still being too friendly to Poles. Now, if they did not treat them as slaves out of conviction, they would be made to treat them as slaves out of fear. The directive went on: 'Any individuals belonging to the German community who maintain relations with Poles which go beyond those deriving from the performance of services or economic considerations will be placed in protective custody…In all cases the maintenance of repeated friendly contacts with Poles must be regarded as failure to observe the prescribed distance.'

At his country house outside Posen, Greiser himself certainly strove to live up to his own ideals. Danuta Pawelczak-Grocholska was a servant in the Greiser household. She remembers him as 'a powerfully built figure. He was a tall man, you could see his arrogance, his conceit. He was so vain, so full of himself – as if there was nothing above him, a god, almost. Everybody tried to get out of his way, people had to bow to him, salute him. And the Poles, he treated them with great contempt. For him the Poles were slaves, good for nothing but work.' Danuta Pawelczak-Grocholska was terrified when first told that she had to work

Right: Albert Forster (on the right) stands next to Arthur Greiser in August 1939 when Greiser still worked for Forster in Danzig/West Prussia. Once Greiser was given his own area to control he complained constantly about his former boss.

German officials in Albert Forster's area determine the suitability for Germanization of the Poles sitting opposite; with Forster's attitude to Germanization, the discussion should not have taken long.

in Greiser's house. 'The very sound of Greiser's name made people shake with fear because they knew who he was.' Greiser had grown up in Poland of German descent, spoke Polish, gone to a Polish school and yet now he was nicknamed the 'Pole hater'. Danuta had already witnessed what he was capable of. In a reprisal action ordered by him, she had seen the Germans shoot twenty Poles in the local village square. 'They shot them solely because they were Polish,' she says. 'It was incredible. That image has stayed with me for so long that whenever I walk through the square, past that place, I see those people. And it was all Greiser's doing.' When he heard the name of his daughter's new employer, Danuta's father said to her, 'You are walking into the lion's den; who knows if you will leave it alive.' Danuta had walked the 6 kilometres from her own home to the Greisers' house in tears. Once there she was put to work cleaning the house – to the 'German' standard: 'You were not supposed to see a speck of dust. Carpet fringes had to be combed in straight lines. God help us if there was one out of place! It was all done to perfection, with exaggerated opulence. On the coldest day of the winter, her ladyship would order the cleaning of the windows for New Year's Eve. Our hands would freeze to the window panes. We blew on our fingers but we had to carry on with the cleaning.' Everything in the seventy-room palace and estate was kept immaculate, all for the use of just Greiser and his wife. 'The orangery, the fishponds, the gamekeeper…. The whole economic base of the place was geared exclusively for the use of these two people. It was luxury, in every respect pure luxury.'

Greiser was not just another conqueror who was exploiting the vanquished in order to live in comfort. He lived this way because, as a German, he believed it was his right. He was at the top of the racial ladder and, as a member of a superior race, he had to be true to the laws of nature and live better than his racial inferiors. Greiser was later to explain his philosophy thus: 'If, in past times, other peoples enjoyed their century-long history by living well and doing so by getting foreign peoples to work for them without compensating them accordingly and without meting out justice to them, then we, too, as Germans, want to learn from this history. No longer must we stand in the wings; on the contrary, we must altogether become a master-race!'

Equally, Greiser felt it essential for the future of the Reich that the racial classification of the incorporated territories was completed diligently and systematically. He was therefore deeply irritated when he saw the casual way in which his neighbour, Albert Forster, was treating the whole question of racial assessment. In a letter dated 16 March 1943, Greiser complained to Himmler about Forster's attitude: '…right from the start I avoided trying to win cheap successes by Germanizing people who could not provide clear proof of their German origin…As I have frequently pointed out in my discussions with you, my ethnic policy is threatened by that pursued in the Reich Gau Danzig/West Prussia in so far as the policy followed there initially appears to many superficial observers to be more successful.'

Himmler replied to Greiser that he was 'particularly pleased' by his work on Germanization. In contrast, Himmler had written a letter of complaint to Forster sixteen months previously, on 26 November 1941 in which he had expressed Hitler's view that: '"I do not wish the Gauleiters of the eastern Gaus to enter into a competition to see who will be the first to report after two or three years, 'My Führer, the Gau has been Germanized.' Instead, I wish to have a population which is racially impeccable and am content if a Gauleiter can report it in ten years' time…." You yourself are such an old National Socialist,' added Himmler, 'that you know that one drop of false blood which comes into an individual's veins can never be removed.'

Himmler (sitting in the front of the car to the left) visits the Lodz ghetto.

The fact that Himmler wrote such a letter to Forster in 1941 but was still hearing Greiser's complaints about Forster in 1943 demonstrates that even Himmler was fallible. As far as Forster was concerned, the only order he was following was the vague instruction from the Führer to Germanize his *Gau*. How he did it was his business. Forster, in his own eyes, was simply pursuing Hitler's vision in the way he thought best. It scarcely mattered to him that Himmler thought he was Germanizing in a way contrary to racial theory; he knew that Himmler could do little about it. Thus, the lack of firm orders and the absence of specific job descriptions defining the scope of any individual's responsibility, all attributes of Nazi administration which had been present in the party from the 1920s, had their bloody impact on the gigantic canvas of Poland.

Nothing better illustrates the conflict between the Nazi lords of Poland, or the inherent lack of a detailed plan for the Nazi administration of Poland, than a row which flared up early in the occupation between Hans Frank, who ran the General Government, and Arthur Greiser. Himmler and Greiser were keen to rid the Warthegau of 'undesirables' as soon as possible and, as we have seen with the tragic story of Anna Jeziorkowska and her family, herded unwanted Poles on to trains which took them to the General Government. Frank protested. The trains arrived and disgorged their human cargo but he had nowhere to put them. 'Night after night trains of evacuees came to the General Government,' says Dr Fritz Arlt, who was a former Nazi Storm Trooper and, in 1940, head of the Department for Population Affairs and Welfare in the General Government (someone who has never, incidentally, been convicted of war crimes). 'The people were thrown out of the trains, whether in the market-place or on the train station, or wherever it was, and nobody cared about it…We received a phone call from the district officer and he said, "I don't know what to do any more. So and so many hundreds have arrived again. I have neither shelter nor food nor anything…" Without doubt, the most awful things were also happening.' The situation was not helped by the antipathy that existed between Frank and SS-Obergruppenführer Friedrich-Wilhelm Krüger, who was the senior SS man in the General Government. Frank believed that since he was in charge of the General Government, then Krüger was subordinate to him. Himmler countered with the view that Krüger was simply 'assigned' to Frank, not 'subordinate'. Hitler never decided who was right.

The disagreement between Frank on the one hand and Himmler and Greiser on the other wasn't just about the administrative difficulties of trains turning up unannounced and leaving thousands of deportees out in the cold. There was a fundamental conflict of ideology between them. Frank wanted the General Government to be the 'granary' of the Reich. He wanted to keep the farmers in their place and to maximize the economic exploitation of the area with as little

inconvenience as possible caused by what he believed were unnecessary transportations. Greiser and Himmler had a bigger vision; the priority for them was not tawdry economic need, but the racial and ideological goal of incorporated territories which were 'pure' and of German blood. If that meant that the General Government would become a dustbin into which all the undesirables of the Reich would be thrown, then so be it.

On 12 February 1940 there was a meeting at Göring's Karinhall estate near Berlin in an attempt to thrash out the difficulties. All the key participants in the dispute were present: Himmler, Frank, Greiser and Göring. Frank allied himself with Göring, who supported him in the meeting. The General Government should become the 'granary' of the Reich, said Göring; the priority must be to strengthen the war potential of the Reich. Himmler protested that he needed space in which to put the incoming ethnic Germans. A compromise appeared to be reached when Himmler stated that he and Frank would 'agree upon the procedures of future evacuations'. Frank was delighted. He thought that Himmler's racial vision of a reordered Poland had received a body blow. Göring's argument that the demands of an ongoing war in France must take priority seemed decisive.

Himmler, however, was not to have his vision dashed so easily. Just as Frank had appealed to Göring, so Himmler decided to appeal to Hitler. A study of the way he did so is particularly instructive because there was no greater manipulator of the Nazi system than Himmler. First, he timed his approach to Hitler perfectly, presenting him with a memo innocuously entitled 'Some Thoughts on the Treatment of the Alien Population in the East' on 15 May 1940, once it was obvious that the Nazis were going to win a great victory in France. In the memo he again called for the General Government to be a dumping ground for undesirable Poles, and since it was clear that the Nazis would now have possession of France and her colonies, he proposed a new solution to the problem of the Polish Jews. Instead of transporting *them* to the General Government, he suggested that they be sent to a colony in Africa. The memo also outlined the methods which would be used to turn the remaining 'unGermanized' Poles into a 'leaderless labouring class'.

Himmler later noted that Hitler read the memorandum and found it 'good and correct'. Furthermore, Himmler felt authorized to tell others that Hitler approved of the memo. Professor Christopher Browning, who has made a

Left: Hans Frank, the keen chess player, on his train in April 1940. He was later to be outplayed in Nazi internal politics by Himmler.

particular study of Nazi resettlement policy in Poland, told me: 'This is the way decisions are made: Hitler does not draw up an elaborate plan, sign it and pass it down the line. What you get is an encouragement to Himmler to fight it out with the others and the ability now to invoke Hitler's approval if they don't give way. And Hitler can still back out later, of course. You see, he's reserving his options, but he's encouraging Himmler, who has anticipated that this is really the sort of long-range thing that Hitler would like.'

Hans Frank now learnt that there had been a change in policy since his meeting with Göring and decided to put the best face he could on it. On 30 May 1940, at a meeting of police chiefs in Cracow, Frank announced the change of policy caused by Himmler's victory. Referring to a recent conversation he himself had had with Hitler, he talked openly of the difficulties of resettling the incoming Poles and of trying to turn them into a leaderless class that could never rise against the Germans again. His speech was extraordinary in its casual brutality even by the standards of the Third Reich: '…we, as National Socialists, are faced with such an incredibly difficult and responsible task that we can only talk about these things in the most intimate circles…The Führer told me that the implementation of German policy in Poland is a matter for the men who are in charge of the General Government to deal with themselves. He put it this way: we must liquidate those people whom we have discovered form the leadership in Poland; all those who follow in their footsteps must be arrested and then got rid of after an appropriate period. We do not need to burden the Reich organization of the German policy with that. We don't need to bother to cart these people off to concentration camps in the Reich because then we would only have trouble and an unnecessary correspondence with their relatives. Instead, we will finish the thing off here. We will do it in the simplest way.' As a result, during the summer of 1940, thousands of Poles, many from the intelligentsia, were simply murdered.

What sort of man makes a speech like that? Hans Frank had been Hitler's lawyer, more used to talking to judges than Nazi executioners. At his enormous and elaborate country retreat outside Cracow we talked to some of Frank's servants and asked them what it was like to work in the household of such a man: 'Wonderful,' says Anna Mirek, a Polish cook, 'even though we worked very hard, sometimes sixteen hours a day, depending on the need, if there were guests. But the atmosphere was jolly, pleasant: people were polite, and even if one was tired it gave one strength…To me Frank seemed a nice man, polite.' Bemused by this response we asked how Anna Mirek reconciled this memory with the knowledge that Frank had been involved in the mass killing of Poles. 'As for those higher political affairs that's something different,' she answered, 'I know nothing about it. I'm not good at it. I'm good at cooking, observing the stars, telling the weather. That I'm good at.'

Zbigniew Bazarnik worked at Frank's country house as a furnace-stoker. 'We all felt quite relaxed here,' he says, 'not, as one used to hear, like in a camp, where one was shaking at the sight of a German.' He did, though, remember one incident which showed a darker side to life in the Frank household. Polish Jews were working at the house doing renovation work in the early years of the German occupation. One day it was discovered that one of the Jews had decided to have a bath in Hans Frank's own bathroom when he thought no one was looking. Mr Bazarnik later learnt what happened to him: 'Here in the courtyard he was pushed into the boot of a small car – an Opel – and they could not fit him in so they broke his arms and legs, took him somewhere outside Krzeszowice and shot him…A sad story but then why he took such a fancy into his head, it is difficult to understand.'

Dr Fritz Arlt knew Hans Frank not as a servant knows a master but as a valued subordinate knows a boss. Dr Arlt worked for Frank in the early years of the war in Cracow. 'If I think about Frank, then I have to say that he was a tragi-comic figure,' says Dr Arlt. 'Frank was a highly intelligent chap. He was a good musician, a pianist.'

Our interview with Dr Arlt was one of the most extraordinary we conducted because even though he was a senior Nazi figure involved in population affairs in the General Government, he said he never knew of the atrocities ordered by Frank and carried out by the SS. Dr Arlt talked of a 'conspiracy of silence' and said that he himself had done his best to implement Nazi policies humanely and that Poles had spoken up in his defence after he had tried to help them. Only once, because we confronted him with a specific document, did I see what I took to be the granite heart of a true Nazi administrator. In Götz Aly's book *Endlösung* a frightening letter is quoted which called for the removal to a concentration camp of ethnic German farmers who were complaining because they were 'homesick'. These ethnic Germans simply refused to accept naturalization. An official letter ordered 'arrangements to be made for the transportation into a concentration camp' of the recalcitrant 'gang leaders' of the homesick farmers. The letter, signed by a *Gauleiter*, bears the dictation mark Dr A – Dr Arlt's initials. 'Yes, it is without doubt the Dr Fritz Arlt who is sitting in front of you now who is named there,' says Dr Arlt when we asked him about the letter. 'What am I supposed to do now?' We asked him what he knew about the concentration camps to which the letter called for the ethnic Germans to be sent. His reply was illuminating. 'This was a regulation passed by Herr Himmler. And I knew about regulations which were in this connection, that people who were not willing to be resettled were to be sent to a concentration camp.' Dr Arlt, of course, had not answered the question. He had simply stated, in effect, that he was 'acting under orders'. When we pressed him and asked what he thought a concentration camp was, he replied: 'What I thought a concentration camp was? Exactly what it says: a camp in which people who somehow or other represented a danger against law and order were concentrated.' We pressed him again, asking if he did not think that this was a severe punishment. 'I'm sorry, but the people knew that they probably would have to expect that. I don't know. I was never a camp administrator.' Here was a man who had been a key part of a process in which homesick ethnic Germans who refused resettlement were consigned to a concentration camp, who had not the slightest remorse about his actions. Indeed, he expected those who questioned him to be satisfied with a response which was that in 1943 all he knew about concentration camps was that they were places where people were 'concentrated'. In our interview with Dr Arlt it was a moment of revelation. Who can tell where coldness and indifference end and criminality begins?

As a group, of course, it was the Jews of Poland who were to suffer most. But in the initial months of the war a racially obsessed Nazi like Greiser perceived himself as having less a Jewish problem than a Polish one. The difficulties of resettling incoming ethnic Germans from the east plus the need to Germanize the Warthegau were his immediate priorities. The Jews were perceived at first as a problem whose solution was imminent, then, as difficulties arose, as one whose ultimate solution could be postponed. As a first interim measure, the Nazis ordered the concentration of Jews in ghettos, the biggest of which in the

Warthegau was Lodz. This was always intended to be a temporary solution until the Jews could be deported, so Greiser and his minions presumed, down to the 'dustbin' of the General Government.

Estera Frenkiel, who came from a Lodz Jewish family, read in her local newspaper in early 1940 that a ghetto for Jews was to be established in the northern part of the city. The streets of Lodz were listed according to the dates by which their Jewish inhabitants had to leave their flats. 'It was just as though a bomb had gone off over our heads,' she says. 'We were used to anti-Semitism. Anti-Semitism was also rife among the Poles…Polish Anti-Semitism was perhaps more financial. But German anti-Semitism was: Why do you exist? You shouldn't be! You ought to disappear!'

The Jews of Lodz rushed to find somewhere to live within the designated area of the ghetto. Housing conditions there were appalling from the very beginning. Out of a total of 31,721 flats, the majority of which consisted of just one room, only 725 had running water. Estera Frenkiel's mother found that the apartment they thought they had reserved, a shop with a small flat attached, was already occupied. 'And then my mother went out on to the street and walked up and down talking to herself: "What shall I do now? Where shall I go with my children? There remains nothing else other than to commit suicide." The people who had taken the flat heard this, called her over and said, "Please, listen. The room and kitchen are enough for us. You can move into the shop."' So the Frenkiel family, with immense gratitude, moved into a shop measuring 12 metres square.

There were rich pickings for those of German descent left in Lodz. Eugen Zielke was an ethnic German who watched an employee of his father's 'take over' a big grocery store in Lodz which had previously been owned by Jews who had now been forced into the poverty of the nearby ghetto. Zielke accompanied his father's employee as he went on to choose an apartment for himself from the accommodation abandoned by the Jewish residents of Lodz. 'The flat was locked up and sealed,' he says, 'but we opened it. It was indescribable. Things were strewn all over the floor, all the clothes. The table in the dining-room was laid for supper, there was bread, there was tea, there was even sausage. But when he saw all that and how it was, he said, "It's not possible! It's unbelievable! What on earth was going on here?"' They both left the apartment, shocked, though not

Scenes of life in the Lodz ghetto. In the middle picture is a man who might well be asking, 'What more can I sell to survive?'

sufficiently so for Zielke's acquaintance to give up the Jewish grocery store he had already accepted from the Nazis.

Greiser asserted that the Jews had 'hoarded colossally'. Therefore, once in the ghetto, they were made to give up their money for food. It was an act of pure gangsterism, a means of plucking all the valuables from the Jews before they were transported to whatever 'dustbin' or reservation was to be their future home. And not only the incoming Nazis benefited from selling food at inflated prices to the Jews trapped in the ghetto. One of Eugen Zielke's relatives participated in the crime, and he himself benefited from it. 'I saw it from the point of view of a businessman,' says Zielke. 'They couldn't nibble on a ring, but if they could get a piece of bread for it, then they could survive for a day or two.' Jewellery would be smuggled out of the ghetto and bought for a fraction of its worth. 'If I got something in my hand for 100 marks and it was worth 5000 marks, then I'd be stupid not to buy it,' says Zielke. 'You don't have to be a businessman – that's what life's about.'

We put the following statement to Eugen Zielke: 'You could say that you became rich on the backs of people in the ghetto, the misery, the poverty of the ghetto dwellers.'

'You can say "Yes" in reply to that question,' answered Herr Zielke. 'The Poles got rich. The Germans got rich. Everyone got rich…some of them with gold and silver and others with food, simply to survive. I already told you. I saw it from another point of view. I saw it as a businessman.'

By August 1940 the Jews trapped in Lodz ghetto had no money left to pay for food, so a decision was forced upon the Nazis. Should they let the Jews starve or should they feed them? The decision-making process, which took place in Lodz that autumn, once again involved minor Nazi functionaries having to thrash out policy for themselves in the face of silence from Berlin. Hans Biebow, a former coffee importer from Bremen, was the Nazi chief of ghetto administration. He came up with a solution to the problem – the Jews in the Lodz ghetto could be made to work and would thus be able to produce goods which could be sold in order to buy food. Biebow's deputy, Alexander Palfinger, disagreed. He believed that the Jews must still be concealing money. Only by the threat of total starvation would the Jews finally reveal their last hoarded gold. If he was mistaken, and the Jews did die, then so be it. 'A rapid dying out of the Jews is for us a matter of total indifference,' he

More pictures of the Lodz ghetto. Notice how in the middle picture the Jewish workers do not even stop working whilst their photo is taken.

Overleaf: Jews carry their belongings through the snow in the initial days of the Lodz ghetto, spring 1940.

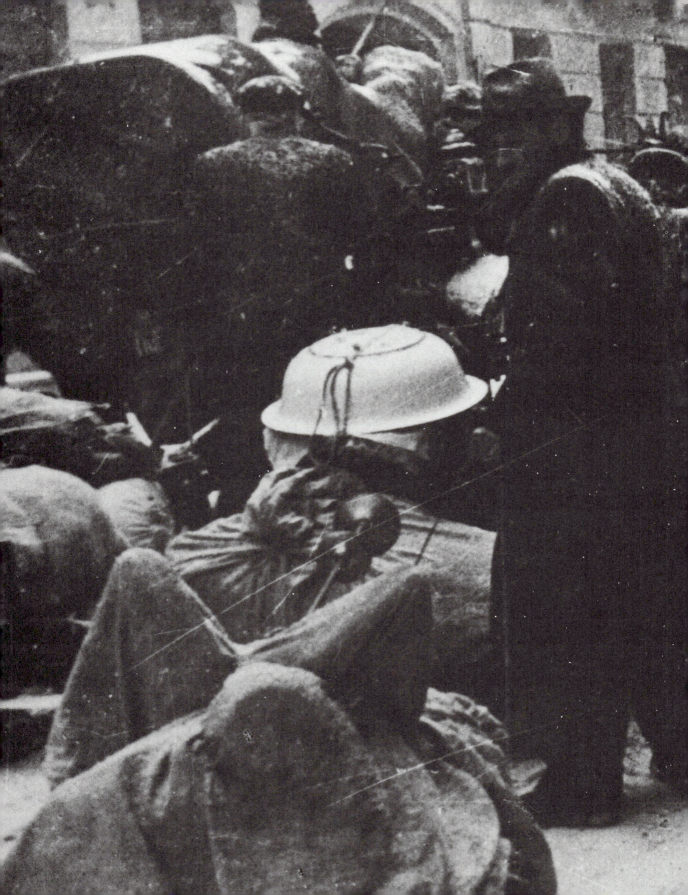

wrote, 'if not to say desirable, as long as the concomitant effects leave the public interest of the German people untouched.'

Palfinger lost the argument. Hans Biebow's immediate superior, Dr Karl Marder, sided with what has been termed Biebow's 'productionist' argument. The Lodz ghetto was now to become a business enterprise. Palfinger left Lodz in disgust. As Professor Browning discovered, Palfinger's 'parting gesture, an obvious ploy to attract attention to what he considered the intolerable coddling

Hans Biebow, ghetto manager of Lodz (on the right), counts the money extorted from the Jews in 1940. Biebow was careful to share the loot around – especially with Arthur Greiser.

of the Lodz Jews, was to order from Berlin 144,000 eggs per week for the ghetto, leaving the embarrassed Biebow to explain that the request had been made without his knowledge'.

Greiser was happy with the proposal that the ghetto become a generator of wealth because he had arranged to pocket the profit from the scheme himself. 'The Jews are going to be providing labour at a set rate,' says Professor Browning, '35 per cent of that is going to go to the Jews themselves so that they can buy food, 65 per cent is going to go into a special account of Greiser's, one that he controls, his slush fund.'

Left: Jews in the Lodz ghetto during the winter of 1940–1.

Estera Frenkiel worked for the Jewish administration inside the ghetto and got to know Hans Biebow well. Her first meeting with him demonstrated at once the schizophrenic attitude of the well-mannered Nazi who had to deal with Polish Jews. Estera Frenkiel remembers how she was introduced to Biebow by another secretary Dora Fuchs: '"This is a new secretary," said Dora. Biebow got up from his chair, came over to me and introduced himself. He shook hands with me. He immediately thought, "What have I done!" and said, "I shake hands only when first introduced."'

Hans Biebow was a man who 'worked towards the Führer' not just for the good of Nazi Germany but for the good of himself. He exploited his position of absolute power over the Jews of Lodz ghetto at every opportunity – sometimes in direct contravention of the strict Nazi rule that Germans should never be physically intimate with Jews. 'One day a 16-year-old girl was engaged in the office,' says Estera Frenkiel. 'She was told to take Biebow some coffee in his office. She gave him the coffee. He saw the pretty girl and touched her up. In all her life the girl had not seen a German man. She had seen Germans from afar, but not close up. She didn't want this. She was still an innocent girl and she fought back. Thereupon he tore off her dress. It is highly likely that nothing happened because she ran away. But he shot at her and hit her in her ear. She bled profusely. She went back to her room and lay down. It was terrible.'

Estera Frenkiel told us this dreadful story – as she told us all her experiences in the Lodz ghetto – dry-eyed while sitting in the Jewish cemetery of Lodz, only yards away from the graves of thousands who had died of the maltreatment they had suffered in the ghetto. I remarked to her after we had filmed the interview that she was one of the toughest and most decisive people I had ever met. She looked at me for a moment and half smiled. 'If I wasn't tough and decisive,' she replied, 'I wouldn't be standing here today.'

As 1940 drew to an end, the Jews in the Lodz ghetto, despite suffering hunger and abuse, had at least not been left to starve to death. From being a temporary measure the ghetto had become a mini-manufacturing camp which had effectively become self-sufficient. It is worth remembering just how the Nazis ended up in this position. For the decision-making process by which the Nazis created a ghetto which could last indefinitely demonstrates the ability individuals had not only to act opportunistically within the Nazi administrative

Previous pages: Jews in the Lodz ghetto move furniture in the spring of 1940. Behind them non-Jews watch through the wire fence of the ghetto.

system but in the process to create new crises which needed to be solved. Since the Nazis were operating expediently in circumstances of crisis, only short-term decisions were made. The Jews were first concentrated in ghettos, something which was intended to be only a brief incarceration, preparatory to shipping them off to the General Government. But Frank objected to large numbers of Poles being simply dumped in his area. Then came the ambitious suggestion that the Jews might be shipped not to the outer reaches of the Nazi empire but to far-flung parts of the world, such as Africa, a solution made possible by the defeat of France and by the expected imminent defeat or capitulation of Britain. This modified proposal allowed Frank to argue that it was a waste of time sending the Jews a few hundred miles down to the General Government first, so they remained even longer in ghettos which had been intended only as temporary holding pens. This allowed the local Nazi administrators to come up with another short-term idea – selling them food as a means of extorting their money. Only when the Jews' money was exhausted did the local Nazis face a real policy decision – whether to let them all starve or not. Once that was answered in the negative, and the plan to allow the ghetto to become a manufacturing base was accepted, the relationship with the Jews changed; they had now become slave-workers employed in semi-permanent camps.

This end result was never 'planned' if by a 'plan' we mean that someone sat down at the beginning and chose to arrive at this destination. Instead of working to a 'plan' the Nazis were taking short-term decisions when each mini-crisis occurred. Crucially, none of these decisions was an 'order' from Hitler. The Führer had communicated broad objectives but local Nazis on the ground made these life and death decisions on their own.

The atmosphere in which the Nazis made each decision was one of contempt for the Poles and hatred for the Jews. In Poland during the early years of the war the Nazis initiated a racial policy the like of which had never been seen before. Hundreds of thousands of people were uprooted and cruelly cast to the wind. But the Nazis had not finished with Poland yet.

CHAPTER FIVE

—

THE ROAD TO TREBLINKA

Images of Auschwitz are among the most familiar on the planet: the row upon row of huts, the emaciated corpses staring out at us from old newsreels. Film exists of Auschwitz because it was a work camp as well as an extermination centre, and this also partly accounts for why there are many more survivors of this camp than the others. But Auschwitz, though a place of nightmares, is not *the* quintessential example of Nazi horror. The Nazis created other hell-like places which were killing factories – pure and simple – designed to produce nothing but corpses. These places, far from German soil, achieved their devilish purpose and were destroyed by the Nazis before the end of the war to hide the enormity of their crime. Such a place was Treblinka. If you visit the site of Treblinka camp today, deep in the isolated Polish countryside, you will stand in a forest and hear only birds. Yet you still stand on a spot which marks one of the lowest points to which human beings have ever descended. The memorial stone at what was the camp boundary is inscribed with the words 'Never Again'. It should also bear another word, written in letters of fire – 'Remember'.

Samuel Willenberg, whom the Germans had caught in a round-up of Jews in Opatów, southern Poland, was in a train rattling towards Treblinka in 1942. Now, crammed into a cattle truck, he heard Polish children shout as they passed different stations, 'Jews! You'll be turned into soap!' As the train snaked through the countryside, Samuel heard other Jews in the cattle truck whisper, 'It's bad. We are going to Treblinka.' Yet still nobody in the truck wanted to accept that a place could exist simply for the elimination of innocent human beings. 'It was hard to believe,' says Samuel Willenberg. 'I was here and still I could not believe it at first.'

Left: An unknown man and boy stare out from behind the wire of Auschwitz (Oswieçim) concentration camp, January 1945. Suffering like this was the logical conclusion of the Nazis' pseudo-Darwinian theories.

The train arrived at Treblinka station, the cattle truck doors crashed open and suddenly there was shouting, '*Schnell, schnell*!' Ukrainians in black SS uniforms herded the Jews off the platform and through a gate into the lower part of the camp. Men were pushed to the right, women to the left. A young Jewish man carrying pieces of string and wearing a red armband approached the men and told them to take off their shoes and tie them together. The young man looked familiar to Samuel. 'I asked him, "Listen, where are you from?" He told me and asked me where I was from. I said, "Czestochowa, Opatów, Warsaw." "From Czestochowa?" "Yes." "What's your name?" "Samuel Willenberg." "Say you are

Women and children queue to be killed in the Ukraine in October 1942. One of the handful of pictures which exist today which bear testimony to the 800,000 or more people who died there. Nothing remains of the extermination camp itself.

a bricklayer," and he left.' That chance meeting and those five words of advice saved Samuel's life. He told the guards he was a bricklayer and so became one of the tiny handful of Jews selected to help in the camp, not for immediate death.

Some 800,000 people (other estimates say more than one million) were exterminated in Treblinka camp over a period of thirteen months between July 1942 and August 1943. It took just 50 Germans, 150 Ukrainians and just over 1000 Jews to accomplish it all. Standing in the clearing where the camp used to be, what strikes one first is its size – a mere 600 by 400 metres. It is a profoundly upsetting moment when one realizes that if people are to be murdered there is no need of space.

The layout of the camp could scarcely have been simpler. The victims arrived on train trucks and were then herded from the station to a central courtyard in the camp where the men were ordered to undress. On one side of the yard was a barracks where the women undressed and where their hair was shaved. 'At that point,' says Samuel, 'the women gained hope, for if they are going to have their hair cut, it means there is going to be some life after, for hygiene is necessary in a camp.' The women did not know, of course, that the Germans wanted to stuff mattresses with their hair. The nakedness of the victims also worked in the Germans' favour. 'A man who takes his shoes off and then is ordered "Strip!" and is naked – that man is no longer a human being, no longer a master of himself,' says Samuel. 'He covers certain parts of his body, he is embarrassed. Suddenly, he has a thousand problems of which he has not been aware in his normal life, which he did not have as he was never forced to walk about naked – except perhaps as a child – among people, among friends. Suddenly everyone is naked! And the Germans, you see, took advantage of that. And on top of that, the lashing, "Quick! *Schnell, schnell*!" At that point one wanted to run somewhere as fast as one could, run somewhere, no matter where.' The men, women and children were harried down a path (the Germans called it 'The Path to Heaven') less than a hundred metres to the gas chambers where they were murdered. Once dead, their bodies were thrown into pits next to the gas chambers.

The whole process, from the arrival of the train to the remains being hurled into the pit, took less than two hours. Most of the victims were never certain where they were or what was happening to them until the last moment. Every effort was made to try and deceive them about their fate. Treblinka station was decorated like a real station with a clock and timetables. The victims were told they had arrived at a transit camp where they would have to take a shower. High barbed-wire fences, in which branches were entwined, wound through the camp so that no one could see what was about to happen to them next.

After the murder of the victims, Treblinka became a vast sorting area. In a huge yard on the east side of the camp Jewish workers, such as Samuel Willenberg, had to sort out belongings which, until moments previously, had been someone's treasured possessions. 'It looked like a Persian bazaar,' says Samuel, 'open suitcases, spread-out sheets, and on each sheet lay different things. Trousers separately from shirts, from woollen things, it all had to be sorted. The

Right: Jewish women in Bessarabia after they had been abused, probably by locals, September 1941.

gold lay separate in the bags…Each of us had a sheet spread out next to him where we put photos, documents, diplomas.' Samuel worked under the eyes of a sadist, an SS guard they called 'Doll'. He had a St Bernard dog called Barry, which he had trained to tear out human flesh, to bite at a man's genitals, on the command 'Man bite dog'. (As the verdict at 'Doll's' later trial stated: 'By the word "man" he meant Barry: the word "dog" referred to the prisoner.') Every moment of the time that Samuel worked in Treblinka until his escape into the surrounding forest seven months later, he risked being killed in an instant, on a whim.

More than fifty years on Samuel Willenberg can still only scarcely comprehend what he saw. 'They alighted on to the platform in the usual manner, as if they had arrived in a health resort. And here, on this small plot of land, was taking place the greatest murder that ever took place in Europe, in the entire world. Before he died, Professor Mering [Samuel's history teacher, who worked alongside him at Treblinka] said, and I will never forget it: "You know, I look at it from the point of view of history." "Excuse me?" I looked at him as if he had gone mad.'

At night Samuel and the other Jews forced to work in the camp would try to make sense of what was happening to them: 'There were discussions, quietly, people asked each other, "Why?" That question, all the time – why? Why? And, "For what crime? Why small children? What have they done? What have I done? What has each of us done?" There was no answer.' These same questions still resonate today. How was it possible that Germans ordered and organized this mechanized extermination? Not just in Treblinka, but in Auschwitz, Belzec, Sobibór and the other death camps. In all history there is no crime to equal it. No one before has ever sought to kill men, women and children on this scale and to justify such killing by the simple expedient 'They were Jews' or 'They were Gypsies' or 'They were homosexuals' – to kill people just because they did not fit, were not wanted. How could it happen? How could a place like Treblinka come to exist on the face of the Earth?

No single cause is itself sufficient to explain it. Rather, there were a number of preconditions without which the final decision to order this mass extermination could not have been made. Chapter One described how anti-Semitism grew in Germany after World War I and how some extreme right-wing parties used rhetoric calling for the Jews to be killed. But before he became

Chancellor of Germany, Hitler himself, at least in his public speeches and writing, never openly called for the Jews to be murdered. His public stance in the 1930s was consonant with calls for the Jews to be excluded from German citizenship and to be forced out of Germany altogether. Many Jews were subsequently pressed into leaving Germany, and this method of dealing with the Nazi-created problem of the Jews was to exist almost until the moment when the killings were ordered.

Yet behind the idea of 'purifying' Germany by ridding it of Jews there had always lain a far more sinister philosophy. As early as 21 March 1933 a Leipzig newspaper had announced: 'If a bullet strikes our beloved leader, all the Jews in Germany will immediately be put up against the wall and the result will be a greater blood bath than anything the world has ever seen.' As Arnon Tamir told us, Nazi anti-Semitism can be summed up in the simple words, 'The Jew is guilty, for everything, always.'

The idea of *blame* is a crucial one. Even the mentally ill, whom the Nazis despised, were never held personally to blame for their own illness. The Jews, however, were always blameworthy: they were held responsible for the loss of World War I and were behind the hideous creed of Bolshevism. It did not matter that this analysis was simply wrong; it was still possible for the Nazis to believe it – after all, Germany had clearly lost the war and suffered as a result. Furthermore, the Nazis said *every* Jew was to blame because, as Nazi propaganda made clear, the Jews were all part of one homogeneous mass, loyal to each other rather than to their Fatherland. If one Jew had committed a crime, then all Jews had committed it.

None of this meant that the extermination of the Jews was inevitable from the moment the Nazis came to power. For most of the 1930s many Jews managed to live relatively peacefully in Hitler's Reich. After the chaotic violence of the early months of the regime and the abortive boycott of 1 April 1933 there was less violent oppression. Segregation and discrimination remained widespread, but many Jews managed to tolerate these everyday abuses. Then, on 9 November 1938, came Kristallnacht. The horror of that night is encapsulated in the experience of 18-year-old Rudi Bamber, who rang the police to report that Storm Troopers were smashing up his family's house, only to realize that they would not help; the police approved of the crime.

Kristallnacht is important in the development of Nazi anti-Semitism because it illustrates once again how the Jews were held collectively to blame for any crime. The Jew who shot the German diplomat in Paris was not treated as an individual criminal, but as one cell in an organism which consisted of all Jews. Rudi Bamber tried to work out why the Storm Troopers had picked on his family. What had they done wrong? But the Nazis did not think that way. *All* Jews were held responsible for any crime committed by any other Jew. It did not matter if they had never met or that they might condemn his crime; one Jew was all Jews.

This all meant that the Jews were in a uniquely vulnerable position in Nazi Germany. On 30 January 1939 Hitler gave a speech which included these words: '…if the international Jewish financiers in and outside Europe should succeed in plunging the nations once more into a world war, then the result will not be the Bolshevizing of the Earth, and thus the victory of Jewry, but the annihilation of the Jewish race in Europe.' At first reading these words seem unequivocal. Hitler talks of the 'annihilation of the Jewish race in Europe' – what could be a clearer promise of the Holocaust than that? But it is not necessarily that obvious. We have already seen how the ghetto managers of Lodz in 1940 knew nothing of any planned extermination; instead, they had initiated a scheme whereby the ghetto was functioning as a slave factory. And another significant clue about Nazi thinking in 1940 exists in Himmler's memo, 'Some thoughts on the treatment of the alien population in the east'. When writing about his plans to educate Polish children only at the lowest level and to kidnap any Polish children who seem to be 'racially first class', Himmler adds the paragraph: 'However cruel and tragic each individual case may be, if one rejects the Bolshevik method of physically exterminating a people as fundamentally un-German and impossible, then this method is the mildest and best one.' Thus to Himmler, writing in the spring of 1940, 'physically exterminating a people' is 'un-German'. Of course, he could have been lying. He could already have known of a secret plan Hitler had hatched to exterminate another group – the Jews. But why would he bother to dissemble in a memo destined for Hitler? Himmler had no difficulty in making inhuman statements once the Holocaust had been decided upon. (In a speech at Posen in October 1943, talking of the 'extermination of the Jewish people', he said, 'We had the moral right, we had the duty to our people, to destroy this

Right: Hitler and Himmler at the annual Party Congress at Nuremberg in 1938. Between these two men the extermination of the Jewish people moved from being a vision to a fact.

people which wanted to destroy us,' and, 'We have exterminated a bacterium because we did not want in the end to be infected by the bacterium and die of it.')

It therefore seems highly unlikely that, despite Hitler's speech in 1939, there was any systematic plan to exterminate the Jews until 1941. But we can never know for sure because we cannot know the content of Hitler's mind – his secret intention. Maybe he longed to implement extermination but was restrained enough to wait until he thought he could do so with impunity. Alternatively, and perhaps more probably, Hitler always loathed and despised the Jews and simply wanted to get rid of them. What form that 'getting rid of' would take was something the Nazis were capable of revising given the circumstances. Initially, the overt policy was clearly one of expulsion. Before the war Adolf Eichmann ran the SS 'Office for Jewish emigration' in Vienna after the Anschluss, which served effectively to steal the Austrian Jews' money before they were allowed to leave. In one sense this was working towards 'annihilating' the Jewish race in Austria.

A grander plan to expel the Jews from Europe took shape in 1940 at the time of the fall of France. At first sight it is an incredible, almost unbelievable plan – to send the Jews to Madagascar. Franz Rademacher, who worked in the German Foreign Ministry, wrote the following memo dated 3 July 1940: 'The imminent victory gives the Germans the possibility, and in my opinion also the duty, of solving the Jewish question in Europe. The desirable solution is: All Jews out of Europe…In the peace treaty France must make the island Madagascar available for the solution of the Jewish question, and must resettle the approximately 25,000 French people living there and compensate them. The island will be transferred to Germany as a mandate…The Jews will be jointly liable for the value of the island. Their former European assets will be transferred for liquidation to a European bank to be set up for the purpose. In so far as these assets are insufficient to pay for the land which they get and for the necessary purchase of commodities in Europe needed for developing the island, bank credits will be made available to the Jews by the same bank.' Outlandish as it appears, this plan was the logical conclusion of the expulsion policy which the Nazis had been following up to this point. The Madagascar version was simply more ambitious: to send the Jews to an island off the coast of Africa and to steal all their money by making them pay for the privilege of going there. And Madagascar was not going to be a tropical paradise for the Jews, it was proposed that the Chancellery of the Führer organize transportation to the island under its head, Philipp Bouhler, the man behind the murderous Nazi euthanasia policy.

In the event, the Madagascar plan came to nothing. A pre-condition of its success was that the sea route to Africa needed to be safe for German shipping. With Britain still in the war, this could not be guaranteed. Of course, when Rademacher wrote his memo in July 1940, the Nazis thought it likely that Britain would shortly be out of the war. Hitler had never wanted to fight the British and was prepared to discuss peace terms – a peace which would have turned Britain into a satellite of the Nazi empire, like Vichy France.

As 1941 dawned, no practical progress had been made on the ambitious Madagascar plan. Deportations of Poles and Jews to the General Government had begun again, but not in sufficient numbers to solve Greiser's problems. Hans Frank still complained that the General Government did not have the resources to take the deportees and the transports temporarily stopped again in March 1941. The squabbling between the competing Nazi barons of Poland over the destination of Polish 'undesirables' seemed never-ending.

By now preparations were in hand for the invasion of the Soviet Union, an event which was to be the catalyst for a radical change in Nazi policy towards the Jews. In a twisted way, the invasion of the Soviet Union – code-named Barbarossa – represented an ideological fulfilment for the Nazis. Now they could grapple with the true enemy Hitler had wanted to confront all along – the enemy that fitted into the great Nazi idea of the Darwinian struggle of nations. On the eve of Operation Barbarossa Hitler wrote to Mussolini, ending the letter thus: 'In conclusion, let me say one more thing, Duce. Since I struggled through to this decision, I again feel spiritually free. The partnership with the Soviet Union, in spite of the complete sincerity of the efforts to bring about a final conciliation, was nevertheless very irksome to me, for in some way or other it seemed to me to be a break with my whole origin, my concepts, and my former obligations. I am happy now to be relieved of these mental agonies.'

Bolshevism and Nazism, the two great competing philosophies, would slug it out to see which should rule the Earth. It was to be the greatest racial struggle in all history. It must have seemed logical to the Nazis, given that background, that this was to be a war conducted with different rules.

In March 1941 Hitler had told his generals that the forthcoming war would be a fight to the death between two ideologies. The army was told that it was at liberty to shoot prisoners and that Communist political 'commissars' must be liquidated. As Nazi propaganda of the time made clear, the Bolsheviks were no ordinary enemy: 'Anyone who has ever looked at the face of a Red commissar knows what the Bolsheviks are like. Here there is no need for theoretical

The Russians fight back against the Germans in the winter offensive around Moscow, 1941. The German–Soviet war was the most brutal conflict the world has seen and had a vital role in the development of the policies which led to the Holocaust.

expressions. We would be insulting animals if we were to describe these men, who are mostly Jewish, as beasts. They are the embodiment of the Satanic and insane hatred against the whole of humanity.'

On the eve of the invasion of the Soviet Union in June 1941 the commander of the 48th Panzer Corps issued the following order of the day: 'We are on the eve of a great event in the war. The Führer has called us again to battle. It is now our task to destroy the Red Army and thereby eradicate for ever Bolshevism, the deadly enemy of National Socialism. We have never forgotten that it was Bolshevism which stabbed our army in the back during the world war and which bears the guilt for all the misfortunes which our people suffered after the war. We should always remember that!'

An atmosphere was thus created in which appalling brutality was to be expected. In sharp contrast to their attitude during the invasion of Poland, the army leadership now openly embraced the Nazi ideological vision of war with the Soviet Union. This time a much more extensive role for the Einsatzgruppen (the German special forces charged with liquidating ideological enemies) was openly acknowledged.

Instructions dated 2 July 1941 tell of the proposed scope of the work of the Einsatzgruppen: '4. Executions. The following will be executed: all officials of the Comintern (most of these will certainly be career politicians); officials of senior and middle rank and 'extremists' in the party, the central committee, and the provincial and district committees; the people's commissars; Jews in the service of the Party or the State...No steps will be taken to interfere with any purges that may be initiated by anti-Communist or anti-Jewish elements in the newly occupied territories. On the contrary, these are to be secretly encouraged.' Reinhard Heydrich, Head of the Reich Main Security Office and close colleague of Himmler, who issued these instructions, is thus openly calling for the execution only of 'Jews in the service of the Party or State', but the fact that purges are to be 'secretly encouraged' and that implicitly such purges may include the killing of women and children shows that there is an inherent contradiction in the instructions, unless the reference to 'Jews in the service of the Party or State' constitutes the bare minimum of Jews to be murdered.

Let us look at how one of the Einsatzgruppen went about its hideous tasks. Einsatzgruppe A was under the command of Police General and SS Brigadeführer Dr Walther Stahlecker. They moved into Lithuania behind the German Army on 23 June 1941 and swiftly reached the town of Kaunas, Lithuania's second city. Given that Lithuania had been incorporated into the Soviet Union against her will in 1939 (as a result of the Molotov/Ribbentrop secret protocol), Stahlecker hoped that the Lithuanians themselves could be persuaded to turn on their former enemies. The Nazi lie that Communism and

Judaism were virtually synonymous had also spread in Lithuania during the two years of Communist rule. According to a report by Stahlecker, 'The task of the security police was to set these purges in motion and put them on the right track so as to ensure that the liquidation goals that had been set might be achieved in the shortest possible time.'

Just after the Germans arrived in Kaunas, a 16-year-old Lithuanian girl called Viera Silkinaite walked past a row of garages just outside the city centre. She saw a group of people gathered around what looked like some drunks having a fight. As she drew closer, she saw that one man was lying on the ground, hardly breathing. Another man was standing above him holding a wooden club. This was not a drunken brawl, but the brutal clubbing to death of unarmed Jews by Lithuanians who had just been released from prison by the Germans. 'I was very frightened,' she says. 'I was lost, worried. I cannot describe my state of mind. Even now I can see that picture in my eyes.' Some of the crowd watching the killing shouted encouragement to the murderers, screaming, 'Beat those Jews!' and one man even held his small child up so that he could see. Viera Silkinaite could scarcely believe that a child was watching: 'What kind of person would he be when he grew up? If, of course, he could understand what he had seen. And what could you expect of such a person who was shouting? It was as if he was going to step into that garage and join the beating.'

Reports survive from some Germans who happened to witness these killings. One, written by an army officer, reads: 'There was a large number of women in the crowd and they had lifted up their children or stood them on chairs or boxes so that they could see better. At first I thought this must be a victory celebration or some type of sporting event because of the cheering, clapping and laughter that kept breaking out. However, when I enquired what was happening, I was told that the "Death-dealer of Kovno [Kaunas]" was at work…In response to a cursory wave, the next man stepped forward silently and was then beaten to death with the wooden club in the most bestial manner….' A German photographer witnessed that, 'After the entire group had been beaten to death, the young man put the crowbar to one side, fetched an accordion and went and stood on the mountain of corpses and played the Lithuanian national anthem.'

After witnessing just a few minutes of the killing, Viera Silkinaite ran off to seek sanctuary in a nearby cemetery. 'I was ashamed,' she says. 'When I went to

Left: A Jewish woman is abused by the citizens of Lemberg (Lvov) in the Ukraine, after the arrival of the Germans in the summer of 1941.

Above: Lithuanians (almost certainly Jews) are marched along the street to their deaths.

Opposite: The 'Death-dealer' of Kaunas holds the iron bar with which he dispatched many of his victims.

Right and below: Photographs of the so-called 'garage' killings in Kaunas. The Germans stood and watched as the Lithuanians did their work for them and killed the Jews.

the cemetery, I sat down and I thought: "God Almighty, I heard before that there were windows broken or something like that done, that was still conceivable, but such an atrocity, to beat a helpless man…it was too much."'

From the first, Einsatzgruppe A was more murderous than the other three groups. We know this because of extensive documentation generated by the groups themselves. Different Einsatzgruppen appear to have interpreted their initial orders in different ways, but even Einsatzgruppe A stopped short of murdering women and children themselves in the initial weeks of the occupation.

Riva Losanskaya, who lived in the village of Butrimonys, roughly halfway between Kaunas and the Lithuanian capital of Vilnius, was 21 years old when the Germans invaded. Until the war she had spent a happy life in Butrimonys with her father, mother and two sisters. They were Jewish, but that was of little consequence before the war as everyone rubbed along together without a problem. 'When the war began,' says Riva, 'although we knew that the Jews were suffering in Poland, we still could not believe that the same thing could happen to us. How could innocent people be detained and killed? My father used to say that without a trial no harm could be done to anyone.' But as the German troops advanced, Riva saw people rushing around shouting 'We must flee!' There were rumours of Jews being killed in reprisals by Germans in the local town and that 'the streets were scattered with corpses'. Riva and her family gathered a few possessions together and travelled ten kilometres to a nearby village where they tried to hide. They still thought that the Russians had been pushed back only temporarily and that the Germans would be swiftly thrown out of Lithuania. Soon, however it became clear that the Russians were not returning and that there was little point, as a family, in trying to hide in another village. 'The people in the village wouldn't give you a crust of bread,' says Riva. 'We had nowhere to go.' So the family returned to Butrimonys, where they lived uneasily in their own house.

Within days of the German occupation, all the Jewish young men of the village were rounded up and taken away. The remaining Jewish villagers were told that the young men had been taken to the nearby town of Alytus, where they had been put to work for the Germans. Riva's father was among those taken after the initial arrests. Days later some locals called on her and her mother and said they had good news. 'These "nice" people with whom we had been on such friendly terms all our life came to us,' says Riva, 'and told us, "We've seen your father, don't cry!" It was Vaitkevicius [a local who has since died], who came to tell us, "Here is a letter we got from him. We'll read it to you and then I'll take a parcel back for him." He had been very friendly with my father. I went to see my neighbours to tell them that everyone was still alive. "Why the tears? My father is still alive and I'm sending him clothes and food via Vaitkevicius." My neighbours said, "Riva, you have such nice friends. Can we pay him to take parcels to our husbands and fathers too?" So we got our parcels ready and gave them to Vaitkevicius who took them all. Other people were collecting up parcels in all the other streets too.' But it was a trick, breathtaking in its callousness. Just before they were killed by the Lithuanian police acting on German orders, the Jewish men had been made to write letters to their families asking for money, clothes and food to be sent to them. Then locals had been given these letters by the police so that they could steal from the victims' families. By the time Riva was told by her neighbours, 'We've seen your father,' he was already dead.

After her father was taken, Riva and her family never spent a night at home. Instead they slept out in the potato fields or in the homes of their neighbours, being careful never to spend more than one night in any one place. Nonetheless, they never went far from their house and still visited it during the day. Then, in September 1941, rumours of a change in policy towards the Jews began to spread around the village. It was said that the Germans had ordered the killing of every Jew in Lithuania, including women and children. 'A woman had even said, "I know that they've already dug the pits,"' says Riva, 'but we thought that maybe the pit was for potatoes…for the war. She was running round the ghetto saying, "They're going to shoot us tomorrow, you must flee!" But the people were thinking, "Perhaps they aren't going to shoot us, perhaps they dug those pits for no particular reason." That's how stupid we were. We didn't imagine that they would come to kill us so fast. The clever Jewish people said that since some kind of holiday was coming, we could relax for a few days.'

As 9 September was a church holiday, many Jews in Butrimonys thought it would be the one day on which their safety was guaranteed. They were wrong. That morning Lithuanian policemen, helped by enthusiastic locals, began rounding up the women, children and old people who constituted the remaining

Jewish women in Latvia are forced to pose for the camera just before they are shot, December 1941. Within months the Nazis would have developed a more efficient way of committing mass murder – the gas chambers of the extermination camp.

Jewish population of Butrimonys. Riva and her mother were part of a column herded along a road out of the village. Their destination was about 2 kilometres away – a pit which had been dug about 200 metres from the road among grassland and trees. The Jews shuffling to their deaths were weak with hunger, many shaken by living rough in the fields. 'I was thinking they'd kill everyone and the survivors would be cursed,' says Riva. 'But right up until the very last moment, I still had a faint vestige of hope.' When they were little over 500 metres from the place of execution, Riva saw a path leading off into the forest on the other side of the road. She dragged her mother towards it and together they hid behind some shrubs. The guards had grown lazy because the rest of the Jews were so compliant and Riva and her mother were not missed. Minutes later they heard gunshots. 'Dogs were barking, perhaps they were frightened by the sound of the shooting,' says Riva. 'My mother said, "They're already shooting!" I said, "No, no, they're dogs." I only said that because I was scared that my mother would go mad.'

That same day Alfonsas Navasinskas was crossing a nearby meadow with a friend, Kosima. 'We saw people being driven along from Butrimonys,' he says. 'Someone on horseback came first and then some policemen and then some ordinary people – a shopkeeper and some clerks who worked in the offices distributing food coupons. They had all gathered together to take the Jews along. They were given sticks and the odd rifle.' Navasinskas and his friend followed the group and watched as the Jews were ordered to lie down on the grass. 'Then along came the men who did the shooting. "Everybody get up," the Jews were told.' Navasinskas noticed that torn banknotes lay scattered on the ground. The Jews had ripped up their money to prevent the killers profiting from them. 'I waited a little and then went closer,' says Navasinskas. 'I could hear them as they shouted, "Choose your space, you so and so!"' He watched as a new group of Jews were ordered to strip at the side of the pit. As they did, some threw their clothes to people they knew in the crowd to prevent their killers from stealing

The SS shoot two prisoners, somewhere in the east. Casual killings like this were widespread on the Eastern Front.

their possessions. Navasinskas later heard remarks by a villager, who had been given an overcoat by one of the condemned Jews just before he was shot: 'Had the Jews survived, I wouldn't have got it. I'll wear it to a dance tonight!' He also heard a Jewish woman tell another local, 'Here's a cardigan, give it to your wife.' The buttons were covered with cloth but they were gold coins from the Tsar's time. The recipient of the cardigan, unaware of its hidden value chucked it in the farmyard with the chickens. In time, the chickens pecked holes in the cloth and revealed the glittering coins to the farmer. 'He has since died, but he told me that to have deserved finding the coins he must have been deemed "good in the eyes of God".'

After he had seen five groups of Jews shot at the pit, Alfonsas Navasinskas went home alone (his friend stayed on to collect the torn-up money). 'I kept turning round to look behind me, wondering whether anybody was coming after me. It was such a horrible feeling. Nobody spoke up for the Jews, nobody said a word. It was as if it were all quite normal.'

Another villager who came to witness the murders was Juozas Gramauskas, then 21 years old. 'The women, children and old men were shot inside the pit,' he says. 'The children were going from person to person, shouting, "Mummy, Daddy, Mummy, Daddy, Mummy!" I think someone was calling for his daughter. And along came a really fat chap with a pistol and…bang, bang! All the grief and weeping was just heartbreaking. Even now, I cannot bear the memory of all the lamenting and crying there. To this day I cannot imagine what was going on.'

The shooting was carried out by Lithuanian soldiers acting under German orders. There were German soldiers present but they simply observed the slaughter. The killing went on until evening, when fires were lit in order to see if there was any movement inside the pit. 'I constantly see it before my eyes, the beasts!' says Juozas Gramauskas.

All this horror is registered in the report of Einsatzkommando 3 simply as follows: '9.9.41 Butrimonys – 67 Jews, 370 Jewesses, 303 Jewish children – (total) 740.' Some villagers remember the execution day as 8 rather than 9 September and recall seeing as many as 900 Jews killed. In the savage circumstances precise record-keeping was hardly practicable.

It is almost impossible to understand how human beings could do this. An easy route, and one that has been taken by some, is to say that those involved were all 'mad', but the evidence scarcely supports this easy conclusion. The diary of a German/Austrian member of an Einsatzkommando, Felix Landau, survives. He was a cabinet-maker by trade, who joined the Nazis in 1931 at the age of 21 and became a member of the Gestapo in Vienna in 1938. He reported to the Einsatzkommando in June 1941, initially for duty in Poland. His diary is an exceptional document because it mixes the horror of his days of killing with sentimental longing for his girlfriend. The entry for 3 July 1941 concludes: 'I have little inclination to shoot defenceless people – even if they are only Jews. I would far rather good honest open combat. Now good night, my dear Hasi [bunny].' The entry for two days later records the shooting of members of the Resistance: 'One of them simply would not die. The first layer of sand had already been thrown on the first group when a hand emerged from out of the sand, waved and pointed to a place, presumably his heart. A couple more shots rang out, then someone shouted – in fact the Pole himself – "Shoot faster!" What is a human being?' The next paragraph begins: 'It looks like we'll be getting our first warm meal today. We've all been given 10 Reichmarks to buy ourselves a few necessities. I bought myself a whip costing 2 Reichmarks.'

On 12 July 1941 he writes: 'Isn't it strange, you love battle and then you have to shoot defenceless people. Twenty-three had to be shot…The death candidates are organized into three shifts as there are not many shovels. Strange, I am completely unmoved. No pity, nothing. That's the way it is and then it's all over.'

Felix Landau's diary shows a man to whom remorse is an unknown emotion. He is a selfish and base human being, but not a madman.

There are many advantages to studying such a diary, not least that it represents the moment with a lack of hindsight. But there is no substitute for the additional insight to be gained by meeting the participants, so we set out to find one of the killers who had operated in Lithuania. Eventually we traced a former Lithuanian soldier who had murdered Jews alongside the German Einsatzgruppe and who spent twenty years in Siberia as a result. Petras Zelionka was born in 1917 and came from a peasant background. His family was not badly off for the region, owning a small farm with two cows. Under the Russian occupation he heard rumours that 'in the security department people were mostly tortured by the Jews. They used to put screws on the head and tighten them, thus torturing the teachers and professors.' He joined the Lithuanian Army

The face of a killer: Petras Zelionka in the uniform of a Lithuanian soldier.

because, as he says, 'I respected Lithuania and I am a real Lithuanian…I was attracted to military things, I liked it very much.'

Petras Zelionka was first involved in the killing of Jews in the Seventh Fort at Kaunas in the early days of the German occupation, during the period when the Einsatzgruppen killed predominantly men. As a guard, he patrolled the ramparts and watched as Jewish men were shot, fifteen at a time, at the edge of a pit which had been dug within the confines of the fort. Earth was thrown on each layer of bodies, then the whole process was repeated until there were no more Jewish men left to kill that day. He recalls that the men went to their deaths with little resistance, 'totally as lambs'.

From the late summer of 1941 the killing widened to include women and children in outlying villages, and Zelionka became one of the murderers himself. His answer to our question, 'When was the first time you had to shoot?' is revealing. 'Where? Where was I? Maybe I was in Babtai? Or maybe near Joniskis, around there…I had to take them somewhere. To take them first from the ghetto and to bring them somewhere.' As the statement he gave to the Russian authorities after the war confirms, Zelionka participated in many mass killings – so many that today he cannot remember where he first committed murder.

Describing a typical day's killing, he told us how soldiers from his battalion would leave their barracks after breakfast, not knowing their destination. There would be the simple command, 'Men, we have to go!' Then they would clamber aboard their lorries and leave. The mood in the lorry he describes as 'not very good. Sometimes I thought I would have to shoot an innocent man.' (His concept of 'innocence' is a diabolical one which excludes all Jews, even women and children.)

Once they reached their destination they would harry the Jews from the village out to the pre-prepared execution site. The Germans would strip the Jews of their 'golden things', such as jewellery and watches, and then order them to lie down. A certain number would then be counted off and taken to the pit, where they were shot. His battalion was assisted by a German detachment. 'You could not do it without the Germans. They had machine-guns. We had just to shoot.'

The murderers were allowed to drink vodka during the killing. With vodka 'everyone becomes braver' says Zelionka. 'When you are drunk, it is different.' Sometimes, after the murders, the Germans would thank the Lithuanians for their help. In his statement to the Russians after the war, Zelionka revealed what he and his comrades did after murdering up to five hundred people in Vikija: 'When we had finished the shooting, we had lunch at a restaurant in Krakes. Spirits were consumed.' Murder did not diminish his appetite.

The murderers were all volunteers. There is no record of anyone being shot or imprisoned for refusing to murder. This is a reality that Zelionka finds hard to accept today. 'You could refuse,' we told him.

'You could shoot and you could not shoot,' he replied. 'But you just pressed the trigger and shot. And that was it, it was not a big ceremony.'

'Did you ever think of refusing to shoot?'

'Now it is very difficult to explain all that, all those things: to shoot or not to shoot. I do not know. The others did it because of their indignation...The Jews are very selfish, how could I say....'

We asked him about shooting women and children. 'Let's say there is a Jew in front of you, not a man, but a woman or a child. A child has certainly never been a Communist. And you shoot that child. What had he done?'

'This is a tragedy, a big tragedy, because...how can I explain it better? Maybe it is because of a curiosity – you just pull the trigger, the shot is fired and that is it. There is a saying, "Youth is foolishness".' Talking later about the murder of children, he remarked, 'Some people are doomed and that is it.'

We tried in vain to get an emotional response from this mass murderer. 'Who was the man you shot first? Do you remember him?' we asked.

'No, I cannot tell you,' he replied. 'There were only the Jews, no one was our countryman. They were all Jews.'

'But were they men, women or children?'

'What can I say? It could be a man, a woman or...after so many years, how can you remember everything that happened?'

I asked our interpreter to press this convicted killer harder about his apparent lack of guilt. Did he not feel any shame? The result was both illuminating and the end of the interview.

'My colleague, an Englishman, asks me to translate this question to you: he says that English people, watching this film, will hardly understand how somebody, a soldier, used to shoot other people like this but he does not feel guilty.'

'They can accuse me, if they want. I was sentenced for twenty years for that. Short and clear. I was guilty and I carried out the sentence of twenty years…penal servitude.'

'But that was an official punishment. What does your *conscience* say?'

'I do not know. I am not going to answer such questions…I am not going to explain or tell you any more.'

So the interview ended.

It was an extraordinary experience to meet Petras Zelionka. It is rare for someone who has committed war crimes as horrendous as this to admit it openly, even if he has served a long sentence for the offence and does not risk prosecution again. Yet here before us was a man who killed alongside the Einsatzgruppen and who did not try either to hide the fact or to glory in it. He sat and talked about committing mass murder in a reserved and matter-of-fact way.

When reading documents relating to the Einsatzgruppen killings, one is always tempted to think that the men who committed them were not really human. Perhaps they were collectively insane. But Petras Zelionka gave every impression of being a sane man. If you met him in the street and were introduced to him, you would not notice anything out of the ordinary. Yet he murdered in cold blood, standing feet away from his victims. Today, when the only mass killers we read about are the crazed murderers featured in the tabloid press, it is important to meet a man like Petras Zelionka who killed more than any tabloid monster and yet sat before us as composed and normal as any grandfather.

Zelionka took part in many murders in Lithuania, but denies having visited Butrimonys. If not him precisely, then it would have been men like him from the Lithuanian Army who killed Riva Losanskaya's Jewish neighbours and from whose guns she herself had such a narrow escape.

In the weeks after the killings at Butrimonys, Riva became increasingly sickened by the behaviour of her fellow villagers, whom she saw profiting from the disappearance of the Jews. She recalls that as soon as she and the other Jews had been marched along to the pits, many of the remaining villagers rushed to the victims' houses to plunder them. 'Even the wives of two priests were fighting with each other,' she says, 'arguing over who was to have what.' Riva learnt that one local woman helped undress the Jews at the execution site and then kept

Overleaf: The Germans hang an unknown woman in Minsk in 1941.

their clothes for herself. 'She didn't even leave their knickers on, their clothes were so precious to her,' says Riva. 'When the Russians came, her children used to go to the cinema wearing those same clothes, sometimes even wearing the Rabbi's clothes.'

Throughout the German occupation Riva and her mother lived in constant fear of denunciation. 'Many people informed the authorities about the ones who had managed to escape,' she says. 'Even the kind-hearted ones did this. One Jew went to see a Russian family hoping that he could stay with them. First, he was given some food, then he was taken to the police and shot along with all the others. Everybody was doing it because they wanted the clothes and they believed that the Jews had lots of gold…But where would all that gold have come from? People didn't even have enough food, they didn't have enough potatoes.'

Riva Losanskaya's life has been spent searching for an answer to the same question posed by Samuel Willenberg in Treblinka – why? 'Fifty years have passed and I'm still wondering how people could do such things. I have always respected intelligence, I love and revere intelligent people. But then I saw them killing…Nobody can explain why the Germans did it. They are a cultured nation and have such a fine literature: Goethe, Schiller, Heinrich Heine….' Even though it was Lithuanian soldiers who shot the Jews of Butrimonys, she blames the Germans more. 'They were the cause of all our unhappiness. The Lithuanians hadn't killed any of us before the Germans arrived.'

The whirlwind of killings the Nazis organized in the first months of the occupation of Lithuania was documented by them in the so-called 'Jäger Report'. This shows a huge increase in the number of Jews killed, especially women and children, from about mid-August 1941. Until 15 August there is no mention of any children killed, but from then on they are killed in their thousands (1609 Jewish children murdered between 18 and 22 August in Kreis Rasainiai alone). Why did this sudden escalation in killings occur? When was the order given for it to happen? If these questions can be answered, they would go some way to helping us understand the decision-making process that led to the Holocaust.

Could the decision to extend the killing have been taken in principle before the invasion of Russia, but not implemented on the ground until mid-August? Professor Browning makes a powerful argument for this case: 'Before the invasion, the Einsatzgruppen were not given explicit orders for the total extermination of the Jews on Soviet territory. Along with the general incitement to an ideological and racial war, however, they were given the general task of liquidating "potential" enemies. Heydrich's much-debated directive of 2 July 1941 was a minimal list of all those who had to be liquidated *immediately*, including all Jews in state and party positions. It is very likely, moreover, that the Einsatzgruppen leaders were told of the *future* goal of a *Judenfrei* [Jew-free] Russia through systematic mass murder.'

But another historian, Professor Philippe Burrin, argues that there is evidence to suggest that the decision to extend the killing could not have been taken before the invasion of Russia. He points to an exchange between Himmler and one of his SS units which started at the end of July. Himmler gave the following order on 30 July 1941 to the 2nd SS Cavalry Regiment in the Pripet Marshes on the south of the front: 'All Jews must be shot. Drive the female Jews into the swamp.' On 12 August Sturmbannführer Franz Magill reported: 'Driving women and children into the swamp was not successful because the swamp was not so deep that sinking could occur. After a depth of 1 metre, for the most part one hit firm ground (probably sand) so that sinking under was not possible.' This communication, like so much of the documentary evidence surrounding the origin of the Holocaust, is open to different interpretations. For Professor Burrin it is evidence that Himmler does not yet feel able to order the killing of women and children. For Professor Browning it is an instruction from Himmler to kill women and children couched in ambiguous terms which the enthusiastic Magill misunderstands.

The debate is important because it goes to the heart of Hitler's motivation in ordering or authorizing the extension of the killing. Browning believes that the impetus for increasing the killing came from a decision Hitler took in mid-July 1941, when he believed that victory over Russia was near. At that point, elated over his conquest, he simply brought forward plans to 'cleanse' the new territories of undesirables. In Browning's words, 'What had hitherto been seen as a future task was now to be implemented immediately.' Burrin sees it differently. He places the decision to order the escalation at late July or August, when Hitler was in a very different mood – raging at news that the German Army was faltering against the Soviets.

Himmler pays a visit to a concentration camp in the east and examines the Russian prisoners. In the conflict in the East the POWs (on both sides) were treated appallingly. The Germans took 5 million Soviet prisoners – only 2 million survived the war.

Whatever timetable one supports – and there are myriad variations on these basic theories – it remains a fact that the killing did increase in ferocity during the summer of 1941 and that the Nazis had moved incrementally towards murder as the potential solution to their self-created 'Jewish problem' throughout the territory they controlled. During August Himmler visited the east and witnessed the Einsatzgruppen killings for himself. He was disturbed by what he saw and sympathized, not with the victims of the crime, but with the 'psychological burden' placed on the killers who had to shoot their victims. This 'care and concern' for the murderers was to result in the development of easier methods of killing, such as the gas van and, eventually, the gas chamber.

By the summer of 1941, we know that there must have been a decision, for whatever reason, to increase the killing in the east. But what of the other Jews in the Reich? What was their intended fate at this time? On 31 July Göring signed a key document – an authorization addressed to Reinhard Heydrich: 'To supplement the task that was assigned to you on 24 January 1939, which dealt with the solution of the Jewish problem by emigration and evacuation in the most suitable way, I hereby charge you with making all necessary preparations with regard to organizational, technical and material matters for bringing about a complete solution of the Jewish question within the German sphere of influence in Europe.'

Yet again, this document is ambiguous and open to different interpretations. For Professor Burrin it contains nothing to make it the 'smoking gun' of the Holocaust, nothing to show that the extermination of the Jews is intended. Since there is explicit mention of the 'final solution' in the context of 'emigration and evacuation', this document might simply be confirmation from Göring that Heydrich's mandate extended throughout the German empire. But others have pointed out that the SS already had enormous powers, so why was this authorization necessary? Perhaps this document is simply part of an ongoing search for a solution to the 'problem' of the Jews. Heydrich is being asked formally to come up with an answer to the problem. All we know for sure is that this document was issued in an atmosphere in which murder was being discussed as a solution to the 'Jewish problem' in the newly conquered territories of the east.

Regardless of the precise meaning of Göring's authorization, another clear decision was taken at some point that summer or early autumn – to extend the killing of Jews beyond the newly occupied territories. We know this not because of a signed and dated order from Hitler, but because it is evident when preparations were launched to widen the killing process and when that killing actually began.

In September 1941 two new measures clearly indicated what the fate of the German Jews would be. They were forced, for the first time, to wear a badge – the yellow star – and their deportation to the east was ordered. Professor Browning establishes that 'Between 15 October and 11 November twenty trains left the Third Reich carrying Jews to Lodz. Five gypsy transports were dispatched to Lodz as well. Other trains subsequently departed for Kovno [Kaunas], Minsk and Riga. When the first wave of deportations came to an end in February 1942, the number of Jewish transports had reached a total of 46. The deportees in all five transports to Kovno [Kaunas] and the first to Riga were massacred immediately on arrival. The rest were granted a very temporary stay of execution, if they could survive the rigours of winter life in the ghettos of Lodz, Minsk and Riga.' Systematic gassing of Jews began at Chelmo, near Lodz, in December 1941. The 'humane' method of killing Himmler had requested after seeing the shootings in August had finally arrived.

Hitler's role in all this is crucial. It is no surprise to learn that a written order authorizing Himmler to proceed does not exist. The Third Reich, as we have seen in countless ways, did not function in that way. Hitler set the mood, had the

Jews are deported from Würzburg in Germany in 1942. Knowledge varied wildly amongst the German Jews about their possible fate – most could probably not conceive that they would be exterminated. Germany, after all, was a cultured and civilized country.

vision, thought the unthinkable; others devised the policy. Hitler wanted it; others did it. Hitler gave more than a clue to his mood in September 1941 when he talked about the fate he wished for Leningrad: 'Petersburg [Leningrad] the "poisonous nest" from which so long Asiatic venom has "spewed forth" into the Baltic must vanish from the Earth's surface.' During this same period, when we know for certain that Hitler felt able to call for a city to 'vanish from the Earth's surface', he was more privately authorizing Himmler to make an entire race 'vanish from the Earth's surface'. A man who speaks with such a combination of baseness and grandiloquence is unlikely to be concerned with the intricate details of how mass extermination is carried out. But without his approval and desire, extermination could not have happened.

That Hitler took the decision to exterminate the Jews can also be deduced from a letter by Heydrich, dated 6 November 1941, about the destruction of synagogues in France. He writes that he organized these reprisals against the Jews 'only from the moment when, at the highest level, Jewry had been forcefully designated as the culpable incendiary in Europe, one which must definitively disappear from Europe'. According to Professor Burrin, the reference to 'the highest level', namely Hitler, 'would have no purpose if the "disappearance" of the Jews were to be an innocent affair'.

Three weeks earlier, on 18 October, Eichmann, further down the chain of command, noted after a telephone conversation with Heydrich, 'No overseas emigration of the Jews.' Thus we know, beyond reasonable doubt, that a decision to exterminate the Jews was taken over the summer or autumn of 1941. But why? What was Hitler's motivation? Why was the decision taken then? Of all the possible explanations, one of two seemingly contradictory ones is most likely. To Professor Burrin the history of Hitler's and the Nazis' dealings with the Jews is one in which, overwhelmingly, the Jews are the scapegoat for anything that goes wrong. Thus, they are to be punished if the war does not go according to plan. The invasion of Russia had already created an atmosphere of murder and inhumanity. Once Operation Barbarossa began to flounder that August, Hitler, in a fit of anger and hatred, vented his frustrations upon the Jews. That he was driven by hatred is consistent with his character as we know it from the end of World War I.

An alternative scenario, painted by Professor Browning, sees Hitler making key decisions about the fate of the Jews at moments of euphoria. In mid-July, when Hitler gives what Browning calls his 'victory speech', he also authorized killings in the newly occupied territories of the east to be stepped up to include women and children. In 'late September and early October 1941, with the capture of Kiev and the great encirclement victory of Vyazma and Bryansk, he approved

German soldiers conduct an execution in a forest somewhere in the east, 1941. Notice the expression on the face of the soldier at the left of the bottom picture. Can he really be enjoying his work?

deportations from the Third Reich'. Browning also points out that Hitler's moods fluctuated wildly during that summer and autumn: periods of anger and frustration were interspersed with peaks of euphoria.

Of course, in the end we can only speculate as to Hitler's frame of mind during the months when the decision to embark on the Final Solution was taken. But perhaps the two interpretations of Burrin and Browning are not as far apart as they seem. The historian Hugh Trevor-Roper has described Hitler as the 'coarsest, cruellest, least magnanimous conqueror the world has ever known'. Even when euphoric he would still act with hatred at his core.

If seeking an understanding of why the Holocaust happened when it did, then one should look for the answer in the following combination: the atmosphere created by the Einsatzgruppen killings of thousands of Jews in the wake of Operation Barbarossa; the vacuum left by the abandoned Madagascar option; and hatred, pure hatred of the Jews, nursed by a World War I veteran who believed that Jews had fatally betrayed Germany during the last great conflict.

On 25 October 1941 Hitler said to Himmler and Heydrich: 'From the rostrum of the Reichstag I prophesied to Jewry that, in the event of war proving inevitable, the Jew would disappear from Europe. That race of criminals has on its conscience the 2 million dead of World War I, and now already hundreds of thousands more.' In a terrifying aside, he added, 'It's not a bad idea, by the way, that public rumour attributes to us a plan to exterminate the Jews. Terror is a salutary thing.'

In the autumn of 1941 the Nazis were embarking on a journey for which there was no precedent. They had decided to exterminate a race. But how were they to do it? The deportations from the Reich that autumn caused great logistical problems, as many were simply crammed into already overcrowded ghettos in places such as Lodz. A more efficient system had to be devised and many basic questions of organization had to be resolved. Who exactly was to be included in the deportations? What should happen to those Germans who were only part Jewish?

The need to resolve these questions resulted in the Wannsee Conference, a meeting chaired by Heydrich on 20 January 1942. Hans Frank knew in advance what was to be proposed, as his state secretary had already had a meeting with Heydrich. This meant that on 16 December 1941 he was able to tell senior officials of the General Government: 'As an old National Socialist, I must state that if the Jewish clan were to survive the war in Europe, while we had sacrificed our best blood in the defence of Europe, then this war would only represent a partial success. With respect to the Jews, therefore, I will only operate on the assumption that they will disappear...We must exterminate the Jews wherever we find them and whenever it is possible to do so in order to maintain the whole structure of the Reich here.'

Frank talks openly of extermination as the fate awaiting the Jews who are about to be deported from the Reich. But the surviving minutes of the Wannsee Conference, which were designed for a wider circulation, were couched in more ambiguous terms. Here the talk is of 'evacuation' as a means towards the Final Solution. But Eichmann, who prepared the minutes, admitted to the Israelis in 1960 that the meeting had openly discussed the practicalities of mass extermination.

This change of policy had been communicated to Hans Biebow, ghetto manager of Lodz, sometime in the autumn of 1941. Now the role of the ghettos changed. They were no longer prison camps but transit camps. In the short term Jews from the Third Reich would be transported into the ghetto, while selected Jews from the ghetto would be sent to the newly created extermination camps. Other transports from the Reich would be sent direct to the extermination camps, depending on their capacity. Inside the Lodz ghetto it was still possible for Jews to believe that the new transports out of the ghetto were simply another deportation to a 'work' camp. Since the talk had always been of imposing forcible emigration on the Jews, this still provided a convenient cover. The Jews of Lodz, however, could see that those transported out of the ghetto were often the least productive ones, although there was never a stringent selection of the sick from the fit. Estera Frenkiel remembers the clearance of the ghetto hospital: 'Whether they were on the healthy side following a routine operation, that was immaterial.' One woman pleaded, 'I only have to stay two days in hospital. I am not ill, I have just had an operation.' But to no avail.

In one of their most heartless acts the Nazis decided to remove children under the age of 10 from the Lodz ghetto. Parents were told to take their children to a collection point, put them on trucks and walk away. 'The children were taken away from their parents,' says Estera Frenkiel. 'Their screams reached the

sky…Every mother went with her child and put it on the cart, pressed it to them. The child screamed and cried. She pressed it to her breast and calmed it down and then went away.' Many mothers decided to leave their husbands in the ghetto and accompany their children to share their fate. One family who had hidden their child in their ghetto flat returned to their room later, to discover the child had suffocated in the confines of his hiding-place.

Working as she did in the office of the Jewish manager of the ghetto, Estera Frenkiel had privileged access to information, some of which she would rather not have learnt. One day a letter arrived, via Biebow's office, asking for information: 'I request that you ascertain immediately whether there is a bone-grinder in the ghetto. Either to be electrically or manually operated.' There was a postscript. 'The Sonderkommando of Kulmhof is interested in such a grinder.'

'One's heart misses a beat,' says Estera Frenkiel talking of her reaction to reading the letter. 'The thoughts come flooding in. What for? Why? For whom? For what purpose?' Rather like the Jews in Samuel Willenberg's train *en route* for Treblinka, even in the face of evidence to the contrary, many of the Lodz Jews simply hoped for the best. But hope on its own was no protection.

Eventually, Estera Frenkiel and her mother were sent to Ravensbrück concentration camp. 'The ghetto was a story in its own right: that was a tale of hunger and starvation – a battle for food, avoiding deportation. But there in Ravensbrück it was hell: neither day, nor night.' She puts her survival down to one thing above all – 'luck'.

In 1942 extermination camps were established at Treblinka, Sobibór, Majdanek and Belzec. Auschwitz, which had existed as a work camp, had its massive new extension at nearby Birkenau also converted into an extermination camp. Mass extermination by gassing had evolved from the killing methods developed for the adult euthanasia programme.

At Auschwitz, unlike Treblinka, a systematic selection was periodically made of those inmates who were to be killed and those who were to be allowed to live, however temporarily. Nazi doctors were quick to grasp the infinite possibilities for human experimentation which this endless supply of human guinea pigs offered them. They devised a series of devilish experiments, the details of which haunt the mind of anyone who has studied the subject. The notorious Dr Josef Mengele once sewed two gypsy children together in an attempt to create Siamese

Previous pages: Corpses of the victims of the Bergen-Belsen concentration camp in northwest Germany, photographed by the liberating forces in spring 1945. Proof that the Nazis created a hell on earth.

twins. Another Nazi doctor, in pursuit of his own warped theory, quizzed a starving inmate about the effect of undernourishment on his metabolism before having him murdered so that he could dissect his internal organs and then judge the anatomical effects for himself. Inmates who tried to escape from the camp could expect to be roasted over giant frying pans when they were recaptured.

The Nazis had now arrived at a destination no one had travelled to before – they had created killing factories where men, women and children could be disposed of in hours. The images of the gas chambers would forever shape and define Nazism. But one should not read history backwards. As we have seen, the journey to the gas chambers was not a simple one. Stages along the route included the anti-Semitism engendered in the wake of World War I defeat; the desire to exclude Jews from German life and the Nazis' belief that Jews were both a dangerous and inferior race; the invasion of Poland, which brought 3 million Polish Jews (considered the worst inferior racial combination) under Nazi control; and finally the decision to kill Communists and Jews in the wake of Operation Barbarossa. No blueprint for the Holocaust existed before 1941: the Nazi regime was too chaotic for that.

Above all, it was the invasion of Russia that caused a radical change in the Nazis' approach to the Jews. Hitler wrote that he felt 'spiritually free' at the time of the invasion, which for a character such as his, meant feeling free to be true to his own emotional view of the world – a world in which, as he said to his generals in August 1939, a human being should strive to 'close your heart to pity – act brutally'. Prior to Barbarossa, there are countless examples where the Nazis restrained their own brutality – the release of the Polish professors, for example – but once Barbarossa began, the Nazis were true to themselves and indifferent to the morals of the world.

They didn't know if it was possible to murder so many people, but twentieth-century technology made it easy.

CHAPTER SIX

—

REAPING THE WHIRLWIND

After the battle of Stalingrad in the autumn and winter of 1942–3, Hitler and the Germans experienced nothing but disaster. So why, when the war must have seemed lost, did the Germans fight on to the end? Why did Germany have to suffer so, and in her suffering inflict destruction on countless others? The answers to these questions contain fundamental truths about Nazism, for this was an ideology which, under its Führer, would sooner destroy itself than surrender. As a result, in the last months of the war, the Nazis came to reap the suffering they had sown.

Until recently historians have concentrated their efforts on examining the major strategic turning points of the war. Only lately has there been much detailed research on the final period of the war when the regime descended into destruction. Between July 1944 and May 1945 more Germans perished than in the previous four years put together; roughly 50,000 German soldiers and civilians died per month. Yet one neighbouring Fascist country in the Axis successfully managed to remove its dictator before the end of the war and so escape further involvement in the conflict.

On 25 July 1943 the Italian Fascist dictator Benito Mussolini had an audience with the king of Italy. He was told that the Grand Fascist Council had voted by nineteen votes to seven to replace him as head of state. Mussolini was arrested as he left the room; thus was the first Fascist dictator bloodlessly removed from power. This prompts the question – if the Italians were capable of seeing the way the war was inevitably going and acting accordingly, why couldn't the Germans?

The first reason, of course, is that there was no German equivalent to the

Left: Women run with their children from the advancing
Red Army, Danzig, March 1945.

Grand Fascist Council which could collectively pass judgement upon Hitler. He had destroyed the normal apparatus of the state which would have served as a check on his absolute power. There were no cabinet meetings, no national assemblies, no party senate, no forums in which Germans could legitimately come together to question the conduct of the war. A system had evolved which protected Hitler not just from being constitutionally removed from office, but from coherent criticism of any sort.

Hitler himself would not seek surrender as the military situation grew ever more desperate. His whole character militated against such action. Consumed by hatred as he was, suicide was always his preferred escape, but only when Nazism had reached the very end of its long and bloody road. He would never capitulate. In order for Germany to be saved her suffering he would have to be removed.

If there was no prospect of removing Hitler from office constitutionally, as Mussolini had been, the only alternative was to remove him violently. Any conspirator seeking to do this would need a privilege rare and precious in those last years of the war – access to the Führer. The only people who were now admitted to Hitler's presence were either members of the Nazi leadership or the Armed Forces. Many obstacles prevented the former from acting against their Führer. Their commitment to Nazism was based on a belief in the supreme ability of Hitler, something which had been inculcated since the Nuremberg rallies of the 1920s. To challenge Hitler meant going against nearly twenty years of subservience and belief. In addition, the Nazi leaders were hopelessly split among themselves by a series of personal enmities. (Goebbels disliked Göring, Göring hated Ribbentrop, Ribbentrop loathed Goebbels.) Finally, most, if not all, of the leadership were implicated in the crimes of the regime, as the Nuremberg trials later showed. They would have had little to gain by removing Hitler and making peace. Just as they had prospered with him, now they would suffer with him.

Only the leaders of the Armed Forces, who came into regular contact with Hitler, could hope to topple him. For many, however, the oath of allegiance they had sworn to the Führer proved too much to overcome. 'It was simply understood,' says Bernd Linn, an officer who served in the east, 'that the soldier has sworn an oath and stood by his oath.' Then there was Hitler's ability to change minds by the power of his own conviction, the effects of which Karl Boehm-Tettelbach, a Luftwaffe staff officer, regularly witnessed at the Wolf's Lair.

On one occasion he drove to a local airfield to collect a field marshal who had just flown in from Paris to brief Hitler on the war on the Western Front. On the drive back to the Wolf's Lair, the field marshal asked Boehm-Tettelbach what mood Hitler was in because, he said, 'I'm going to give him hell. He should know what's going on in France.' On the return journey to the airfield the field marshal said, 'Boehm, excuse me, I was mad today but I made a mistake. Hitler convinced me that it was justified and I'm wrong. I didn't know what he knows. So therefore I feel very sorry.' As Boehm-Tettelbach says today, 'The flair Hitler had was unusual. He could take somebody who was almost ready for suicide, he could revive him and make him feel that he should carry the flag and die in battle. Very strange.'

It wasn't just Hitler's powers of persuasion, or the oath of allegiance, that kept many of the army in line: it was the often unspoken knowledge of what was happening in the east. That the war against the Soviet Union was to be a war unlike any other had been trumpeted from the start of the campaign. Despite the protestations to the contrary of many surviving ex-Wehrmacht and Waffen-SS soldiers today, the evidence is overwhelming that participation in atrocities in the east was widespread.

Walter Fernau was a 22-year-old corporal in the Wehrmacht when he fought in the bitter retreat from Moscow during 1942. He had reason to be grateful to the Russians because for a short period he was quartered with a Soviet family who were friendly and hospitable towards him. 'They even let me sleep together with the grandfather on the top of their oven,' he says today. But another NCO from his regiment, billeted with Russians nearby, was not so grateful to the civilians who gave him shelter, as Walter Fernau witnessed. 'All of a sudden I heard two salvoes from a sub-machine-gun firing out and I imagined it was partisans or something, so I went into the house with my sub-machine-gun. And then I saw that for no reason at all, this NCO had shot the two old Russians who lived in the house with his sub-machine-gun. I had a go at him, I said, "How can you do something like that?" Well, and then he said, and he'd certainly had too much to drink, "The only good Russian is a dead Russian!" I said, "But surely not these poor old people, you know!" But he just wouldn't go into it. Well, it was a sad business of course.'

Adolf Buchner served in an SS unit on the Eastern Front, near Leningrad, and he too witnessed the consequences of Hitler's desire to fight a war of

annihilation. Under the guise of suspecting particular villages of sheltering 'partisans', Buchner's unit would set fire to wooden houses with flame-throwers and then shoot anyone who emerged. 'These were defenceless people and perhaps they could have been gathered together and brought to a camp and given a chance to survive, but this was sheer brutality, totally stubborn. Anything that moved – bang! There were children among them too. There were no scruples, everybody was a target.' Adolf Buchner denies shooting women and children himself, but he does admit shooting at the men who emerged from the burning houses. 'What can you do?…It feels like being hypnotized, you cannot really describe it.' The brutality of the German soldiers even extended to shooting stray children. 'The child has to be fed, so they'd sooner simply get rid of it. Put it in a ditch and the matter was over and done with.' Once, when a school was being stormed, Buchner said to his comrades, 'Don't you feel sorry for the children?' 'Why?' came the reply. 'A child might also be holding a weapon.'

Still troubling Adolf Buchner today is the knowledge that some of his German comrades enjoyed the killing: 'Was there any need, for example, to shoot the children in front of the women and then shoot the women after that? That happened too. That is sadism. There were officers like that, they liked sadistic things, they liked it when the mothers were screaming or children were screaming – they were really hot for that. In my view these people are not human…to see a child crying "Mummy" or "Daddy"…a human being capable of thought who is capable of doing such things, I cannot get it into my head that such things exist, but they do.'

Adolf Buchner is clear about the extent of German participation in the atrocities in the east. 'Virtually all units were involved….It did not matter whether it was Wehrmacht or SS, both of them.'

Academic research confirms Buchner's statement that participation in mass killings or other atrocities was widespread, probably universal. Arduous checks have been carried out on the Wehrmacht records and the records of the survivors, which has led Professor Michael Geyer to the conclusion that almost every single Wehrmacht unit was involved in some form of mass killing. 'A certain unit may indeed have escaped any of this,' says Professor Geyer, 'but that unit is almost a miraculous unit on the Eastern Front or in the Balkans. And it is curious that the miracle always happens when there are no records.'

Left: A Russian 'partisan' hangs from a lamppost, 1941.
Germany would now suffer the Soviet revenge.

Almost all the Wehrmacht officers we interviewed who served in the east vehemently dispute such findings, but one or two, when pressed, made some interesting admissions. First, they were at pains to say that they did not take part in the extermination of Jews. Then they emphasized the undoubted atrocities the Russians committed on Germans. Only then did they admit that their unit may have been involved in the killing of 'partisans' in actions like those described by Adolf Buchner.

During the war German soldiers habitually used racist terms to describe the enemy in the east – 'dirty, sub-human creatures' who were like 'wild ducks who have to be shot' – terms which are simply unacceptable today. This may be one of the reasons why so many of our interviewees found it difficult to refer to the crimes which the Germans undoubtedly committed. 'After 1945 no one can say [such things] any more,' says Professor Geyer, 'so their language disappears and there is a blank spot where at one point they said "wild ducks".' Another way of rationalizing the atrocities, which is denied veterans today, was only to hint at what one had witnessed. According to Professor Geyer, soldiers often did this in letters home: 'They say, "Something very outrageous happened to me yesterday, it's so unbelievable I cannot possibly tell you because it would upset you to know...." And then they can go on for very long passages explaining how upsetting this would be if they actually told what happened. And in the process of writing how upsetting it was, they forget the story.'

The feeling that they were part of a conflict which was uniquely cruel and barbarous in modern times must have been widespread among German soldiers in the east. In Chapter Four we saw how Wilhelm Moses, a driver with the Wehrmacht in Poland, was haunted by the hanging of Jews during the early months of the war. Yet Poland saw only a small number of Jews openly killed compared with the number who died following Operation Barbarossa. Not surprisingly, there are many more accounts of Wehrmacht soldiers witnessing the killing of Jews from June 1941 onwards than there were before. Hundreds of thousands of Jews were killed relatively openly by Einsatzgruppen actions in the east. SS officer Bernd Linn learnt about these killings through a friend in the SS Order Police. The friend said to him, 'I am not going back to the unit.' Linn warned him that this would be desertion and asked why he didn't want to go back. His friend refused to give the reason, but he later met his friend's girlfriend who said he had shown her pictures of Jews being shot. Bernd Linn's friend had participated in the murder of Jews in the east.

Knowledge that Germans were involved in these crimes could provoke one of a number of responses within the army élite: officers could genuinely believe in the Nazi propaganda that they were fighting a nation of sub-humans who deserved all they got; or such knowledge could make officers more frightened of

A German soldier examines the body of a Prussian refugee – allegedly murdered by the Soviets.

defeat and more desperate to keep fighting so that the crime could be hidden; more rarely, it could provoke a desire to see such crimes stopped and the chief criminal, Hitler, brought swiftly to account. Hans von Herwarth fell into the last group and was unique among all the German soldiers we talked to. Not only did he admit to knowing about the abuses being committed in the east, but he actually resolved, along with his friend Count Klaus Schenk von Stauffenberg, to do something about it.

Hans von Herwarth first learnt about the mass executions in the summer of 1942, when an officer who had personally witnessed the atrocities reported them to him. When he realized what was happening, he made a decision: 'We must get rid of Hitler. It confirmed my view that he was a devil of a person and that he had to be destroyed.' He met von Stauffenberg a year or so later: 'I met him when he was in hospital in Munich, and there was a burning fire, you know, a holy fire in this man. He said, "Well, I have to recover, I have something to do."' As von Herwarth says, 'There were quite a lot of people who were willing to kill Hitler, but there was no possibility to bring them into contact with him.' Von Stauffenberg, however, had both the opportunity and the will, being a staff officer at the Wolf's Lair.

On the morning of 20 July 1944 Karl Boehm-Tettelbach woke late in his bedroom at the Führer's headquarters near Rastenburg in East Prussia. After working through the night he felt too groggy to attend the situation briefing with Hitler at midday. At 12.45, as he walked into his own office, there was the sound of a distant explosion. One of his colleagues rushed up and said, 'Did you hear that big boom?' 'Yes,' replied Boehm-Tettelbach, 'it's probably one of the deer.'

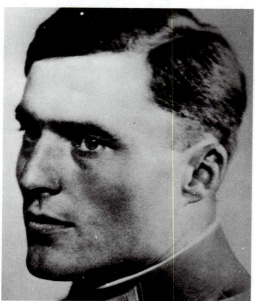

Count von Stauffenberg. The man who tried to kill Hitler on 20 July 1944.

The area around the Wolf's Lair was heavily mined and four or five times every night deer or rabbits in the forest would set off an explosion. This time, however, it was not a mine in the forest which had detonated, but a bomb in Hitler's own briefing room.

In the most famous act of resistance in the history of the Third Reich, a bomb placed by Count von Stauffenberg had exploded in an attempt to assassinate Hitler. Had the conference been held, as usual, in Hitler's command bunker with its concrete walls, instead of in the wooden hut to which it had been re-scheduled, Hitler would probably have died in the explosion. As it was, the wooden walls of the hut exploded outwards and dissipated the force of the blast, allowing Hitler to escape with minor wounds.

Countless books have been written about the incident. Many, especially those written in the immediate post-war years, point to the 20 July plot as a glorious, albeit doomed, episode in German history. But that was not how it was perceived at the time. A study of letters sent back from frontline troops in the weeks immediately after the bomb plot shows a very different reaction. The censor's report, based on an examination of 45,000 letters, concludes: 'The treachery of the conspiratorial clique is rejected by all as the greatest crime against the German people.' Obviously, knowing that letters were censored, it would have been foolhardy for any soldier to record anti-Hitler sentiments in his correspondence, but equally there was no obligation to condemn the bomb plot either. The letters point to an overwhelming feeling of betrayal. After all, the German officers who had conspired against Hitler had broken their oath.

Hans von Herwarth has little sympathy for those officers who accuse him of breaking his oath to Hitler and who used this as a reason not to join in the bomb plot: 'That's a very cheap excuse,' he says. 'Hitler broke his oath twenty times, fifty times, he broke his oath to Germany.'

I asked Karl Boehm-Tettelbach what he would have said to von Stauffenberg had he been approached. 'I would have said, "I am going to report to Hitler that you want to kill him."' More than fifty years later he still appears angry about von Stauffenberg's actions. 'I don't approve,' he says simply. He objects to the 20 July bomb for a variety of reasons: von Stauffenberg broke his oath of allegiance to Hitler ('Nobody approached me', he says, 'because they knew that I wouldn't break my oath'); simply killing Hitler would have accomplished little ('Himmler must be replaced, Göring must be replaced and many, many other people, because just blowing up Hitler is nuts'); and, crucially, von Stauffenberg did not sacrifice himself in order to ensure that Hitler was killed ('That's what the Palestinians do now').

After the bomb went off and failed to kill Hitler, the Nazi revenge was swift and brutal. Some seven thousand people were arrested and by April 1945 five thousand of them had been executed. Anyone who had even been approached to take part in the conspiracy was executed; it was no defence to say that one had refused to take part. At breakfast, the day after the bomb exploded, Karl Boehm-

The aftermath of the bomb at the Wolf's Lair. No wonder, seeing this destruction,
that Hitler felt divine providence had saved him.

Tettelbach witnessed the Nazis' revenge as he sat next to a shaking army colonel. 'He was so nervous, I said, "What's wrong with you? You're so nervous!" His hand was trembling and coffee was spilling and he said, "I just don't, I can't say." And at that moment, during breakfast at 9 o'clock, two SS men came and said, "Colonel, please come along." And by that night he was dead, because he did not participate but he was approached by von Stauffenberg.' Hans von Herwarth was lucky. Even under torture, those who knew he had supported the bomb plot did not give his name. As he says today, 'I owe my life to them.'

We know that knowledge of atrocities in the east played a part in motivating the bomb plotters. Equally, we know from recent academic research that soldiers on the Eastern Front generally knew of the atrocities. What is less certain is how much the ordinary population of Germany knew in the final years of the war.

What we do know is that German society changed fundamentally during the war. Previously it had been a country whose government *preached* the values of racism: now it was a country which *benefited* from racism. As Professor Geyer says, 'Within Germany about 30 per cent of the industrial and agricultural labour force was foreign – forced labour, POWs, or even concentration camp inmates that were parcelled out basically on the principle of expendable labour.' And the disturbing conclusion historians such as Professor Geyer come to about the racist state Germany had become is that 'the Germans

Forced labourers from the east (identified by their armbands) work in a German factory during the war.

not only experienced it but by and large liked it'. The arrival of a huge class of people in Germany who were by definition inferior to the lowest German was plainly of benefit. At the very least, it enabled Germans to feel that they were superior and that the Nazi propaganda was correct – they were a 'master race'. The lowly German worker could become a foreman; the housewife could have servants. Society had changed in a profoundly racist way. This is the background against which one must judge the statements of Germans on the home front that they knew nothing of what was happening in the east. For not only did every German experience the racial propaganda of the Nazis, but almost all of them experienced the consequences of racism in the form of the 'sub-human' workers who were everywhere. How hard it must be in such an environment not to feel superior, not to think that these people are less than oneself. When Polish workers shuffled by in their rags, how could the Germans not feel superior? After 1945 it was hard for Germans to express openly such feelings of superiority, especially once detailed knowledge of the Holocaust became commonplace. The vocabulary of racism was denied to those on the home front, just as it was denied to the soldiers who had fought the enemy.

It is not too fanciful to imagine that the same Germans who benefited from living in a racist state would fear what life would be like once the slaves regained their freedom. If Germany fell, surely the oppressed would seek revenge on their oppressors? Anyone who benefits from a crime seeks to avoid the moment of reckoning.

If fear of eventual judgement for participating in a racist slave state played any part in the decision of ordinary Germans to follow the regime until the end, there remains a crucial question to answer – how many ordinary Germans knew during the war that the Jews were being exterminated? If one takes at face value the evidence from the many interviews we filmed with German civilians of the period, the answer is clear – none. When asked what she thought was happening to the Jews, Gabriele Winckler, a secretary, gave a typical reply: 'People always told us they were going to Madagascar or somewhere, some barren country. God knows what rubbish they talked, and then I really didn't think much more about it all.' Alternatively, our interviewees would say that they thought the Jews were being deported east to work. Johannes Zahn, a financial expert, says, 'I knew that the Jews were being put into work camps, but I didn't know that they were being systematically killed. But I do have to say honestly that if I had known about it then, I wouldn't have done anything about it…nobody in their right mind runs straight into the machine-guns.'

Our interviewees often expressed great indignation at relatively minor injustices meted out by the Nazis, such as forcing German Jews to wear yellow stars prior to their deportation. 'Terrible! Terrible!' says Erna Kranz, then a young woman living in Munich. 'In the street parallel to us we had a Baroness Brancka who was married to a baron, but was a Jewish shopkeeper's daughter from Hamburg...and she had to wear the Jewish star. I was sorry about that, it was so terrible because this woman was such a nice woman, that's what you felt. But really, just like today when you walk away from people in need, you can't help everywhere, it was the same then. You said what can we do? You couldn't do anything, could you? We were forced to do nothing and accept that a single person who wasn't at fault could be persecuted.' A lesson learned from such testimony is that the small injustice in front of one's nose can have a greater impact than a much larger injustice which occurs out of sight – even if that larger injustice is suspected. Thus the Nazi plan to transport the Jews *away* from Germany was an inspired act of evil.

The more we posed the question, 'When did you know about the extermination camps?' to our interviewees, the more it became clear that the question invited a black-and-white answer – either the interviewees knew during the war or they didn't – when it seemed the true answer must be in shades of grey. Professor Geyer believes there were at least three levels of recognition among the ordinary German population concerning the fate of the Jews. The first level was the simple one of 'visual' knowledge. It was clear that the Jews were no longer there. 'Neighbours were no longer neighbours,' as Professor Geyer puts it. 'They definitely knew and somehow acquiesced to the fact that their Jewish neighbours would no longer be present.' Every German would have recognized the fate of the German Jews at this level. At the other extreme, specific knowledge of the extermination camps must have been confined to relatively few people. None of the extermination camps operated within the pre-war boundaries of Germany, and even among the higher levels of the Nazi hierarchy there existed a euphemistic language to describe what was actually taking place in them (the code word 'evacuation', for example, used in Eichmann's memorandum of the Wannsee Conference). Those with the second level of recognition knew that something 'bad' was happening to the Jews. This is the most interesting level of knowledge and the one that is hardest to quantify. Once the Jews had disappeared from the towns and villages, it was possible for ordinary Germans not to think about what was happening to them. But if they *did* think about it, surely it must have been obvious that the Jews were going to a terrible fate? Jews had been public victims of Nazi persecution since the boycott of 1933. Hitler had announced in 1939 that a world war would mean the 'annihilation' of Jews in Europe. Knowledge of atrocities in the east, even if not specific knowledge of anti-Semitic actions, must have been widespread back on German soil if one accepts that the vast majority of German Army units were involved. The majority of Germans who thought about it even for a moment must have realized that, at the least, 'something bad' was happening to the Jews.

A Nazi report (by the SD, the intelligence branch of the SS run by Reinhard Heydrich) from Franconia in southern Germany, dated December 1942, demonstrates that the Nazis themselves were concerned about the effect on the population of knowledge about the killing of Jews in the east: 'One of the strongest causes of unease among those attached to the Church and in the rural population is at the present time formed by news from Russia in which shooting and extermination of the Jews is spoken about. The news frequently leaves great anxiety, care and worry in those sections of the population. According to widely held opinion in the rural population, it is not at all certain that we will win the war, and if the Jews come again to Germany, they will exact dreadful revenge upon us.'

But there was only sporadic resistance within Germany to Nazi persecution of the Jews. One of the most famous acts was conducted by Hans and Sophie Scholl, both students at the University of Munich, who produced leaflets during the war calling for German youth to 'rise up immediately' to build a 'new, spiritual Europe'. They called the treatment of the Jews and the killing of the Polish intelligentsia 'the most terrible crime against human dignity'. They were both denounced, tortured and then executed. Sophie Scholl confided to another prisoner that she thought her execution would be the sign for thousands of other Germans to question the actions of the Nazis. Significantly, on the day of her execution, 22 February 1943, the students of Munich University demonstrated their loyalty to the Nazi regime. As the historian Ian Kershaw argues, 'Not only was resistance to Hitler carried out – inevitably one might say – without active support from the mass of the people, but even passive support was largely lacking for those risking everything to overthrow the system.'

The citizens of Germany had only to walk as far as their local cinema to see one more reason not to support brave individuals like Sophie and Hans Scholl and to keep on fighting. The Nazi newsreels showed in graphic terms how the country was fighting a life and death struggle against the enemy they all feared most – Russia. Fear at what would happen to Germany if the hated Bolsheviks triumphed was a powerful incentive to support the war and, in doing so, to support the Nazi leadership.

From the first moment of Operation Barbarossa the German Army had stimulated desire for revenge in the Russians. Atrocities were committed by both sides against captured troops. Russian prisoners of war were treated abominably – of 5 million captured by the Germans, only 2 million survived the war.

'What did the German soldier fight for and, one has to ask, against what?' says Graf von Kielmansegg, a German staff officer. 'For me this is the decisive reason: all those who had been in Russia at least knew what Germany could expect if Bolshevism came to Germany…If it had only been England and France, we would have stopped earlier in a simplified manner. Not against Russia.' As Hermann Teschemacher, who served on the Eastern Front, puts it: 'We told ourselves that there's a storm over Asia and it will come over Germany, and then brutal extermination, mistreatment and killings would follow, we knew that. So we defended ourselves to the end and remained loyal to the oath…The worst would have been if Bolshevism stormed over Germany – then the whole of Europe would be lost. But first and foremost we thought about ourselves and our families and that is why we defended ourselves to the end.'

Fear and hatred of Bolshevism had been at the core of Nazi ideology since the days of the Räterepublik in Munich in 1919. How much greater that fear and hatred were when there seemed the danger, perhaps even the likelihood, that the hated Bolsheviks would soon be on German soil. So great was the perceived danger that hundreds of thousands of non-Germans used it as a justification for joining the Waffen-SS after 1941. Contrary to popular belief, recruits did not have to be German to be ideologically committed members of Himmler's SS. Jacques Leroy was a young Belgian who had been impressed with the 'nice behaviour' of the occupying German forces and who resolved to join the Waffen-SS because he 'wanted to fight Communism and Bolshevism'. We asked him if he was not, therefore, a traitor. 'What is a traitor?' he angrily replied. 'What is a traitor, sir? Can you be a traitor at the age of 16? I didn't wear a Belgian uniform. You are a traitor when you fight ideas which are not those of Europe, which are not popular. When you take on ideas from abroad, you are a traitor. The word traitor never once came into my mind...I was fighting Communism.'

More than fifty years after the end of the war, Jacques Leroy is still openly racist. Even today he retains many of the views that his colleagues in the Waffen-SS held so dear. 'The difference between the people whom you call *Übermenschen* [superior races] and the ones whom you call *Untermenschen* [inferior races] is that the people who are the *Übermenschen* are the white race. That's why at the moment so many foreigners want to come to white race countries...In those days we were proud to belong to the white race.'

Jacques Leroy fought in some of the bloodiest battles on the Eastern Front, motivated by his racism and his hatred of Communism. At the battle of Teklino on 14 January 1945 his Waffen-SS unit came upon more than three Soviet regiments hidden in a forest. The SS attacked and lost 60 per cent of their men. At one point Leroy saw a Russian kneeling behind a birch tree and then suddenly he felt 'an electric shock' through his body. He dropped his rifle and 'at that moment I saw blood dripping on to the snow. I was bleeding, it was my eye which had been hit by a bullet.' Leroy's injuries cost him an eye and an arm, but after a few weeks in hospital, he pleaded to rejoin the SS, and was allowed to do so: 'Of course I had lost an arm and an eye but you know, when you're very young, one isn't affected by troubles in the same way that an older person might be.' When we asked why he wanted to rejoin the SS he replied, 'So as not to fall into mediocrity and to stay with my comrades...I don't like mediocrity, I don't like doing nothing, being idle and not having any aim in life...otherwise, what is your life for? Life is not about watching television all the time! You have to think, you have to see, you must have a goal.'

The Waffen-SS soldiers who fought the Russians for every step of territory as they advanced into the Reich included Bernd Linn, who was to take part in an engagement that in many ways symbolizes both the bravery and the futility of the Nazi armed resistance – the Battle of Halbe, fought on 29 April 1945, just days before the end of the war. Linn's unit was ordered to 'break through regardless of losses' – a futile order given that everyone knew that the war was lost.

'There was the sound of gunfire from every side,' says Linn, talking of the 'Hell of Halbe'. In the heart of the battle he came across a German tiger tank, damaged so that it was unable to move and yet still firing its machine-gun.

Overleaf: A German soldier gives a thumbs-up sign to a Frenchman who has volunteered to fight for the Germans against the Soviet Union. The Nazis dreamt of an alliance of the west against the east.

'Behind it was a lieutenant with a leg missing, but he wasn't dead yet. I went to him and said, "Is there something that you want?" And the lieutenant said, "Yes, please put my leg next to me." I wanted to take him with us in the vehicle and he said, "We have been ordered to break through regardless of losses. Please put my leg next to me."' As the men fell dead, German Red Cross nurses took up arms. Bernd Linn handed one a bazooka. 'Then the Russians shouted, "Surrender!" "Certainly not!" I said, "We're breaking through."' We pressed Linn to say why he fought on till the last. The nearest he came to making us understand was when he said that as a committed Nazi he thought it was simply his fate.

Conditioned as they were by Nazi propaganda about 'sub-human' Russians and the barbaric atrocities the Communists were allegedly capable of committing as they came west, the German troops' resistance is perhaps not so surprising. After all, what alternative did they have? Only surrender to a group who, they had been told, would treat them appallingly, and to whom the Germans had already done terrible things themselves. Since every soldier had been told from the beginning of hostilities against Russia that this was a war like no other, now, to surrender must be to experience a suffering as a Prisoner of War like no other. But it was more than fear which kept the Germans fighting in the east – hope also played a part. The dream that Britain, the United States and France would ask Germany to join them in a crusade against Communism was one which persisted in the face of all evidence to the contrary and the Allies' continued insistence on unconditional surrender.

Yet these cannot be the only reasons why German soldiers continued fighting to the end. In Italy, the country which opted out of the war in 1943, German troops continued fighting fiercely until the official surrender in May 1945. Facing their so-called 'honourable' adversaries – the Americans and the British – they could have deserted in droves if they had wished. And lest one imagines that desertion was considered 'un-German', it is worth remembering that one estimate is that as many as a million German soldiers deserted during World War I. Yet this didn't happen, even in Italy, during World War II.

The Nazis were born out of World War I and the pain of what they saw as a shameful defeat: one cannot overestimate the German desire not to see a repetition of November 1918. The German soldiers in Italy, just as much as the German soldiers fighting the ideological enemy in the east, were vividly aware of the circumstances of defeat in 1918. The Nazi élite themselves had an overwhelming desire not to relive these circumstances. Indeed, it is not too extreme to imagine that the decision to proceed with the Holocaust might have been partly inspired by a desire to ensure that Jews were not able to 'profit' from World War II as they had 'profited' from World War I. Ludicrous as these beliefs about the Jews were, they were clearly held by many Nazis and were, almost unbelievably, occasionally expressed to us even today. The German Army may not have been able to prevent the Allies advancing, may not even have been able to prevent them defeating Germany, but what *was* in their power was to ensure that the manner of their defeat in no way resembled the humiliation of World War I. This time German soldiers would not be surprised to hear the announcement of the surrender.

As the war drew to a close, Hitler remained a crucial presence in the German soldier's mind. During the last months Walter Fernau became a National Socialist Guidance Officer (NSFO) and gave propaganda speeches to soldiers in Germany, telling them why they should fight on. 'It was my task to address the troop at the company level, no bigger, to call on them to see it through,' he says. 'This accordion player appeared before the troop and then songs were sung, seamen shanties, and this created a wonderful atmosphere. And then I said, "Men, we haven't come together just to sing songs here. I have to tell you something about this entire situation in which we find ourselves. If we take a look at the military situation as it is at the moment, then we know that the Americans or the English are at our border. We know that the Russians are marching towards Berlin and we know that in the south the Americans have passed Rome. And furthermore, masses of planes are flying day and night over our country and dropping bombs on our cities. And none of us knows at this moment whether his family has already fallen victim or if his house is standing. If we are to judge the overall situation now, then I can only express it in simple soldier's language: 'It's all shit!' But in exactly the same way that we judge the military situation, so too must our Führer see it as the supreme commander. Perhaps he knows that it is even worse than we know today. But perhaps he knows that it is better. And he still demands of us today, however, that we continue to do our duty, that is, some of us must perhaps even be prepared to die or to be heavily wounded. And he can only demand that of us if he can

expect a good end to the war." And then I said to the soldiers, "Do you want to chuck your rifles in the corner today and go home? And then when the war is over and Hitler comes and says, 'Well, you've thrown away your weapons! I wanted to find a good ending!' We do not want to expose ourselves to this reproach.'" His view of Hitler at the time was simple. 'For us the Führer was, let us say, an idol.' This leads Walter Fernau to give a simple answer to the question – why did German soldiers desert in droves in World War I yet fight to the end in World War II? 'In the First World War there was no Hitler.'

The fact that German soldiers continued fighting to the end, though tragic in terms of human loss, may have had one positive benefit, according to Hans von Herwarth: 'The new *Dolchstosslegende* (stab-in-the-back legend) would otherwise have come true...Many of the women in Germany had lost their sons or their brothers and they couldn't imagine that all this was in vain, that they were killed for the wrong reason, they couldn't believe it.' If Hitler had been assassinated in 1944 and peace had immediately followed, in later years it would have been possible to argue that Germany would not necessarily have lost the war if she had fought on. Counterfactual history is by definition unprovable and the speculation would have been intense. In that last year of the war would the Western Allies have finally turned on the Russians? Would the Germans have developed their 'wonder weapons', including the V1 and V2 rockets, to a point where they could have made a real difference? The debate would still be raging, especially in ultra-right-wing circles. Ironically, the fight to the end may have prevented another Hitler being born from this war, albeit a new Hitler justly burdened with the legacy of the Holocaust.

Yet the benefits to Germany of peace in 1944 would have been immense, not just in terms of soldiers spared from death at the hands of the enemy, but in terms of German civilians who would have been saved from death at the hands of the Nazis. In that last year of the war, Nazi terror inside Germany spiralled out of control. One shocking case from the Würzburg archives illustrates how the Nazis turned on ordinary Germans as the war seemed lost. Karl Weiglein, a farmer in Zellingen, a village a few kilometres from Würzburg, was 59 years old in 1945 when he was called up to fight in the Volkssturm, the local defence force. He was assigned to a company led by a local teacher, Alfons Schmiedel, a fanatical Nazi who also led the local Hitler Youth. On 25 March, at about two o'clock in the

Left: The aftermath of the fire-bombing of Dresden, February 1945. Destruction like this reinforced, for many Germans, the need to fight to the end.

afternoon, the whole battalion lined up for a roll-call in the village square and listened to a short speech from Dr Mühl-Kühner, the battalion commander, who said that with the war coming closer, regulations would be tighter and anyone who didn't obey orders would be shot. A group in the first battalion, including Karl Weiglein, replied "Oh-oho!". Around the same time some anti-tank obstacles were removed from a nearby road, and a false rumour went around that Kurt Weiglein had something to do with it. On Tuesday 27 March the Nazis blew up a bridge connecting Zellingen with the neighbouring village of Retzbach in order to prevent the advance of American troops. Weiglein, whose house was near the bridge, said to one of his neighbours, 'Those idiots who have done this, Schmiedel and Mühl-Kühner, ought to be hanged!' Schmiedel overheard the remark and reported it to Mühl-Kühner.

The next evening the Fliegendes Standgericht (Flying Court Martial) of Major Erwin Helm arrived in Karlstadt. These courts had been formed to enforce discipline in the face of Germany's imminent defeat and had the legal powers of a formal court martial. The one headed by Major Helm was particularly notorious and referred to by locals as a 'lynching unit'. Major Helm was well known for his brutality and sadism; he had been overheard saying to a 17-year-old boy, 'Have you already chosen the twig you want to hang from?' On another occasion he had said to his officers, 'Look at this chap's neck, it's really tempting!'

Major Helm and Mühl-Kühner decided to execute Karl Weiglein as an example to others. He was promptly fetched from the police station in Zellingen and the Flying Court Martial convened at midnight. Helm ordered one of his lieutenants, Engelbert Michalsky, to chair the proceedings. Two local farmers, Anton Seubert and Theodor Wittmann, were brought in as 'assessors'. Walter Fernau, who by now was another of Helm's lieutenants, was ordered to act as prosecutor: 'Helm said, "You can take over the prosecution. It's a very straightforward case. I'll get the execution squad together."' He had written the death sentence before the trial even started. But then there was a hitch. The two local farmers, Seubert and Wittmann, refused to sentence Karl Weiglein to death. Helm solved the problem by dismissing them, later threatening them with a court martial themselves. Karl Weiglein was found guilty, and Walter Fernau knew that the death sentence was the only possible outcome: 'Even if you now think I am a brutal dog,' he says, 'I really cannot say to you that at the time I thought that it was too harsh…The judicial authority decides that this is the case with a flying court martial, and I cannot then say, "Wouldn't it be better to give him three or six months in prison?" That would almost have been like saying to the soldiers, "Now all of you here commit some sort of crime, come up before the Flying Court Martial…you will spend six months locked up and in that time the war will be over and the others will die and you won't." Do you understand it

German soldiers shoot 'deserters', April 1945. That spring the Nazis turned on their own countrymen in an unprecedented way.

then? Even today some people, lots of people, will confirm that such situations demand harsh measures, even though it's not to my taste. But I cannot make the laws.' Crucially, Walter Fernau talks of a link between the horrors he had seen in the east and his own attitude to the work of the Flying Courts Martial. 'I saw so many deaths of my own comrades in the war that you do get a rather thick skin as a result…Shooting people and seeing them fall too, that is terrible. But over time one becomes accustomed to it. If you are in Russia and see the Russians running about and coming towards you and then they come closer and then maybe they have attached their bayonets, well, then you shoot one after the other and are delighted when they drop. Dreadful! Can anyone understand that today, one being happy when another falls?'

At 1.30 a.m. Karl Weiglein was taken out to the pear tree Helm had selected for the hanging. He was made to wear a sign around his neck which read: 'Sentenced to death because of sabotage and destruction of fighting strength.' The pear tree was only 5 metres from Weiglein's home and he called out to his wife, 'Oh Dora, Dora, they are hanging me!' She opened the kitchen window and shouted at Helm and the others, 'Leave my husband alone! He hasn't done anything to you!' Michalsky shouted back, 'Shut up and close the window!' Her husband was hanged in front of her by Helm with the assistance of his lance-corporal. Even Walter Fernau, hardened as he was by his experiences in the east, was upset by the circumstances of Karl Weiglein's execution: 'One can describe it as shame…It's terrible for a woman like that to witness her own husband, to whom she has been married for maybe forty years or more, being hanged in front of their door.' The body was left hanging at the tree for three days until Easter Sunday, guarded by two soldiers.

After the war, and on reflection, Walter Fernau expressed his sorrow at what had happened: 'I spoke about it in my last statement, that I was so terribly sorry, but in such an event where people are simply executed it really is too banal afterwards to say, "I am sorry" or "I regret it." You can do that if you knock the mirror off a car; you can say, "I am sorry" then "What does it cost?" But not when a person is dead. And then I ask, what can be done at all? And that is the big question, which is still open today, what can I do?'

Many of the perpetrators of this killing escaped conviction. Of those who were punished, Major Helm was given a life sentence by an East German court in 1953, but since the East German secret service, the Stasi, wanted him to work for them in West Germany, he was released after three years. Walter Fernau was sentenced to six years in prison for his part in the court martial, and served more than five.

Such horrific tales of oppression in Germany are not uncommon in the final days of the war. In Penzberg, in the foothills of the German Alps, local inhabitants defended their coal mines against destruction from Hitler's scorched earth policy.

The US Army was only a day away, but a Nazi execution squad was dispatched from Munich and coldly shot the leaders of the opposition. They then drew up a list of those considered 'politically unreliable' and had them hanged.

In the face of such terror the majority conformed. Johannes Zahn, for example, says, 'I personally reproach Hitler greatly, after it was clear that the war could not be won, for not immediately saying, "OK, I give up, I will make peace, I will withdraw, I admit that I'm weaker." He should have done this, but unfortunately he did not have the greatness of character.' Men like Zahn were not the sort to resist, purely for pragmatic reasons: 'When there is a clique like Stalin's or Hitler's, when they are in power, they have all the means at their disposal and are determined to use these means of power ruthlessly. Everyone says, "There's no point. I won't risk anything," because anybody who risks anything will be killed. We saw that with the July affair. Even the people who were trained to kill and to exercise violence weren't able to do it, so how could a harmless civilian sitting in his chocolate shop selling sweets, how can he fight against something like that?' Zahn operated a simple policy of self-preservation: 'Fight them? I wouldn't have risked it. I put my tea-cosy over the telephone so as to survive these times. That's what the majority decided, that was their plan: shut up and see that nothing happens to you.' When, during an interview with one German who 'went along' with the regime, I questioned such sentiments and asked why there had been so much compliance, he angrily replied, with an element of justification, 'It's easy for you, isn't it? You've never been tested.'

In the last months of the war Karl Boehm-Tettelbach left Berlin and was ordered north to Neustadt-Flensberg. On the way he and his fellow officers stopped to meet Himmler. This was to be Boehm-Tettelbach's last meeting with the SS chief and, despite the Reich crumbling around him, Himmler could scarcely have been more charming: 'Himmler saw that I was really hungry and frozen and he wanted me to have tea and warm up a little bit, and then noticed that I was in my summer underwear, in just my short shirt, and he didn't like that and he said: "Now look here, you are going to Flensberg. In Flensberg there is an SS supply store and there you get a shirt and underwear for colder days." I went there when I arrived and with Himmler's signature out of his notebook they gave me three shirts and three SS underwear shirts…There is still one shirt which my American daughter wears when it's really very, very cold. That's from Himmler.'

Boehm-Tettelbach's anecdote demonstrates how even in the last moments of the war, with the knowledge that he would be known to history as one of the creators of the Holocaust, Himmler was still able to project the image of a senior officer who had polite concern for the welfare of his fellow Germans.

The leading Nazis thus held on to real power until the very end. Yet Hitler's own physical condition deteriorated severely over the last two years of the war: his left arm shook as a result of the July 1944 attack, and he felt dizzy and sick for hours at a time. His personal physician, Dr Morrell, filled him full of quack remedies; Albert Speer, the Nazi Armaments Minister, had the impression that Hitler was burning out. Despite all this, Hitler was still obeyed by his loyal entourage. True, there were some acts of disobedience, such as Speer refusing to implement Hitler's 'Nero' order at the end, which called for the destruction of Germany's infrastructure in order to leave the Allies with nothing but ruins. Nonetheless, even Speer professed loyalty when questioned. In Hugh Trevor-Roper's words, 'Hitler still remained, in the universal chaos he had caused, the sole master whose orders were implicitly obeyed.'

On 30 April 1945, just before 3.30 p.m., as Soviet soldiers raised the Red Flag over the Reichstag in Berlin, Hitler killed himself. Only with his death did his power over the Nazi Party came to an end. The Nazis and their leader were motivated at the core by hatred and had created a structure within which the most evil ideas in modern history could grow and flourish. In the end Hitler's own hatred had turned on the Germans he ruled and, like a fire, had ended by consuming itself – a fitting and predictable end for Hitler and the Nazi Party. Born of crisis and hatred they had died in crisis and hatred.

In their twelve-year reign the Nazis had demonstrated just what human beings can do if they take the brute beasts of the animal kingdom as their role models and are inspired by words like, 'Close your hearts to pity. Act brutally'. Of course, it can be exciting to behave in such a way; to take from the weak, to destroy the inferior and to clothe oneself in the riches of conquest. But the Nazis proved this base philosophy leads to ruin (perhaps, if such a course was ever embarked upon by a nation which possesses nuclear weapons, to the ruin of the entire world). For all time the story of the Nazis will act as a terrible warning.

Shortly after Hitler's death, at the formal German surrender, Karl Boehm-Tettelbach observed the signing of the document which meant that Germany had

Right: The Führer meets a member of the Hitler Youth in March 1945. Broken as he was, Hitler was still in command.

Soviet soldiers shelter behind a sign which says, in Russian, 'Onwards Stalingraders, the victory is close!', in the Kreuzberg district of Berlin, April 1945.

lost her second world war in less than thirty years. These were the thoughts that went through his mind: 'I had to raise the question, "Was it worth it, to start a war with all these losses on all sides; the Russian side, the German side, the American and English and French?"…I said to myself, "You've got the wrong profession. From now on, think of something else. And don't think of being a soldier again."'

After the war Karl Boehm-Tettelbach ran the Nuremberg office of the American airline Pan Am.

Right: The grave of a German soldier is marked by a cross and three helmets as holidaymakers sunbathe by one of the lakes in Berlin in the summer of 1945. The war was over. It couldn't be forgotten.

REFERENCES

INTRODUCTION

p.9 'That which has happened…' Jaspers, Karl, *The Origin and Goal of History* (Yale Universiy Press, 1953). Quoted in Kershaw, Ian, *The Nazi Dictatorship* (Edward Arnold, 1985)

CHAPTER ONE

p.14 'Hitler is lonely…' Laffin, John, *Hitler Warned Us* (Brassey's, 1995), p.31

p.14 'It is only…' Ibid., p.33

p.14 'Dear Führer…' Noakes, J. and Pridham, G. (eds), *Nazism: A Documentary Reader 1919-45* (University of Exeter Press, 1984), Vol.2, p.572

p.14 'Who is this man…' Kershaw, Ian, *Hitler* (Longman, 1991), p.33

p.14 'no noticeable influence…' Bundesarchive Lichterfelde, file R43, I/2696

p.23 'The picture which…' Hamann, Brigitte, *Hitler's Wein* (R. Piper GmbH, München, 1996)

p.24 'Nobody knows…' Bayrisches Hauptstaatsarchiv, Abt IV, p.3071

p.25 'Since I am…' Fest, Joachim, *The Face of the Third Reich*, (Penguin Books, 1972), p.211

p.25 'Brutality is …' Ibid. p.208

p.25 'I joined the…' Ibid. p.115

p.26 'It is absolutely…' *Marktbreiter Wochenblatt* 26 Oct.1923, Bayrisches Hauptstaatsarchiv, Microfiche 1, Akt. Minn73725

p.26 'What shall we…' Zentrum für Antisemitismusforschung, Technische Universität Berlin (pamphlet originally published by Dr Heinrich Budor, Leipzig)

p.29 'Gentlemen, it is…' Noakes and Pridham, Vol. I, p.35

p.36 'He suddenly…' *Hitler's Table Talk* (Oxford University Press Paperback, 1988, p.39

p.42 'Hindenburg declared…' Meissner, Otto, *Staatssekretär*, (Hoffmann und Campe Verlag, 1950), p.240

p.44 'party's fortunes…' Bessel, Richard, *The Rise of the NSDAP and the Myth of Nazi Propaganda*, Wiener Library Bulletin, 1980, Vol. 23, no. 51/51

p.46 'all preparations…' von Papen, Franz, *Der Wahrheit eine Gasse* (Paul List Verlag, Munich, 1952), p.249

p.46 'Even when…' Diary note made on 2 Dec. 1932 by Lutz Graf von Schwerin-Kroszigk, Reichs Finance Minister, quoted in 'Preparations for the military emergency under Papen' by Wolfram Pyta, Militärgeschichtliche Mitteilungen MGM51 (1992), p.141

CHAPTER TWO

p.51 'Everyone is …' Noakes and Pridham, p.169–70

p.56 A kind remark…These facts about Blomberg are quoted in Fest, Joachim, *Hitler* (Harcourt Brace Jovanovich, 1974), p.453

p.57 'Most of his…' Speer, Albert, *Inside the Third Reich* (Orion, 1995), p.84

p.57 'In the eyes…'Ibid. pp.194–5

p.57 'Everyone who…' Kershaw, Ian, 'Working Towards the Führer', *Contemporary European History*, Vol.2, Issue 2 (Cambridge University Press, 1993), pp.103–18

p.61 *Gone with the Wind*: for more on the reasons for Goebbels's obsession with this film see *Selling Politics* (BBC Books, 1992) by the present author

p.64 Professor Robert Gellately. What follows is

based on an extensive BBC interview at the Würzburg archives with Professor Gellately. See also his book *The Gestapo and German Society* (Oxford University Press, 1991)

p.70 'It must be acknowledged...' Gellately, *The Gestapo and German Society*, pp.55-6

p.80 The Children's 'Euthanasia' Programme: this chronology is based on documents in Noakes and Pridham, Vol.3, and on Professor Noakes's advice to us for the section of the script of episode two of the television series *The Nazis – a Warning from History*, which dealt with the workings of the Chancellery and the child euthanasia policy

CHAPTER THREE

p.87 'Let's learn...' *Hitler's Table Talk*, p.15

p.87 'What India was...' Ibid., p.24

p.88 'The next five...' Noakes and Pridham, Vol.2, p.263

p.88 'I desire...' Wistrich, Robert S., *Who's Who in Nazi Germany* (Routledge, 1995), p.202

p.89 'I have never...' *Hitler's Table Talk*, p.635

p.89 'We are taking...' Noakes and Pridham, Vol.3, p.615

p.90 'At the present...' Ibid., Vol. 3, p.614

p.92 'happiest day...' Ribbentrop, Joachim von, *The Ribbentrop Memoirs* (London, 1954) p.41

p.93 'he bought...' Wistrich, p.202

p.93 'The Duce says...' Ibid., p.202

p.96 'The standard...' Noakes and Pridham, Vol.2, p.278

p.96 'Hence all...' Memo from Hitler, August 1936. Ibid., Vol.2, p281

p.101 'The Führer...' Ibid., Vol.3, p.680

p.102 'in order not...' Ibid., Vol.3, p.680

p.102 'day-dreaming...' Taylor, A.J.P., *The Origins of the Second World War* (Hamish Hamilton, London, 1961), Ch.2

p.103 'I have worked...' Noakes and Pridham, Vol. 3, p.696

p.103 'the behaviour...' Ibid., p.688

p.106 Fritsch was forced...See Fest, *Hitler*, p.543

p.107 'Führer wants...' Ibid., p.544

p.108 'I have just...' Noakes and Pridham, Vol.3, p.739

p.108 'All reports...' Fest, *Hitler*, p.546

p.114 'Germany's future...' Fest, Joachim (ed.), *Himmler's Secret Speeches* (Propyläen Verlag, Germany, 1974), p.49

p.116 'the commonest...' Cooper, Duff, *Old Men Forget* (Rupert Hart-Davis, 1953)

p.120 'Now Poland...' Noakes and Pridham, Vol. 3, p.739

p.123 'Herr von Ribbentrop...' Author's interview with Hans Otto Meissner, 1991

CHAPTER FOUR

p.126 'race of rulers...' *Hitler's Table Talk*, p.19; 1 Aug. 1941

p.126 'they had ten...' Browning, Christopher, *The Path to Genocide* (Cambridge University Press, 1992)

p.126 'I, for my part...' Personal correspondence, Greiser to Himmler, 21 Nov. 1942 (Berlin Document Centre)

p.131 'It is misguided...' Noakes and Pridham, Vol.3, p.938

p.131 'starts making...' Ibid., p.940

p.142 'It will require...' Ibid. p.954

p.145 'If, in past...' Public statement, June 1942; Institut für Zeitgeschichte, DokI–176, p.29

p.145 'right from the...' Noakes and Pridham, Vol.3, p.949

p.146 'My Führer...' Ibid., p.949

p.149 'agree upon...' Browning, p.13

p.150 'we, as National...' Noakes and Pridham, Vol.3, p.965

p.152 'arrangements to...' Letter, 19 Jan.1943 (Berlin Document Centre, BDC, SS-HOI/4701)

p.153 Out of a total... Dobroszycki, Lucjan (ed.), *Chronicle of the Lodz Ghetto 1941–44* (Yale University Press, 1985), p.37

p.155 'A rapid dying...' Browning, p.36. See also this book (pp.28-56) for a detailed description of the decision-making process which led to the establishment of factories in the Lodz ghetto.

p.159 'parting gesture...' Ibid., p.37

CHAPTER FIVE

p.170 'By the word…' Klee, Ernst, Dressen, Willi, and Riess, Volker, *Those Were The Days* (Hamish Hamilton, 1991; first published by S.Fischer Verlag GmbH 1988), p.293

p.171 'If a bullet…' Burrin, Philipp, *Hitler and the Jews* (Edward Arnold, 1994), p.38

p.172 'We had the…' Noakes and Pridham, Vol.3, p.1200

p.174 'The imminent…' Ibid., p.1075

p.176 'Anyone who…' Bartov, Omar, *The Eastern Front* (Macmillan, 1985), p.83

p.176 'We are on…' Ibid., p.84

p.177 '4. Executions…' Noakes and Pridham, Vol.3, p.1091

p.179 'The task of…' Klee, Dressen and Riess, p.27

p.179 'There was a…' Ibid., p.28

p.179 'After the…' Ibid., p.31

p.187 'I have little…' Ibid., p.90

p.187 'One of them…' Ibid., p.90

p.187 'Isn't it strange…' Ibid., p.96

p.194 Until 15 August… Ibid., p.51

p.194 'Before the…' Browning, p.101

p.195 'Driving women…' For a full discussion of the debate see Browning, *The Path to Genocide*, and Burrin, *Hitler and the Jews*.

p.197 'To supplement…' Noakes and Pridham, Vol.3, p.1104

p.198 But others…Ibid., pp.1104–5

p.198 'Between 15 October…' Browning, p.116

p.199 'Petersburg…' Quoted in Irving, David, *Hitler's War* (Hodder & Stoughton, 1977), p.311

p.200 'would have no…' Burrin, p.124

p.200 'No overseas…' Ibid., p.129

p.200 'late September…' Browning, p.121

p.202 'It's not a…' *Hitler's Table Talk*, p.87

p.203 'As an old…' Noakes and Pridham, Vol.3, p.1126

CHAPTER SIX

p.217 'The treachery…' Kershaw, Ian, *The Hitler Myth* (Oxford University Press, 1989), p.218

p.223 'One of the…' Kershaw, Ian, *The Persecution of the Jews and German Popular Opinion in the Third Reich* (Yearbook of Leo Baeck Institute 1981, Vol.26), p.284

p.223 'not only was…' Kershaw, Ian, *The Nazi Dictatorship*, p.177

p.231 One shocking case… This file was originally selected for us by Professor Gellately and then the research was completed by BBC Assistant Producer Detlef Siebert

p.232 The two local… Walter Fernau still disputes the assessors' version of what they said happened inside the courtroom. It was, after all, the assessors' evidence that helped convict him for participating in the court martial at his own trial after the war

p.236 'Hitler still…' Trevor-Roper, Hugh, *The Last Days of Hitler* (Macmillan, 1947)

p.236 'Close your hearts…' Noakes and Pridham, Vol.3, p.743

BIBLIOGRAPHY

There are more books on the Third Reich than any other subject in modern history. It is easy to be overwhelmed with material; so, bearing that in mind, here is a very brief selection of useful books.

SOURCES TRANSLATED INTO ENGLISH

Goebbels Josef, *My Part in Germany's Fight*, trans. by Dr Kurt Fielder (Hurst & Blackett, 1935)
   The propaganda minister's own self-serving account of the Nazis' rise to power. See also the collection of his diary entries, *The Goebbels Diaries*, trans. and ed. by Louis P. Lockner (Hamish Hamilton, 1948); for those with German, the four-volume *Die Tagebücher von Josef Goebbels* (K.G. Saur Verlag, 1987)

Hitler, Adolf, *Mein Kampf* (Houghton Mifflin Co., 1971; first pub. by Verlag Frz. Eher Nachf GmbH, 1925)
   Hitler's 'testament' written in Landsberg prison. Almost unreadable, but still worth the effort.

Klee, Ernst, Dressen, Willi, and Riess, Volker, *Those Were the Days* (Introduction to English edition by H.R. Trevor-Roper) (Hamish Hamiliton, 1991; first pub. by S. Fischer Verlag GmbH, 1988)
   This collection of Holocaust-related documents is a valuable insight into the attitudes of the period.

Noakes, Jeremy, and Pridham, Geoffrey (eds.), *Nazism: A Documentary Reader 1919–45* (University of Exeter Press). *Vol 1: The Rise to Power 1919–34* (1983), *Vol 2: State, Economy and Society 1933–39* (1984), *Vol 3: Foreign Policy, War and Racial Extermination 1933–45* (1988).
   This three-volume collection of documents with commentary is a monumental achievement. It should be essential reading for anyone seriously interested in the study of Nazism. The fourth and final volume (*Germany at War: the Home Front 1939–45*) is forthcoming.

Hitler's Table Talk (Introduction by H.R. Trevor-Roper) (Oxford University Press, 1988; first pub. in the UK by Weidenfeld & Nicolson, 1953)
   One of the most important original sources we have for Hitler's thinking.

OTHER BOOKS

Bartov, Omar, *The Eastern Front* (Macmillan, 1985)
   The conflict with the Soviet Union.

Bessel, Richard, *Life in the Third Reich* (Oxford University Press, 1987)
   An interesting collection of essays.

Bloch, Michael, *Ribbentrop* (Bantam Press, 1992)
   Biography of the Nazi almost all the other leading Nazis hated.

Bracher, Karl Dietrich, *The German Dictatorship* (Penguin Books, 1973; first pub. by Verlag Kiepenheuer & Witsch, 1969)
    An attempt to explain how the Nazi dictatorship worked.

Broszat, Martin, *The Hitler State* (Longman, 1981; first pub. by Deutscher Taschenbuch Verlag, 1969)
    A brilliant examination of the functioning of the Nazi state.

Browning, Christopher, *Fateful Months* (Holmes & Meier Publishers Inc., 1985)
    The piecing together of the decision-making process that led to the Holocaust.

Browning, Christopher, *The Path to Genocide* (Cambridge University Press, 1992)
    This collection of Holocaust-related essays is full of insights.

Browning, Christopher, *Ordinary Men* (HarperCollins, 1992)
    The haunting story of Reserve Police Battalion 101.

Bullock, Alan, *Hitler, a Study in Tyranny* (rev. ed. Odhams, 1964)
    His masterpiece, first published in 1952.

Bullock, Alan, *Hitler and Stalin, Parallel Lives* (HarperCollins 1991)
    Comparative lives of the two dictators.

Burrin, Philippe, *Hitler and the Jews* (Edward Arnold, 1994)
    A compulsively readable theory on the origins of the Holocaust.

Grunberger, Richard, *A Social History of the Third Reich* (Penguin Books, 1974; first pub. by Weidenfeld & Nicolson, 1971)
    An attempt to answer the question – what was it like living in Nazi Germany?

Fest, Joachim, *The Face of the Third Reich* (Penguin Books, 1972; first pub. in the UK by Weidenfeld & Nicolson, 1970.)
    A series of pen portraits of leading Nazis.

Fest, Joachim, *Hitler* (Weidenfeld & Nicolson, 1974; originally pub. by Verlag Ullstein, 1973)
    A dazzling study of Hitler's personality.

Frei, Norbert, *National Socialist Rule in Germany 1933-45* (Basil Blackwell Ltd, 1993; originally pub. by Deutscher Taschenbuch Verlag GmbH & Co. KG, 1987)
    The internal history of the Third Reich.

Gordon, Harold J., *Hitler and the Beer Hall Putsch* (Princeton University Press, 1972)
    The story of the failed revolution in Munich.

Gellately, Robert, *The Gestapo and German Society*, (Oxford University Press, 1991)
    His ground-breaking work on the Gestapo.

Kershaw, Ian, *Hitler* (Longman, 1991)
    The best short biography of Hitler.

Kershaw, Ian, *The Hitler Myth* (Oxford University Press, 1989)
   How Goebbels and others created the 'myth'.

Kershaw, Ian, *The Nazi Dictatorship* (Edward Arnold, 1985)
   A guide through the historiography.

Koch, H.W., *Aspects of the Third Reich* (Macmillan Education Ltd, 1985)
   Essays by British and German historians.

Merkl, Peter, *Political Violence under the Swastika* (Princeton University Press, 1975)
   The attitudes and beliefs of those who followed the Nazis.

Mommsen, Hans, *From Weimar to Auschwitz* (Polity Press, 1991)
   Perceptive essays from one of Germany's most distinguished historians of the Nazi period.

Padfield, Peter, *Himmler* (Macmillan, 1990)
   Biography of the Reichsführer SS.

Sereny, Gitta, *Albert Speer, His Battle with Truth* (Macmillan, 1995)
   The new biography of Speer, which lays bare the extent of his own guilt.

Speer, Albert, *Inside the Third Reich* (Orion, 1995; first published in the UK by Weidenfeld & Nicolson, 1970)
   Hitler's architect's own story – should be read in conjunction with Gitta Sereny's biography (see above).

Turner, Henry A., *German Big Business and the Rise of Hitler* (Oxford University Press, 1985)
   Hitler and the industrialists.

Trevor-Roper, Hugh, *The Last Days of Hitler* (Macmillan, 1947)
   The standard work on the last days; immensely readable.

Welch, David, *Propaganda and the German Cinema 1933–45* (Oxford University Press, 1983)
   The standard work on Goebbels' films; full of surprising information.

Willenberg, Samuel, *Revolt in Treblinka*, (Zydowski Instytut Historyczny, 1992; first pub. in English as *Surviving Treblinka*, Basil Blackwell, 1989)
   The harrowing story of Samuel Willenberg.

Wistrich, Robert S., *Who's Who in Nazi Germany* (Routledge, 1995; first pub. by Weidenfeld & Nicolson, 1982)
   A useful reference book.

NOTES ON EYE-WITNESSES

DR FRITZ ARLT

Joined the Hitler Youth in 1929 at the age of 17, and became a Nazi Storm Trooper in 1932. He gained a PhD in 1936. Between 1939 and 1940 he was head of the Department for Population Affairs and Welfare at the Internal Affairs Office of the Government General. In 1940 he became head of the Reich office for the Consolidation of German Nationhood in charge of the administration of the resettlement policy. In 1943 he transferred to the Waffen-SS.

RUDI BAMBER

Born into a Jewish family in Nuremberg in 1920, he was educated in a mixed school until 1936. In 1933 his parents became the caretakers of the B'nai Brith Lodge premises in Nuremberg; from 1935 they ran a Jewish café and guest house in the city. His father, who had won the Iron Cross during World War I, was murdered by Storm Troopers on Kristallnacht. In July 1939 Rudi Bamber managed to escape from Germany.

ZBIGNIEW BAZARNIK

Aged 14 at the start of the war, he worked as a handyman and assistant electrician at Hans Frank's estate at Krzeszowice outside Cracow from May 1941.

GERDA BERNHARDT

The sister of Manfred Bernhardt, a mentally disabled boy murdered at Aplerbeck psychiatric hospital in Dortmund during the Nazi's Children's 'Euthanasia' Programme. Only in 1989 did the whole truth about the killings at Aplerbeck become known.

CHARLES BLEEKER-KOHLSAAT

Born in 1928 into a wealthy ethnic German family in Posen, in a part of Poland that had been German before World War I. He later became a member of the Hitler Youth and witnessed the resettlement of the incoming ethnic Germans.

KARL BOEHM-TETTELBACH

Born in 1910, he joined the Luftwaffe before the Nazis came to power and trained as a pilot secretly in Russia. He was adjutant to Field-Marshal von Blomberg during the Fritsch/Blomberg crisis of 1938. During the war he served at the Führer's headquarters in East Prussia, the Wolf's Lair; he was present in the compound at the time of the 20 July 1944 assassination attempt on Hitler.

PROFESSOR MIECZYSLAW BROZEK

As a young assistant professor in classical philology at the Jagellonian University in Cracow, he was arrested in November 1939 along with other academics as part of the Nazi plan to deprive Poland of intelligent people. He was imprisoned in various concentration camps, including Dachau. He and the surviving professors were released as the result of international pressure at the end of 1940.

ADOLF BUCHNER

Born in 1923 in Munich, he later trained in agriculture at Marktoberdorf. He was arrested in 1942 after being denounced for listening to foreign broadcasts. In February 1944 he was called into the SS-Pionierbataillon Dresden for 'probation at the front'. He participated in 'cleansing' villages near Leningrad.

PAUL EGGERT

Coming as he did from a broken home, Paul Eggert was forcibly sterilized by the Nazis when he was 11. He later spent three months in the children's ward of Aplerbeck psychiatric hospital where he witnessed the 'disappearance' of many of the children.

IRMA EIGI

An ethnic German from Estonia, she (at the age of 17) and her family arrived in the Warthegau in late 1939 as part of the first group of Baltic Germans to be resettled in 'Germany' under the terms of the secret protocol to the Nazi-Soviet Pact.

JOSEF FELDER

Born in 1900, he was a Social Democrat MP by the time Hitler became Chancellor in January 1933. After the Nazis came to power he was arrested and sent to Dachau. Released after eighteen months in the camp, he had to remove himself from politics for the duration of the Nazi rule of Germany.

WALTER FERNAU

Born in 1920 in Melsungen. As a member of the 14 Panzerjäger-Kompanie of his regiment, he took part in Operation Barbarossa and was wounded during the retreat from Moscow. He became a lieutenant in 1944, and in the spring of 1945 he joined Major Helm's unit which was charged with assembling scattered soldiers and later with 'Flying Courts Martial'. He became Helm's adjutant and was appointed NSFO (National Socialist Guidance Officer). In many of the Flying Courts Martial he acted as prosecutor.

ESTERA FRENKIEL

Born into a Jewish family in Lodz she, along with other Lodz Jews, was forced by the Nazis to move into the designated 'ghetto' area of the city in the spring of 1940. She managed to get a job as a secretary working in the ghetto administration and was thus able to meet Hans Biebow, the Nazi who was the ghetto manager. When the ghetto was closed she and her mother were transported to Ravensbrück concentration camp.

JUOZAS GRAMAUSKAS

Born in 1920, he lived in the village of Butrimonys in Lithuania. In September 1941 he witnessed the massacre of women and children by units of the Lithuanian Army acting on German orders.

BRUNO HÄHNEL

Born in 1911, he joined the youth wing of the Storm Troopers in 1927 before working as a regional leader of the Hitler Youth in Westphalia until 1945.

HANS VON HERWARTH

Born in 1904, he joined the German diplomatic corps in 1929. From 1931–9 he worked in the German embassy in Moscow and witnessed the signing of the Nazi–Soviet Pact. From 1939–45 he served in the Wehrmacht.

FRANZ JAGEMANN

Born in 1917 into a German family (but with a Polish father). He served as a 'supply translator' from July to October 1940 in the Warthegau.

ANNA JEZIORKOWSKA

Born in 1929 into a Polish family in Posen, she and her family were brutally evicted from their flat in November 1939 and transported in animal freight wagons to the General Government.

WALTER KAMMERLING

Born into a Jewish family in Vienna in 1923; as a 15-year-old he witnessed the Anschluss and the mistreatment of Jews on the streets of Vienna. He managed to leave Austria in October 1938.

JOHANN-ADOLF GRAF VON KIELMANSEGG

Born in 1906, he joined the German Army in 1926. In 1939 he became a member of the General Staff.

EMIL KLEIN

Born in 1905, he participated in the march through Munich during the Beer Hall *Putsch* and was later decorated with the Nazi 'blood order'. He joined the Storm Troopers in the early 1920s and became a Nazi propaganda speaker after 1925.

ERNA KRANZ

Born into a middle class Bavarian family, as a teenager she participated in the Night of the Amazons Pageant in Munich in 1938.

MARIA THERESIA KRAUS

Born in 1920, she is a former neighbour of Ilse Sonja Totzke who died in a Nazi concentration camp after being the victim of denunciations. One of the denunciations attacking Miss Totzke (in the Würzburg archives) is signed by Resi Kraus.

JACQUES LEROY

Born in 1924 in the French-speaking part of Belgium, he joined the Waffen SS after the fall of France. He rejoined his unit after losing an arm and an eye and was decorated with the Knight's Cross on 20 April 1945 for his bravery in the defence of Nazi Germany.

EUGENE LEVINÉ

Born in 1916, he is the son of the Jewish Räterepublik politician Eugene Leviné who was executed in 1919. He later joined the German Communist Party and escaped from Germany in 1933.

BERND LINN

As a boy, growing up in Bavaria in the 1920s, he witnessed the arrival of the so called 'eastern Jews'. He later joined the Waffen SS and fought on the Eastern Front during the war.

DR GÜNTER LOHSE

He joined the German Foreign Office and the Nazi Party in the 1930s. He witnessed the consequences of Hitler's chaotic method of government.

RIVA LOSANSKAYA

Born in 1918, she is one of only sixteen Jewish survivors from the massacres at the village of Butrimonys in Lithuania.

ANNA MIREK

Twenty-seven years old at the start of the war, she worked as a cook at Hans Frank's estate at Krzeszowice outside Cracow.

WILHELM MOSES

As a driver in a Wehrmacht transport regiment he participated in the invasion of Poland and witnessed atrocities committed by the SS Germania.

ALFONSAS NAVASINSKAS
At the age of about 20 he witnessed the massacre of the Jews in Butrimonys in Lithuania. He comes from a relatively wealthy peasant family.

DANUTA PAWELCZAK-GROCHOLSKA
She joined the domestic staff of Arthur Greiser's county house outside Posen in 1942. She was one of only six Polish women working in Greiser's mansion – the rest of the servants were German.

ALOIS PFALLER
Born in 1910, he joined the Communist Youth Movement in the late 1920s. Trained as a painter and decorator, he suffered periods of unemployment during the German Depression. He was arrested by the Nazis in 1934 and was imprisoned in various concentration camps until his release in 1945.

ROMUALD PILACZYNSKI
Born in 1927 into a middle-class Polish family in Bydgoszcz, in what became part of Albert Forster's domain after the Nazi redrawing of Polish boundaries. His family were reclassified as 'third category' Germans.

OTTO PIRKHAM
Austrian diplomat who witnessed the meeting of Hitler and the Austrian Chancellor Kurt von Schuschnigg on 12 February 1938 at the Berghof.

DR HERBERT RICHTER
Born in 1899, he fought as a German soldier during World War I. In 1924 he joined the German Diplomatic Corps, and later served in Rome, Bombay and Colombo.

DR JUTTA RÜDIGER
From 1937–45 she was Reich Leader of the League of German Girls (the BDM). As a child she witnessed the French occupation of the Ruhr.

MANFRED FREIHERR VON SCHRÖDER
Born in 1914, he joined the Nazi Party in November 1933. In 1938 he entered the German Foreign Office. From 1937 to 1938 he was a member of the SS Cavalry Unit and, from May 1942 to August 1943, served in the Wehrmacht on the Eastern Front.

SUSI SEITZ
Born in 1923, she was not quite 15 when she stood cheering in the crowd which welcomed Hitler into the Austrian town of Linz in March 1938. She went on to become a leading member of the Austrian Hitler Youth.

VIERA SILKINAITE
A native of Kaunas in Lithuania, at the age of 16 she witnessed the murder of Lithuanian Jews in the 'garage' killing in Kaunas in the early days of the German occupation.

FRIDOLIN VON SPAUN
Born in 1900, he volunteered to fight in the right-wing Bavarian Freikorps Oberland after World War I and saw action with the Freikorps in Poland. After Hitler came to power he worked to promote Nazi propaganda in Germany.

REINHARD SPITZY

Born in Austria, he joined the SS and the staff of Joachim von Ribbentrop in the 1930s. During the war he served in German intelligence.

ARNON TAMIR

Born in 1917 in Stuttgart, he went on to be active in the Jewish Youth Movement. In 1938 he was one of a large number of Jews deported to Poland by the Nazis, but subsequently managed to escape to Palestine.

HERMANN TESCHEMACHER

Active in right-wing politics in the 1920s, he later joined the Nazi Party. During the war he fought on the Eastern Front.

WOLFGANG TEUBERT

Joined the Nazi Storm Troopers in the east of Germany during the late 1920s. During the war he served in the German Army on the Eastern Front.

PROFESSOR STANISLAW URBANCZYK

An academic at the Jagellonian University, Cracow, he was imprisoned by the Nazis at Sachsenhausen concentration camp. He was released after 14 months, at Christmas 1940.

SAMUEL WILLENBERG

Born in 1923 into a Jewish family in Poland, in 1942 he was sent to the Nazi death camp at Treblinka. In 1943 he managed to escape and, after a series of adventures, eventually joined the Polish underground and fought against the Nazis.

GABRIELE WINCKLER

She was a secretary in Germany during the 1930s.

PROFESSOR JOHANNES ZAHN

Born in 1907, he gained a PhD in Law in 1929. From 1933 to 1934 he worked at the Central Association of German Banks and in 1935 became Managing Director of the German Institute of Banking. From 1939–45 he served in the Wehrmacht; during this period he was also German administrator of English and American banks in Belgium.

PETRAS ZELIONKA

Born in 1917 into a poor Lithuanian peasant family, in 1941 he joined the 3rd/13th Lithuanian Auxiliary Police Battalion. As a ghetto guard he witnessed killings in the 7th Fort in Kaunas and later murdered victims himself in numerous other actions. In 1948 the Soviets sentenced him to twenty-five years in Siberia.

EUGEN ZIELKE

An ethnic German from Lodz in Poland whose father ran a food shop. In 1940, when he was in his early 20s, he benefited from trade with the Jews who were imprisoned in the Lodz ghetto.

ACKNOWLEDGEMENTS

There are two people I feel I must thank above all others. The first is Michael Jackson, former Director of BBC Television. Without his support and encouragement there would be no television series and no book.

The second person to whom I owe a particular debt of gratitude is Professor Ian Kershaw who was historical consultant on the series. Before anyone else worked on the project, Ian and I spent the best part of a year developing the series' structure. I knew in advance of his reputation as one of the most brilliant scholars of the Third Reich, whose forthcoming major biography of Hitler is eagerly awaited here and in Germany, but I soon learnt that he is also the most tolerant and forgiving of colleagues. His contribution to this project cannot be overestimated, nor can our gratitude to him.

Many other production people worked on the television series *The Nazis – a Warning from History* on which this book is based. I am glad to have this opportunity of thanking them all for their skill, dedication and patience. Tilman Remme was associate producer on the series and his work was of the highest quality. He himself was a model of painstaking efficiency, charm and support. Detlef Siebert, SallyAnn Kleibel, Sue McConachy and Corinna Stürmer were assistant producers; all are superb journalists. We also benefited from the craft skills of some of the finest people working in factual television: the film editors Alan Lygo and Jamie Hay, the camera team of Martin Patmore and Richard Manton, the graphic designer John Kennedy, Adrian Wood, who scoured the film archives of the world for us, and Joanne King who trawled the photo libraries.

Ann Cattini was the series' unit manager and Venita Singh Warner, Laura Davey and Harriet Rowe, the production assistants; all were enormously supportive. My own secretaries, first Stephanie Harvie then later Kate Gorst, were a great help too. In Germany Marita Krauss, Friederike Albat and Volker Riess were extremely helpful. In Poland Wanda Koscia did a fine job for us, and in Lithuania excellent work was completed by Saulius Berzinis and Alicija

Zukauskaitè. At BBC Books Sheila Ableman was always staunch in her commitment to the project and Martha Caute saw the manuscript through into production with great care.

The head of documentaries, Paul Hamann, was always encouraging, as was the new controller of BBC2, Mark Thompson.

I also remain profoundly grateful to my American co-producers, Arts and Entertainment Network, in particular to Brooke Bailey Johnson, Michael Cascio, Charlie Mayday and Michael Catz. No one ever had more talented or more supportive colleagues across the Atlantic.

Two further groups of people I can only thank collectively. If I thanked them all individually, I would fill many pages with hundreds of names and yet still be worried that I had left someone out. They are the interviewees who gave us their memories, feelings and opinions, and the academics who gave us their advice and helped us sceptically to examine the responses of our interviewees. Making a series like this is a privilege in many ways, not least in the opportunity it gives to meet and question those who have extraordinary knowledge and those who have had extraordinary experiences. More often than not, these people show great kindness to their questioners. I thank them all and I hope they will accept that my thanks are no less genuine for being collectively expressed.

My wife Helena and Professor Kershaw both read this book in draft form and I am grateful for their comments. But notwithstanding the enormous amount of helpful advice I have received on this subject over these last years, the opinions and judgements expressed in this book are entirely my own.

This book is dedicated to my son and my daughter with their father's love.

LR

INDEX

PICTURE CREDITS

Frontispiece: Bildarchiv Preussischer Kulturbesitz; page 11 BPK; p12 AKG London; p16 Dirk Halfbrodt; p18-9 Bayerische Staatsbibliothek; p20 l&r Leviné family; p23 Süddeutscher Verlag; pp24, 25 BS; p26 BPK; p28 SV; p29 AKG; p32 BPK; pp34, 39; pp40, 43 Bundesarchiv, Koblenz; p45 AKG; p48 Ullstein Bilderdienst; pp50, 52 AKG; p54 SV; p56 Karl Böhm - Tettelbach; p58-59 Ullstein; p63 Bundesarchiv; p65 BBC TV; pp66, 67, 70 BPK; p72 AKG; p75 Bamber family; pp77,78 BPK; p79 AKG; p80 Ullstein; p81 Bernhardt family; pp82, 87 BPK; p88 Bundesarchiv; p90 SV; p91 AKG; p94 BPK; p96-7 AKG; p100 BPK; p104 Ullstein; pp109, 111, 112-3 AKG; p115 BPK; p117 Bibliothek für Zeitgeschichte, Stuttgart; p121 AKG; p124 SV; p126 AKG; p127 BS; p128 SV; p131 Ullstein; pp134, 135 AKG; p137 Ullstein; pp143, 144 SV; p146 AKG; p148 Ullstein; p154-5 Jewish Museum, Frankfurt p156-7 AKG;; pp158, 159, 160-1 BPK; p164 Novosti; p166-7 Ullstein; pp169, 172 BPK; pp176, 178 AKG; p180-1 Zentrale Stelle der Landesjustizverwaltungen, Ludwigsburg; p184 BPK; p185 Ullstein; p188 Petras Zelionka; p192-3 Kaunaus War Museum of Vytautas the Great; p196-7 SV; p199 AKG; p201 t+b Kaunaus War Museum of Vytautas the Great; pp204-5, 208 AKG; p212 BPK; p215 AKG; pp216, 218, 220, 226-7 Ullstein; p230 AKG; p233 Ullstein; pp237, 238 BPK; p239 AKG.

Abbreviations: AKG = AKG London; BPK = Bildarchiv Preussischer Kulturbesitz; BS = Bayerische Staatsbibliothek; SV = Süddeutscher Verlag